No. 2692
$27.95

DESIGNING AND PROGRAMMING
PERSONAL EXPERT SYSTEMS

CARL TOWNSEND AND DENNIS FEUCHT

TAB BOOKS Inc.
Blue Ridge Summit, PA 17214

FIRST EDITION
FIRST PRINTING

Library of Congress Cataloging in Publication Data

Townsend, Carl, 1938-
Designing and programming personal expert systems.

Bibliography: p.
Includes index.
1. Expert systems (Computer science) 2. Micro-
computers—Programming. I. Feucht, Dennis. II. Title.
QA76.76.E95T69 1986   006.3'3   85-30407
ISBN 0-8306-0692-0
ISBN 0-8306-2692-1 (pbk.)

Contents

Acknowledgment   vii

Introduction   viii

PART I: EXPERT AND KNOWLEDGE SYSTEMS   1

1 Introduction to Artificial Intelligence   3

What Is Thinking? 3
The Human Mind 4
The Organization of Information in the Brain 6
The World of Artificial Intelligence 9
  Knowledge Representation—Problem Solving—Expert and Knowledge Systems—Natural Language
  Interfaces—Learning—Cognitive Modeling—Vision and Robotics
Where We Are Today 15
Exercises 16

2 Introduction to Knowledge Systems   17

What Is a Knowledge System? 17
Features of a Knowledge System 20
Using Knowledge Systems 20
  Medical Diagnostics—Prediction—Planning—Interpretation—Monitoring and Control—Mechanical
  and Electrical Diagnosis—Instruction
Applications for Knowledge Systems 22
Limitations of Knowledge Systems 23
Advantages of the Knowledge System 24

Personal Computers as Knowledge Systems 25
Heuristic versus Algorithmic Computing 26
Symbolic versus Numeric Processing 27
Divergent versus Convergent Reasoning 28
Summary 28
Exercises 28

3 The Components of a Knowledge System   **30**

The Production System 30
The Rule Memory or Rulebase—The Working Memory or Database—The Inference Engine or Rule
Interpreter—The Knowledge Acquisition Module—The Natural Language Interface—The Explanatory
Interface
Control Strategies 40
Backward and Forward Chaining—Improving the Search Efficiency
Commercial Production Systems 42
Using Tools 43
Computer Languages for Knowledge Systems 45
The Human Brain 45
Exercises 47

4 Representing Knowledge   **48**

The Animal Game 48
Knowledge Representation with Rules 49
Frame Representations 53
Semantic Network Representations 56
First-Order Logic Representations 57
Logical Concepts—Prefix Predicate Calculus (Predicate Logic)—The Syntax of Predicate Logic
Blackboard Systems 62
Representation by Example 62
Using an Example 63
Exercises 64

5 Introduction to Knowledge Engineering   **65**

Defining the Domain 66
Identifying the Problem—Identifying the Objects in the Domain—Identifying the Relationship of
Objects—Expressing Knowledge in a Language—Identifying Key Problem Areas in the Application
Domain—Creating the Representational Theory—Structural Hierarchy—Behavioral or Causal
Hierarchy—Functional Hierarchy—Deep Knowledge versus Shallow Knowledge—Representing
versus Implementing Knowledge
Acquiring Knowledge 75
Exercises 76

PART II: BUILDING KNOWLEDGE SYSTEMS   **77**

6 Forth: A Versatile Expert Systems Language   **79**

Words and the Dictionary 80
Passing Data Using the Stack 81
Hierarchical Decomposition and Modularity 82
Forth Arithmetic 83
Stack Manipulation 86
Accessing Data 87
Flags, Logical Operators, and Numerical Comparisons 89
Forth Control Constructs 90
The Return Stack 95
String Handling 96
Text Streams 97
Forth Word Structure 97
Dictionary Management 98

The Forth Virtual Machine 100
Defining- and Compiling-Words 102
Disk Words 108
Exercises 109

7 Introduction to List Processing   110

Why Emulate LISP? 111
Static versus Dynamic Memory Management 112
What Is a List? 112
Primitive List Operations 114
List Identifiers and List Pointers 116
Printing Lists 116
List Input 118
List-Processing Data Types 120
What Is NIL? 120
Property-Lists 121
Association-Lists 122
EQUAL versus EQ 123
Destructive List Operations 124
Other List Functions 124
Exercises 128

8 Programming Techniques   129

Recursion 129
Garbage Collection 136
Implementation of Destructive List Functions 138
Destructive List Functions and Reference Counting 139
Exercises 140

9 A Prolog Knowledge System   141

Logic Programming in Prolog 141
A Prolog Interpreter 145
Implementation of SEARCH 149
Deduction Trees 155
Breadth-First and Heuristic Search 156
Unification 157
Exercises 164

10 Advanced Concepts   166

Prolog Built-In Predicates 166
Procedural Attachment and Pattern-Directed Invocation 167
Nonmonotonic Reasoning 168
Object-Oriented Programming 169
Metareasoning: Reasoning about Control 171
Uncertainty and Evidence 173
Forth Vocabularies 175
Parallel Computation 178
Exercises 179

11 Learning and Pattern Recognition   181

Learning 181
Pattern Recognition 183
  Hyperplane Properties—Minimum-Distance Classifiers
Pattern Recognition and Learning 196
Exercises 204

Appendix A: Source Listing   205

Appendix B: **The Diagnosis Routines**   **222**

Appendix C: **Forth Vocabulary**   **227**

Appendix D: **Expert System Tools**   **235**

Appendix E: **Expert Systems**   **240**

Glossary   **243**

Resources   **250**

Index   **254**

Acknowledgment

The authors wish to express their grateful appreciation to Tektronix and Mike Freiling for help and support in writing this book.

Introduction

"The coming age of artificial intelligence is expected to impact jobs of white-collar workers the way industrial automation altered the blue-collar ranks."
John Diebold

"A database contains data; a knowledge base contains both data and assertions about those data. It seems a natural extension of what we have today. At the very least, computers will become interactive consultants to the professions—especially medicine."
James Martin

T HE DEVELOPMENT OF EXPERT SYSTEMS IS ONE OF THE MOST EXCITING DEVEL-
opments in the history of the computer; research, researchers, and products in this area are growing almost exponentially. In 1980 expert system research was almost entirely confined to the universities. In 1981 Japan announced it intended to leap-frog U.S. computer technology, developing a fifth-generation computer that would revolutionize the entire industry. Scientists in the United States have taken a more distributed approach—approximately 50 percent of the Fortune 500 companies already have launched their own expert system research. Some of the companies are working together to build extremely complex knowledge systems that are beyond the resources

of any single company. About 10 percent of these companies have actual applications in use or development.

If you are waiting to purchase a laser disk at your local store to make your computer an in-resident expert, you will still have to wait a long, long time. Technologically this may be achieved in only a few years, but our culture is nowhere near ready for the changes such a laser disk would initiate. More realistically, in the near future you can expect to see these expert systems as tools, used by men and women who are already experts, to enhance their knowledge and work.

This book is intended as an introduction to these thinking machines of the future. Together we will explore the basic ideas of thinking and intelligence, the basic concepts of a knowledge system, and how knowledge systems are built. You will also find the complete program listings here for a small knowledge system with which you can begin your own adventure using nothing more than your home or business computer.

The first part of this book is intended as an introduction to artificial intelligence and knowledge systems. It is presented as a tutorial, guiding you through the technical background assuming a minimal knowledge of artificial intelligence. You will find plenty of examples, and if you do want to explore further you can use the references in the Appendix. Chapter 1 is a basic introduction to artificial intelligence, and Chapter 2 introduces the knowledge or expert system. Chapter 3 describes a particular type of knowledge system—the production system. Chapter 4 is an overview of different ways of representing knowledge, beginning with the production system structure already described in Chapter 3. Chapter 5 will introduce the basic concepts of building the knowledgebase.

The second part of the book describes a complete knowledge system that can be built using the Forth language. Chapter 6 is an overview of the Forth language, which is the language environment used for building the knowledge system in this book. Chapter 7 is an introduction to list processing, the heart of symbolic processing. Chapter 8 is an introduction to programming techniques. Chapter 9 is an overview of Prolog, which is the actual language used to implement the knowledge system. Chapters 10 and 11 explore a variety of advanced topics.

The backmatter contains a complete glossary, a resource listing, the source listing for the knowledge system developed in the text, an overview of expert system products currently available, a Forth vocabulary, and additional code to make the Prolog knowledge system into a rule interpreter.

The knowledge system in this book can be used as a shell to work with small knowledgebases to solve a variety of problems, including the examples of the first part. The second part also introduces some more advanced concepts that can be applied if you have some expertise in programming. The listing for the knowledge system in the text is written using Forth-83. Both the Apple II and IBM PC disks are available from the publisher and contain the Forth interpreter that is needed for that particular implementation. If you wish to enter the listing yourself, the "Resources" section lists some inexpensive Forth interpreters and compilers that can be used.

Enjoy the adventure.

PART I

EXPERT AND KNOWLEDGE SYSTEMS

T HIS FIRST PART OF THE BOOK WILL INTRODUCE YOU TO THE BASIC CONCEPTS of artificial intelligence and knowledge engineering. This part is intended as a tutorial, and you will find examples and exercises to help you in this learning experience. If you need further help in any topic, you can use the Appendix to locate resources that can give you additional information.

For this part of the book, you will need very little mathematical or programming experience. Most terms and concepts are introduced as they are needed. Even if you have had some knowledge engineering experience, you should still take the time to scan the first chapter and read the remaining chapters in this part to become familiar with the terminology that will be an integral part of the second part.

CARL TOWNSEND

Chapter 1

Introduction to Artificial Intelligence

F ROM THE BEGINNING OF TIME, PHILOSOPHERS AND SCIENTISTS HAVE TRIED TO explore the human mind and create artificial forms of intelligence. Some of the earliest examples were the fictional Greek gods, behaving as humans who had infinite resources of beauty, intelligence, and power, hundreds of years before the time of Christ. By the fourteenth century, man had learned to create clocks decorated with automated figures that nodded, marched, struck gongs, and bowed at predetermined moments— the beginning of robotics. By the nineteenth century, scientists had learned to harness intelligent machines for productive purposes, creating a printing press that printed the Bible in less time than it would take several hundred scribes.

WHAT IS THINKING?

The development of thinking machines has always been a subject of diversity and mixed emotions. Many see the thinking machine as a form of power, a path to prosperity and wealth, and a means of transcending man's own limitations. Others view the same machines as the biblical Baal—an idol, a false god, wicked and evil. In truth, however, the "thinking" machine is really amoral. Unlike a human, the machine cannot decide to do right or wrong. All machines in existence today make decisions using basic rules that are explicitly or implicitly stored in the machine by some human. If a machine is said to be intelligent, it is because it appears, at least to some degree, to make decisions in a way similar to that a human would use.

A classic interpretation of the meaning of intelligence was developed by A.M. Turing a little over three decades ago. The problem is defined in terms of an "imitation game" based on a popular British parlor game of the time. In Turing's version of the game, a man or a woman (A) and an intelligent machine (B) are put in separate rooms; an interrogator (C) is permitted to communicate with each. The object of the game is for the interrogator to determine which of the two is a human and which is a machine. If the interpreter cannot determine which is which, the machine is said to be "intelligent." The interrogator, of course, must try to develop some dialog strategy in which he (or she) could determine if the object (or witness) is actually learning and creating or simply repeating knowledge, parrot-fashion. Here is an example of Turing's classic dialog:

INTERROGATOR: In the first line of the sonnet which reads, "Shall I compare thee to a summer's day," would not "a spring day" do as well or better?
WITNESS: It wouldn't scan.
INTERROGATOR: How about "a winter's day?" That would scan all right.
WITNESS: Yes, but nobody wants to be compared to a winter's day.
INTERROGATOR: Would you say Mr. Pickwick reminded you of Christmas?
WITNESS: In a way.
INTERROGATOR: Yet Christmas is a winter's day, and I do not think Mr. Pickwick would mind the comparison.
WITNESS: I don't think you're serious. By "winter's day" one means a typical winter day, rather than a special one like Christmas.

Such a sustained dialog would certainly be impossible for any current machine or machine in development today. The question still remains, however: Could such a machine eventually be developed?

THE HUMAN MIND

The thinking process of the human mind is incredibly complex. A single cell in the human eye is capable of processing in 10 milliseconds the equivalent of 500 simultaneous nonlinear differential equations a hundred times. The Cray-1 supercomputer, currently the fastest computer in the world, would take several minutes to solve the same equations. As there are 10 million or more cells in the human eye, each interacting with the others, it would take at least 100 years on a Cray supercomputer to simulate what happens in the eye each second.

For the human mind, external data enters the system through one of the five senses (such as vision) and is temporarily stored in short-term buffer memories for analysis. Another memory system in the brain, a long-term memory, stores symbols and symbolic relationships that are used for interpreting the new information in the short-term memory (Fig. 1-1). The long-term memory stores not so much facts and data as it does objects and the relationship between these objects, i.e., symbolic patterns. Large amounts of data are constantly being "dumped" into the short-term memory, and we are constantly analyzing and filtering this information to determine what is important and how it relates to patterns already stored in the long-term memory.

Perhaps even more amazing is the fact that scientists have yet to discover the physical location of *any* type of memory in the brain. Evidence suggests that whatever memory is in the human brain is incorporated into the structure at whatever point the

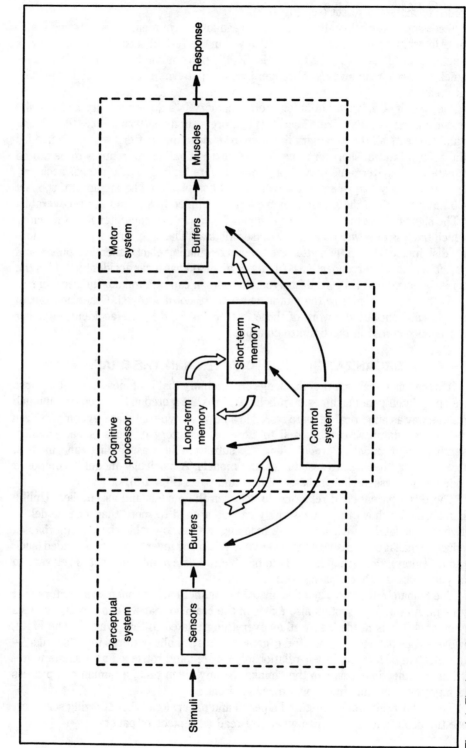

Fig. 1-1. The human knowledge processing system.

5

stored information is to act (see Fig. 1-2).

Accessing information already stored in the long-term memory is extremely efficient. Almost any piece of data can be retrieved in the 70-millisecond processing cycle and acted upon. This enables us to "instinctively" pull our hand away from a hot stove or quickly steer our car away from danger by using patterns already stored in the long-term memory.

The *storing* of information in long-term memory is a different story and is quite time-consuming. It takes about 7 seconds to store a single pattern in long-term memory and to create all the necessary linkages to retrieve that pattern when it is needed in the future. Data in short-term memory requires about 15-20 minutes to be stored completely in long-term memory. If a person suffers brain damage in a car accident, long-term memory may seem to recover almost completely. The memory of the last 15-20 minutes before the accident, however, is completely lost and not recoverable.

The short-term memory could be compared roughly to a computer RAM memory in which the loss of power completely erases all data. The long-term memory is more like a disk memory, with the patterns stored in circulating electrochemical pulses and physical neuronal interconnections. In fact, if a person has a car accident in which the brain is damaged and neurons destroyed, the person can often make full recovery as long as the speech center or the motor neurons are not destroyed. Other neurons in the brain can continue the work of those lost or damaged by the accident, enabling patterns once stored in the brain to continue.

ORGANIZATION OF INFORMATION IN THE BRAIN

It is the functional aspect of this long-term memory that is of most interest to those developing intelligent machines. Symbolic patterns are stored in this memory in much the same way as numerical data are stored in a network-type database. A computerized network-type database can be used to store an inventory of parts, subassemblies, assemblies, and models. Parts "belong" to subassemblies, assemblies, and models. Subassemblies "belong" to assemblies and models. A particular model is composed of one or more assemblies, subassemblies, and parts (Fig. 1-3).

There is a parent-child relationship between the models and assemblies. Unlike a human family, however, an assembly can be a child to more than one model. A network-type database has a complex indexing system to enable the user (perhaps a production manager) to manage the inventory. When any inventory item is needed (such as an assembly), the manager needs to be able to retrieve all data that is relevant to that part (subassemblies, parts, etc.)

The human brain stores symbols instead of numerical data such as inventory part numbers. An indexing system also exists in the brain so that we can rapidly retrieve any symbol that is needed, as well as everything related to that symbol. The brain, however, goes one step further and organizes the symbolic patterns into "chunks"—any collection of facts and their relationships stored and retrieved as a single unit—with interconnections between the chunks. At any given time, a human can process and interpret a maximum of four to seven chunks.

To see how this works, first find a pencil and paper. Read the following sentence, close the book, and try to write what you read on a piece of paper:

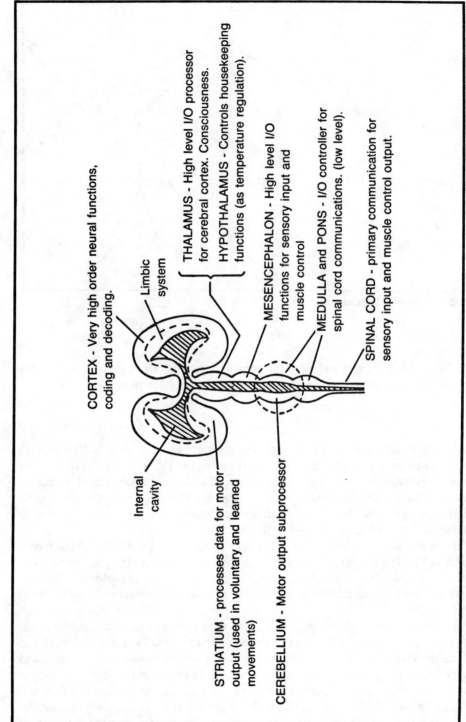

CORTEX - Very high order neural functions, coding and decoding.

Limbic system

THALAMUS - High level I/O processor for cerebral cortex. Consciousness.

HYPOTHALAMUS - Controls housekeeping functions (as temperature regulation).

MESENCEPHALON - High level I/O functions for sensory input and muscle control

MEDULLA and PONS - I/O controller for spinal cord communications. (low level).

SPINAL CORD - primary communication for sensory input and muscle control output.

Internal cavity

STRIATIUM - processes data for motor output (used in voluntary and learned movements)

CEREBELLIUM - Motor output subprocessor

Fig. 1-2. Hierarchial organization of the human brain.

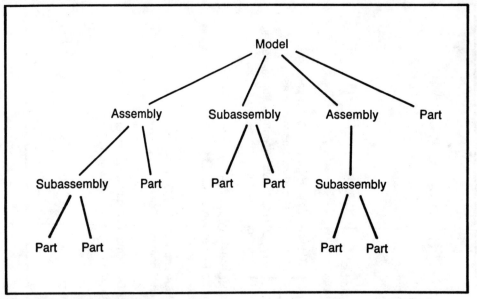

Fig. 1-3. The network database.

Nlonmy zrzynkz imn wnbnm gvss.

Now check what you wrote and see how many characters you wrote correctly—probably from four to seven. Now repeat the experiment with the following sentence:

Expert systems are never dull.

Check your results. Did you get all the characters correct this time? Both sentences have the same number of characters and are the same length. What was the difference? In the second case you "chunked" your objects (the letter symbols) into five chunks, and you actually had to remember only the five chunks and their relationship—quite within the range of the human mind. In the first example, you had to remember 29 chunks, far beyond the capabilities of the mind.

Using this same strategy, a chess master can recall the position of all the pieces on a chessboard after a brief look. He or she does not remember the position of every piece on the board, but rather chunks the board into collections of positions. The master remembers only the chunks, and from this can recreate the entire board with unerring accuracy.

It is this chunking ability that distinguishes the expert in a particular subject area, or *domain*, from someone who is not an expert. The expert has extensively developed the ability to organize a large amount of data in a particular domain into chunks and has created hierarchical linkages between the chunks to access this data and apply it to new perceptions as they arrive at the brain. A typical expert in a specific field will know 50,000 to 100,000 chunks that can be applied to decisions in their specific domain of expertise. The accumulation and indexing of this much data in the human mind takes from 10 to 20 years.

8

THE WORLD OF ARTIFICIAL INTELLIGENCE

The science of artificial intelligence is rather broad and has, in effect, been explored from the beginning of time; the modern beginning can be dated perhaps from 1956. In that year Claude Shannon of the Bell Telephone Laboratories and Marvin Minsky of the Massachusetts Institute of Technology met at Dartmouth College with other information science pioneers for the unveiling of the world's first expert system—Allen Newell's Logic Theorist. Today the science of artificial intelligence spans a growing list of emerging disciplines: knowledge representation, problem solving, expert systems, natural language interfaces, learning, cognitive modeling, strategy games, vision, and robotics (see Fig. 1-4). Artificial intelligence is a subfield of computer science, and is concerned primarily with symbolic reasoning and problem solving.

Knowledge Representation

Knowledge representation is perhaps the most important area of artificial intelligence research. It is the cornerstone on which all the other disciplines are built. For this reason, two chapters in this book (Chapters 4 and 5) are devoted to the subject. Knowledge pertains to objects, relationships, and procedures in some domain of interest. "Skill" is having the right knowledge and using it effectively. The human brain is very adept at symbolic processing, but fails miserably in numerical processing against even small calculators. Can computers mimic the symbolic processing of the human brain? If so, how could this be done?

The longer-range quest for knowledge representation research is to find a general theory or method for representing any knowledge. As yet, scientists have no general theory of knowledge representation. Such a theory would make possible the capture of commonsense knowledge that we use all the time and apply it to the solution of new problems, even though we do not know what the knowledge itself might be. In order to do this, however, we need first to have a way of representing commonsense knowledge—and this is the problem of knowledge representation.

Problem Solving

Problem solving is finding a way to get from some initial situation to a desired goal. Humans do it very effectively using deductive logic (reason), procedural analysis, analogy, and induction. We can also learn from own own experiences. Computers, at least at the present time, generally solve problems only by deductive logic and procedural analysis.

The type of problem determines the method best suited for its solution. Problems that lend themselves to procedural analysis are generally best solved using a computer. Inventory control, accounting, and cash flow analysis are all examples of procedural problems that computers can solve faster and more reliably than humans. Problems involving analogy or induction are generally best solved without a computer. Problems that are solved using deductive reasoning are possible candidates for expert and knowledge systems, the subject of this book.

Some problem-solving research has centered on the development of efficient game-playing hardware and software for complex games that require a combination of

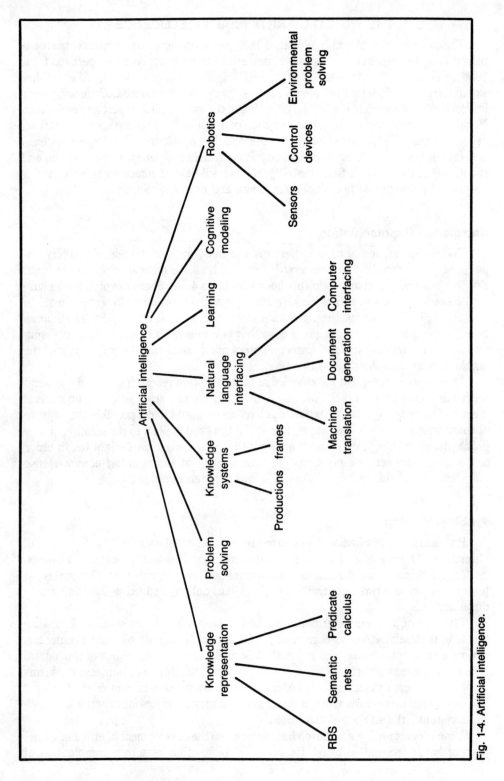

Fig. 1-4. Artificial intelligence.

10

problem-solving skills, such as chess and checkers. Software has already been developed for personal computers that can play chess at an intermediate level, and mainframe chess programs can compete at a master's level.

Strategies for problem solving can also be explored by developing games that challenge the creativity or skill of the player or mimic the problem-solving aspects of the human mind. Some of the factors to be considered in the design of a game include:

Assumption. The basic paradigm of the game will involve certain key decisions:

1. Should the game be win/lose (such as chess), or win/win?
2. How many players are involved?
3. Is the game deterministic (no dice or random-number generation), partially deterministic, or nondeterministic?
4. Is perfect information available (such as in chess), or should some of the information be hidden (such as in a card game)?

Representation. How will the game be represented? In chess, representations are needed for the game pieces, their position on the board, and their value. In some cases, the game may include a fantasy world that is an extension of the real world. The "rules" of this fantasy world can be defined by the game creator.

Goal. What is the basic goal of the game? In chess, the goal is to checkmate the opponent. Some means must also be provided for detecting this goal state. The goal may be visible to the player (such as in chess) or hidden (such as in Infocom adventure games).

Rules of the Game. What are the legal moves available in the game? In chess there are certain moves that are available for each type of piece, as well as certain pattern moves (such as castling) available under certain conditions. The rules may be visible (as in chess) or hidden (as in Infocom adventure games).

Control Strategy. In a computer game representation, the computer must be provided with some means of determining the next (and best) move.

Expert and Knowledge Systems

Expert and knowledge systems are a class of computer programs that can advise, analyze, categorize, consult, and diagnose. They address problems that normally require the expertise of a human specialist. Unlike computer programs that use procedural analysis to solve problems, expert systems attempt to solve problems in specified domains (specific fields of expertise) using deductive reasoning. Such systems are often capable of solving problems that are unstructured and poorly defined. They cope with the lack of structure through the use of *heuristics,* which are "rules of thumb" that can be used to solve a problem when a lack of knowledge or time prevents a more complete analysis. Knowledge systems are the primary subject of this book.

Natural Language Interfaces

Machines use their own language in representing knowledge and problem solving. Language can be defined as the symbols used to represent knowledge (*semantics*) and the rules for processing the symbols (*syntax*) and solving problems. Humans work most efficiently using special languages that evolve to meet the needs of a specific culture. When traveling is in a foreign country, one must constantly convert his or her knowledge to the language of that country. In the same way, the traveler gains more knowledge by converting knowledge in the foreign language to that of his or her own native language and then storing it in his or her knowledge base. The modern traveler may use a small pocket electronic translator for help in communicating.

Using an intelligent machine is much like traveling in a foreign country. The machine has its own language, and we often find ourselves trying to express our definition of a problem in terms that the computer can understand. In the same way, the solution reached by the computer is in a foreign language unless it can be translated back to the user's own language.

If the rules of the language conversion (in both directions) can be expressed as a collection of knowledge (symbols and procedures), it is logical to assume that it is possible to develop a technique for a computer to understand the definition of the problem in a human's language and then to communicate the problem solution in the human's language. This is a major subject of natural language interface research. The two primary goals of natural language research are to understand how humans communicate and to create machines with human-like communication skills. This involves four key areas:

Machine translation—Using a computer to translate information from one language to another.

Information retrieval—Using computers to access information on a particular subject from a larger database. Currently this is limited to keyword retrieval. Computers cannot locate information that is similar in context or analogous.

Document generation—Using computers to convert documents in one form or specialized language to that of another. (For example, the automatic conversion of a technical manual on how to use a computer to a manual in a language that could be understood by a doctor who was a generalist).

Computer interfacing—To simplify the interactive interface between the nontechnical user and the computer.

Natural language interfacing is important because it is needed in building expert systems for nontechnical users. Robots and other mechanical forms of artificial intelligence sometimes include extensive natural language interfacing to make them easier to use.

Some of the most interesting examples of natural language interfacing are the Infocom games available for most personal computers. Some of these games use an extensive vocabulary of over 1000 words and permit the user to communicate with the computer using a subset of the English language (Fig. 1-5).

Learning

The parent of a handicapped child may experience growing impatience at a child's lack of ability to learn a simple procedure that must be repeated hundreds of times before it is learned. A good teacher, in contrast, has a remarkable ability to stay with a child through the large number of times it may be necessary to repeat a simple procedure to learn the multiplication tables, a language, a skiing maneuver, or ride a bicycle.

With a computer as the student and the user as the teacher, it is just as aggravating for the user to be required to repeat constantly an initialization each time a program is used, or to repeat a series of steps to accomplish a desired result. Why can't the computer learn even the simplest procedure?

```
Here begins a transcript of interaction with

WISHBRINGER
Interactive Fantasy for Beginners
Copyright (C)1985 Infocom, Inc. All rights reserved.
Release 68 / Serial Number 850501

>LOOK AROUND

South of bridge
This is the south side of a covered bridge that spans the Festeron River.
Paths lead of to the east and west, and a road leads south to the village.

>WALK TO THE WEST

River Outlet
This is where the lake empties into the Festeron River.  A road leads south
along the edge of the lake, and bends east to follow the river bank. A narrow
trail leads upward to the top of Lookout Hill.

>CLIMB UP THE HILL

Lookout Hill
You're standing at the summit of a high, barren hill.  Looking east, you can
see Festeron Village nestled among the trees.  A narrow trail winds down the
north side of the hill, towards the river.

Crowning the hill is the stump that must have been a very large and majestic
oak tree.

A horseshoe is lying in the grass near the stump.

>PICK UP THE HORSESHOE

Taken.

>INVENTORY

You're holding a horseshoe, a gold coin, a piece of chocolate, a conch shell,
a dead seahorse, a violet note and an umbrella.

>LISTEN TO THE CONCH SHELL AND THEN BLOW INTO IT

You can hear the rush of the ocean surf.

The conch shell makes an embarrassing sound.

>SIT ON THE STUMP

The stump affords an excellent view of the surrounding area.

>GO DOWN THE HILL

(climbing off the stump first)
River Outlet
```

Fig. 1-5. Natural language game interface (courtesy Infocom).

This chapter was written using Microsoft Word™. With this program, it is possible to develop several dozen formatting procedures for characters, paragraphs, and titling that could be repeated for each document (chapter) and even for other books. You can "teach" these to the program through the use of "style sheets." Once taught, they are accessible with no more than a few keystrokes. The spelling corrector, in addition, seems to have a type of native intelligence. If I misspell a word, I can tell the checker to find the word it thinks I meant to use, saving a trip to the dictionary. New words can be learned and added to the electronic dictionary.

Today there is a growing awareness that the ability to learn must be added to almost every application program a user might employ. A decade ago, most of the data processing in a company was done in a data processing department by programmers. The programmers were, in effect, a priesthood between the mysterious computer and those who used the data and made decisions.

The personal computer has, effectively, begun to change the relationship between the user and the computer, and thus the role of the programmer. Rather than forcing a user to learn the intricacies of the program operation, the computer must learn the intricacies of how the user communicates a particular problem to the computer. Products such as spreadsheet programs, database managers, and word processors will be adding more artificial intelligence capabilities (learning, natural language interfaces, and knowledge system aspects) as the price of memory and technology continues to drop. This does not eliminate the need for programmers, but rather changes their role in how they relate to the computer and the user.

Cognitive Modeling

Cognitive modeling involves the development of theories, concepts, and models that are used to study the human mind and how it functions. The results not only help in the diagnosis and cure of mental diseases, but also help us in understanding the problem-solving process. This does not lead, necessarily, to the conclusion that the best computers are modeled on the human mind. It does help us, however, in defining what type of computers are needed, how computers can be designed to extend the human thinking process, and how to help us to be more efficient in solving problems.

Vision and Robotics

From the early automata of the fourteenth century, man has been fascinated by the idea of building electrical and mechanical devices that could function as a human. Perhaps the most famous of the early automata was Vaucanson's duck (1738) that could beat its wings, drink water, eat grain, and even excrete using an elaborate digestion process.

Today robots have already relieved the industrial worker of many routine jobs, performing almost flawlessly without coffee breaks or sick leave, and never striking. At an IBM production facility in the sixties I watched as machines designed and built the next generation of computers with almost no human intervention. Today the Macintosh and IBM PC computers are built this same way.

Robotics is that branch of artificial intelligence research that is concerned with enabling computers to see and manipulate objects in their environment. Robotic research is primarily directed in three areas:

1. The development of sensors (particularly visual sensors) and the understanding of sensing systems.
2. The development of manipulators and the controls for these systems.
3. The development of heuristics for object- and space-oriented environmental problem solving (planning).

In the future, robots will become more intelligent. Isaac Asimov, writing in 1950, developed the now-classic "Three Laws of Robotics," which became the nucleus of many of his robotics stories that teased us with the social and ethical issues of using robots:

1. A robot may not injure a human being, or, through inaction, allow a human being to come to harm.
2. A robot must obey the orders given to it by human beings except when such orders would conflict with the First Law.
3. A robot must protect its own existence as long as such protection does not conflict with the First or Second Law.

WHERE WE ARE TODAY

Expert systems on mainframe computers can already mimic experts of some knowledge domains. Digital Equipment Corporation (DEC) uses expert systems to analyze prospective customer needs for computers and to configure systems to meet those needs. This has already proven cost-effective, saving the company $200,000 per month. Even more important is the improved quality of the installation procedure. For example, before using expert systems the lack of a $10 cable in an installation could critically delay a customer's use of the system and cost DEC many dollars in installation time. The use of a computer-controlled installation procedure, tailored to the unique system and listing all the necessary components and procedures, insures correct installation the first time. PROSPECTOR, another expert system, has located a molybdenum deposit worth $100 million that none of the nine experts who helped build PROSPECTOR's knowledgebase had been able to find. MYCIN does medical diagnosis that is comparable to the expert.

Most researchers consider personal computers to be too limited in their computing capability for most types of productive expert systems. Artificially intelligent machines require megabytes of memory and fast processors. Processes may need to be occurring in parallel with other processes. The languages used with computers still reflect, perhaps too much, the procedures that are more relevant to numerical processing rather than the symbolic processing techniques required for the solution of many problems. Natural language interfaces to most application programs are almost nonexistent except for a few primitive products such as Microrim's CLOUT and Excalibur's Savvy. Industrial robots have begun to invade the industrial scene, but it will be years before household robots become as common as pets.

But researchers remain undaunted. The reason is easy to understand. The rapid drop in the cost of technology and the development of new processors and languages more adaptable for symbolic processing will soon make artificial intelligence cost-effective for the solution of many problems. The better expert systems took 10 man-years or more to develop. In other words, much of what will be realized on personal computers in the next decade is already in the minds of developers in the laboratories today. Even with today's primitive technological tools, we can begin to create the models and dreams of the future. The theories, models, software, and hardware we create today will become steps to systems that can do productive work in the future.

One example of how artificial intelligence techniques will influence personal computer software in the future is Ansa's new database manager called Paradox. This program is not marketed as a knowledge system, but rather uses artificial intelligence techniques to control a hidden agenda. Using this approach, Paradox can easily be used by someone without database, programming, or knowledge engineering experience to solve knowledge problems. The user defines the problem by given examples, and Paradox then uses heuristics (see Chapter 2) to write its own procedure to solve the problem.

EXERCISES

1. Repeat the chunking exercise mentioned in this chapter with the following sentence. Look at the sentence for 10 seconds, then close the book and write it on a piece of paper:

   Knowledge engineering is a very young science and still lacks adequate standards.

   Now try the same experiment with this nonsense sentence:

   Able time work often loves Sam science discipline lacks adequate strange color.

   In the first case, you were probably sucessful in remembering all the words, even though there were 12 chunks—quite beyond the range of short-term memory. Why was this possible? Why did you fail with a sentence of the same word length in the second case? What does this say about how we chunk knowledge?
2. What makes knowledge valuable? What determines the value of knowledge?
3. What are some particular functional aspects of the human mind in an professional expert? In a problem-solver? In a creative person? In a teacher? Which of these can be improved with discipline and learning, and which are an inherent part of the personality from birth?

Chapter 2

Introduction to Knowledge Systems

T HE DEVELOPMENT OF KNOWLEDGE SYSTEMS IS A PARTICULAR BRANCH OF AR-
tificial intelligence that is concerned with the application of computers to the solution of problems that normally require the use of human expertise. In this chapter you
will gain some insights on the uses and limitations of knowledge systems as well as
gaining some understanding of the basic concepts of symbolic processing.

WHAT IS A KNOWLEDGE SYSTEM?

Edward Feigenbaum, a leading researcher in knowledge systems at Stanford
University, has defined an expert system as:

"... an intelligent computer program that uses knowledge and inference
procedures to solve problems that are difficult enough to require significant human expertise for their solution."

Artificial intelligence is still a young science, and few standards exist. This book
will make no distinction between expert and knowledge systems, using the above definition to apply to both. In a *knowledge system,* the rules (or *heuristics*) that are used for
solving problems in a particular domain are stored in a *knowledgebase.* Problems are
then stated to the system in terms of certain facts that are known about a particular
situation. The knowledge system then attempts to draw a conclusion from the facts
using the knowledgebase (see Fig. 2-1). *Heuristics* are the rules of judgment that are
used to make decisions from known facts.

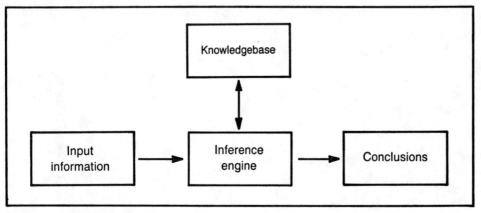

Fig. 2-1. The knowledge system.

For example, the following facts that might be determined about a patient for a medical diagnosis:

> The salivary glands are swollen.
> There is a high temperature.
> There is very little saliva.
> The lymph node in the neck is enlarged.
> It is very painful or impossible to suck on a lemon.

From this a doctor might determine that the patient has the mumps. The same decision could be reached using a computerized knowledge system if the proper rules (heuristics) were stored in the system. We could then say that the quality of an expert system is determined by the size and quality of the knowledgebase (rules or heuristics). The system functions in a cyclic mode: selecting (requesting) tests or data, making observations, interpreting the results, assimilating knowledge, making temporary hypotheses using rules, and then selecting more tests or data (Fig. 2-2). This continues until there is enough information for a conclusion.

The simpler knowledge systems function in a dialog, or what is called a *consultation mode*. After the system is started, it asks the user a series of questions about the problem, each of which can be answered by "yes" or "no." The answers are used to establish facts from which the conclusion can be drawn (Fig. 2-3).

At any given time, three types of knowledge exist in the system:

1. *Structural knowledge*—This is the static knowledge about domain of interest. As new knowledge is obtained, this knowledge does not change.
2. *Structural dynamic knowledge*—This is dynamic knowledge about the domain. This changes as more information is learned about the domain. In the previous example, the relationship of the four facts to the conclusion is structural dynamic knowledge.
3. *Working knowledge*—This is knowledge that applies to a specific problem or consultation. In the previous example, the fact that the patient has a high fever is working knowledge.

18

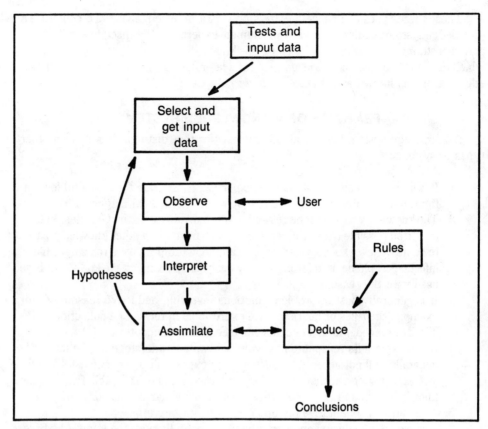

Fig. 2-2. Using the knowledge system.

```
(Initial dialog establishes patient name, age, culture site, and
other specifics)

9) Was a smear examined at the time the specimen for the pending
csf culture was obtained?
YES

10) Were any organisms seen on the smear of the specimen submitted
as pending csf culture?
NO

11) Have there been POSITIVE cultures yielding organisms about
which you will NOT be seeking advice?
YES

12) Do you suspect the patient may have an infection at a site
from which you have not obtained culture specimens?
NO

13) Is the patient receiving therapy with any antimicrobial agent?
```

Fig. 2-3. Sample of a portion of a knowledge system consultation session.

These three types of knowledge are stored in a knowledgebase. To construct a knowledge system requires interviewing human experts in the discipline of interest and then storing, organizing, and indexing this knowledge into the knowledgebase from which the knowledge can be retrieved easily at a later date. A person who builds knowledge systems is known as a *knowledge engineer.*

FEATURES OF A KNOWLEDGE SYSTEM

A knowledge system has certain characteristics that distinguishes it from other types of systems:

1. It is limited to a specific domain of expertise. A program that is useful for configuring computer systems would not work for medical diagnosis.
2. The knowledgebase and the reasoning mechanism are distinct entities. In fact, it is often possible to use the reasoning mechanism with other knowledgebases to create a new expert system. For example, a program used to analyze blood infections could be used for pulmonary analysis by changing the knowledgebase used with the reasoning mechanism.
3. It is generally best at problem solutions involving deductive reasoning. For example, the rules or heuristics are expressible in terms of a collection of IF-THEN antecedents and conclusions (see the next chapter).
4. It can explain its reasoning in a way that can be understood by the user. We generally will not accept the answer of an expert unless we can ask "Why?" and expect a logical answer. In the same way, we should be able to query the knowledge system as to how it reached a particular conclusion.
5. The output is qualitative (as opposed to quantitative).
6. It is modular in design and can grow incrementally with the knowledgebase.

USING KNOWLEDGE SYSTEMS

Applications for knowledge systems can be grouped into several major categories: medical diagnostics, prediction, planning, interpretation, monitor/control, mechanical and electrical diagnostics, and instruction.

Medical Diagnostics

Diagnostic systems are used to relate behavioral faults with the causes of the behavior. The most famous medical diagnostic system is probably MYCIN, which is used for the diagnosis and treatment of meningitis and bacteremia infections. It was originally developed at Stanford University during the mid-seventies. The system now performs at the level of a human expert, and the development has been extended to other medical disciplines.

Prediction

Prediction systems are used to predict future results from a given state. Summa's "Winning on Wall Street" software can help you analyze the stock market and uses statistics and algorithms to help plan future investments. It is *not* a knowledge system;

it uses procedures and algorithms like any traditional computer program. Although there is yet no knowledge system available that can enable you to make plenty of money on the stock market, prediction systems *can* be used today for weather forecasting, agricultural analysis, and traffic flow prediction. Even a personal computer can do very accurate local weather forecasting using a simple knowledge system.

Planning

Planning systems are used to achieve specific goals when many variables are involved. At the Dallas Infomart, first-time computer buyers can sit at any of 13 work stations in the lobby and receive a free 15-minute consultation that advises them on the right computer system for their needs and budget. The system uses the Texas Instruments *Personal Consultant* and was designed by Boeing Computer Services Company of Seattle. Boeing is also using expert systems to plan a deep-space station (as well as for diagnosing airplane engine problems and repairing helicopters).

Digital Equipment Corporation's XCON is an expert system that is used to configure and reconfigure VAX systems to customer specifications. DEC is now developing a larger XSEL system (which includes the XCON knowledgebase) that will be used by salespeople to assist customers in configuring their systems. Unlike XCON, XSEL is interactive.

Interpretation

Interpretation systems are able to establish certain conclusions from observed data. PROSPECTOR, one of the more famous of the interpretive systems, has been programmed with the knowledge of nine experts. Using their combined expertise, PROSPECTOR has been able to locate ore deposits worth millions of dollars, deposits that eluded all nine of the experts. Another interpretive system, HASP/SIAP, infers the locations and types of ships in the Pacific Ocean using acoustic sensors.

Monitoring and Control

Knowledge systems can also be used as intelligent monitoring systems to make decisions using data from many input sources. These systems already exist for nuclear power plants, aircraft traffic control, and medical monitoring. They can also be used in financial monitoring of a corporation to help management make critical decisions faster.

Mechanical and Electrical Diagnosis

Knowledge systems can be used for the repair of mechanical and electrical systems (automobiles, diesel locomotives, etc.) as well as for debugging a variety of problems in computer hardware and software. Several years ago, General Electric realized that their resident expert in diesel locomotive repair was retiring within a few years; they needed to capture his expertise before he left. Their decision was to build an expert system around the engineer's knowledge during his last few years on the job.

Instruction

Knowledge systems can also be used as a part of computer-aided tutorials. The system represents another system's (student's) performance, and then interprets the system's (student's) behavior. The knowledgebase of the performer is then altered, based on the performance. One example is the computerized strategy game that increases its complexity and skill level automatically as the player grows more proficient at the game.

One of the most interesting of the learning expert systems was Douglas Lenat's EURISKO system, which used simple heuristics. It was entered to the national war game Traveller T.C.S., in which the object is to design a fleet that can defeat an opponent under a rigid set of rules. EURISKO produced a fleet of small, fast attack vessels and one ship that was extremely fast and tiny. EURISKO won, and continued to win for three years in succession—despite the fact that the rules were changed each year in an attempt to prevent it from winning.

Most expert systems include expertise that classifies them as really more than one type. An instruction system, for example, may include both diagnostic and planning aspects. It diagnoses the learner's abilities in key areas and then plans its tutorial based on this diagnosis. A control system may include monitoring, diagnostic, predictive, and planning features. A home security control system might monitor an environment, diagnose what has happened (*a window is broken*), predict what will happen (*a burglar is planning to enter the house*), and plan an action (*call the police*).

APPLICATIONS FOR KNOWLEDGE SYSTEMS

Certain applications are more suitable for solutions with knowledge systems than others:

1. Knowledge systems should be used primarily when the data and knowledge are reliable and do not change with time.
2. The space (or domain) of possible solutions should be relatively small.
3. The problem solution should involve formal reasoning. Knowledge systems today are still poor alternatives when the problem solution must be reached by analogy or abstraction (the human mind is much better at this). Traditional computer programs are better than knowledge systems when the problem solution involves a procedural analysis. Knowledge systems are best at problem solutions that use formal reasoning.
4. There should be at least one acknowledged expert, who should be able to explain his or her knowledge and the methods used to apply knowledge to the problem.

Table 2-1 is a comparison of application domains that are suitable and unsuitable for expert systems. In general, the following types of tasks should not be done with expert systems:

Mathematical applications—These generally are solved using formulas and procedural analysis.

Table 2-1. Overview of Knowledge System Domains.

Suitable	Unsuitable
No procedural algorithm exists, but heuristics are available.	Algorithmic solution exists.
Only a few experts exist.	No experts or many experts exist.
Available data is noisy.	Precise facts and procedures known.
Diagnostic, interpretive, or predictive.	Calculative.
Problems solved using formal reasoning.	Problems solved using procedural reasoning, analogy, or intuition.
Knowledge is static (does not change with time).	Knowledge is dynamic (changes with time).

Perceptual problems—Perceptual problems are generally solved using numerical techniques.

Problems in which no knowledge exists—If no knowledge exists, it would be impossible to create the knowledge base.

LIMITATIONS OF KNOWLEDGE SYSTEMS

Even the best of today's knowledge systems that operate efficiently on the larger mainframe and minicomputers have limitations when compared with the human expert:

1. Most of today's knowledge systems are not very user-oriented. Unless you've had some experience with knowledge systems, you will find them difficult to use effectively. Many can only be used by the expert who created the knowledgebase.
2. The question-and-answer dialog generally used by such systems to reach their conclusions is often slow. With MYCIN, for example, the doctor can (and often must) make a decision more quickly than can be done using MYCIN.
3. The knowledge system's ability does not degrade gracefully at the edge of the system's expertise.
4. The biggest problem still remains that of getting the knowledge of the expert into a codified form that can be understood and used by a computer effectively.
5. Today's knowledge systems do not learn and lack common sense. A house cat

can learn it should not be on the couch and a child can learn that it will get wet if a glass of water is spilled; yet, if I spill coffee on a computer console, there is not even enough common sense in the computer to move the keyboard out of the way.

6. Expert systems cannot be used with large domains. They should be limited to domains in which an expert can reach a conclusion in anywhere from a few minutes to a few hours.

7. Expert systems cannot be used in domains in which no expert exists (such as for astrology).

8. Expert systems can only be used for tasks that are primarily cognitive. Tennis and bicycle riding would not be applicable, but you might use an expert system to analyze football teams.

9. Human experts can generally apply intuition and common sense to solve problems when no formal solution or analogy exists. A bank executive, for example, once visited a South American bank that had applied for a loan and spent days analyzing their books. By all formal reasoning, the bank appeared a good candidate for a loan. The executive, however, recommended that his bank reject their loan request because of his experience and intuition about the request. A few weeks later the South American bank went bankrupt.

A career analysis system in which the number of "solutions" consists of thousands of job opportunities with many variables that change with time would not be a good application for a knowledge system. It would be better to use a database with a natural language interface.

ADVANTAGES OF THE KNOWLEDGE SYSTEM

The knowledge system has several advantages over the human expert:

1. The knowledge system is not biased.
2. The knowledge system does not jump to conclusions.
3. The knowledge system applies a systematic process, considering all details, often working to the best possible alternative.
4. The knowledgebase can be very, very large. A medical doctor has a limited knowledgebase, and if the data is not retrieved constantly and repeatedly it becomes lost in the human mind and inaccessible. A rural doctor, for example, may fail to recognize a specific disease because it is rare or he has never seen it before. This would not be true of a computerized expert system. Once stored, the knowledge is always accessible.
5. Knowledge systems are not "noisy." An expert is easily influenced by knowledge and perceptions that do not relate to the specific problem being analyzed. Knowledge systems, unencumbered with knowledge outside of the domain of interest, are inherently less noisy.

Knowledge systems may eventually become recognized by users as a type of publishing medium—a new way of recording and disseminating knowledge. As with any other type of computer program, they do not replace the human mind in solving problems but are more like the lever, enabling the user to solve problems faster and more effectively than could be done without the computer. The knowledge system does not replace the expert; rather, it is a tool in the expert's hand.

PERSONAL COMPUTERS AS KNOWLEDGE SYSTEMS

Knowledge systems almost invariably require large amounts of computer memory and fast processors. Most of the computer memory is used to store the knowledgebase and the heuristics that are used to reach the conclusions. The actual "program" is quite small. (In later chapters, when you actually begin using the knowledge system described in this book, you will discover that the entire program takes only about 30,000 bytes of computer memory on the IBM PC—far less than most word processors, spreadsheet programs, or database managers on this same computer.)

Large amounts of memory are needed, however, to store the knowledgebase for knowledge systems. A personal computer with 640,000 bytes of memory might be limited to a few hundred rules and about two dozen conclusions. At the current time this limits personal knowledge systems (such as the one in this book) to very small domains, developing prototypes for larger systems, and teaching knowledge system concepts. Here are some possible applications for a knowledge system on a personal computer:

- ☐ Calculating postage and the best way to mail packages based on the weight and destination.
- ☐ Analyzing alternative phone services for the service with the lowest cost for a particular application.
- ☐ Automotive repair diagnosis.
- ☐ Analyzing customer computer needs and configuring small computer systems.
- ☐ Local weather forecasting.
- ☐ Security systems.
- ☐ Solar heating systems.
- ☐ Analyzing trip reports for corporate deductions.
- ☐ Analyzing personal investment strategies.
- ☐ Electrophoresis interpretation.

The size of the knowledgebase does not necessarily determine the cost-effectiveness of the system. Sholom M. Weiss and Casimir A. Kulikowski, at Rutgers University, and Robert S. Galen at Columbia University collaborated on the development of a microprocessor-based electrophoresis interpretation system in 1980 that used only 82 rules. This system was found to produce results that were 100 percent acceptable.

The limitations of personal computer knowledge systems are imposed by the memory size and processor speed, and are really only a temporary constraint. Today the development of knowledge systems on personal computers is rapidly evolving, with now over a hundred companies aggressively developing microcomputer knowledge system products to meet the needs of users.

There are some interesting parallels between the development of knowledge systems for personal computers and the development of database managers for these same systems a few years ago. When the first database management systems were designed for personal computers, designers used software that was already operational on the larger computers and tried to convert these products to the microcomputer. These products all failed against a relatively new type of database management system called dBASE II—which did not even conform to the standard definition of a relational database manager. Many of the theories used with the larger machines were applicable, but the concept of *how the database manager was used* was radically different.

In the development of productive knowledge systems for personal computers, one wonders if history is repeating itself. As this is written, one of the most popular knowledge system products for the personal computer is Expert-Ease, a knowledge system that functions quite differently from the standard definition of a knowledge system. The winner (or winners) in the product race may well be those who have the creativity to search for new methods of systematically applying knowledge and knowledge engineering techniques to problems. Almost all of today's expert systems require programming expertise to use. If expert systems are ever to become useful tools for businesspeople and specialists, they must evolve to a form that is a natural extension of the language and methods of the expert rather than the programmer.

HEURISTIC VERSUS ALGORITHMIC COMPUTING

At present, the computer is used primarily to solve problems in which a definite procedure exists for the solution of the problem. Such a procedure is said to be an *algorithm.* An *algorithm* is a systematic procedure that can be used to solve a problem. It guarantees a correct outcome, and will repeatedly give the same solution. The calculation of your monthly payment for a car loan, for example, involves the use of such an algorithm or defined procedure. Certain input data is required: the amount of the loan, the number of monthly payments, and the interest rate. From this, the procedure (algorithm) can calculate the monthly payment. The same input data always gives the same output result, and there will always be an answer.

In contrast, repairing your automobile involves the use of another approach to problem solution. Suppose, for example, your car does not start one morning—the starter motor does not even turn over. Since the starter motor does not turn over, you assume the electrical system is at fault. You would then try to find what part of the electrical system is not working: the starter motor, regulator, battery, or alternator. If you suspect the battery, you would check the battery connections, the water level, and the battery charge. Eventually you find the specific cause of the problem.

In solving this problem, you used *heuristics,* techniques that improve the efficiency of a problem-solving process, even though their use cannot be strictly justified. Heuristics reduce the time required to solve the problem by reducing the search path in a large problem space. In the automotive example, there would be no need to check the radiator water level, since the initial steps rule out the cooling system as the problem. Although heuristics do not guarantee a solution, they can be used to reduce the time required to solve extremely complex problems. Heuristics are rather like filters for a pattern-matching process, enabling the system to focus on a few key patterns to save time in the problem-solving process.

The automobile repair problem does not lend itself to a solution using procedural methods such as those generally employed by conventional programmers. The nature of the problem is much different from that of calculating the monthly payment for a car loan. The automobile repair problem is relatively unstructured, and it is almost impossible to define any procedure that could be used to complete the repair with assurance. We could consider the automotive repair problem as a search through a defined state space, with each state a candidate for partial solution to the final solution. Each time we move to a new state, we hope we are moving closer to the final goal, but there is no guarantee we are actually moving to our goal. We can, however, define a heuristic that can help us to minimize our movements through the state space and, with luck, ensure that each movement takes us closer to the ultimate goal of getting the car started.

During the early days of artificial intelligence research, most of the research was directed toward developing heuristics for solving problems that were not well-defined. The focus is changing. Most of the knowledge system research today is on developing means of identifying and organizing (or "chunking") knowledge into a form that can be used to solve poorly structured problems that elude even the experts.

SYMBOLIC VERSUS NUMERIC PROCESSING

Almost all of our computers today are very adept at numeric processing and can outperform even the human mind when the reliability and speed of numerical processing is at stake. The human mind, in contrast, is far more adept at the processing of symbols than even the best computers.

A human chess player uses symbolic processing to win the game. The board is evaluated by viewing it as a collection of symbolic patterns or chunks. The player compares these patterns against chess patterns already stored in his or her long-term memory. Human players work toward creating certain patterns on the board that have value toward creating a checkmate. The chess-playing computer, in contrast, is slow and inefficient at symbolic processing, and tries to win by analyzing a large number of possible moves (a feat at which it is much better than the human) and using some heuristics to minimize the number of moves that must be analyzed.

The development of expert systems is an attempt to develop symbolic processing capability that humans use to solve problems on the computer to equal the expert within a limited domain. A *domain* is identifiable related knowledge.

Systems also can be categorized as *prescriptive* or *descriptive*. The computerized chess program uses prescriptive processing, using predefined algorithms and procedures to evaluate each move and then choose the move that has the best value. Heuristics are used to reduce the number of moves that must be evaluated. In a descriptive system, in contrast, problem-solving is driven not by procedures but by knowledge that is stored in a knowledgebase. A procedure may exist, but it is not explicit. This concept will become clearer in the next chapter. Most computer languages such as BASIC, Pascal, C, and Fortran are all designed to support prescriptive problem solving. As we shall see in Chapters 6 and 10, it is necessary to develop special languages (and hardware features) if we wish to support descriptive problem solving.

We can define a *symbol* as any component of a knowledge structure. Here are some examples of symbols:

Four
Jack

Sparrow
3.1416
Daughter

One important precursor of any artificial intelligence work is the development of formal languages for symbolic computation. In Chapter 4 you will see how such formal languages can be used to express symbolic relationships.

DIVERGENT VERSUS CONVERGENT REASONING

Traditional computer systems are best at divergent reasoning. Using a small amount of input data, these computers can produce an almost infinite amount of output data (results). Humans and knowledge systems are best at convergent reasoning—producing a few results from a large amount of data. A scientist, for example, may spend years analyzing knowledge about a subject to draw a single conclusion that may win a Nobel prize.

SUMMARY

The knowledge system is a distinctive type of computer system that differs in many ways from the traditional computer system. It uses declarative processing, symbolic processing, and convergent reasoning (see Table 2-2). The emerging architecture for these computers has yet to be defined, but will involve parallel processing, in contrast with the sequential processing of today's computers. The most significant contribution of expert systems will be the codification of knowledge and help in understanding the processes used to solve problems, particularly problems that are poorly structured and defined.

EXERCISES

1. In each of the following applications, tell whether a knowledge system or traditional computer system is more applicable and why:

   a. Inventory Control
   b. Computer Repair
   c. Classification of biological entities (birds, flowers, etc.)
   d. Menu planning
   e. Blood chemistry analysis interpretation for nutritional deficiencies
   f. Curriculum planning
   g. Investment analysis (financial planning)

2. Identify an application with which you are familiar that requires an expert today. Could this expert use an expert system to solve problems in this application? Why or why not?
3. Imagine an application in which the knowledge available to the expert continues to grow until it is beyond the capability of the human mind to use effectively. What

Table 2-2. Feature Comparison: Traditional Computers and Knowledge Systems.

Traditional Computer Systems	Knowledge Systems
Procedure-driven control flow	Data-driven control flow
Numerical processing	Symbolic processing
Divergent reasoning	Convergent reasoning
von Neumann architecture	Non-von Neumann architecture
Algorithmic processing	Heuristic processing
Maintained by programmers	Maintained by knowledge engineers
Sequential processing	Interactive and parallel processing
Structured design process (linear)	Interactive design process (cyclic)

happens to the knowledge at this point and what happens to how it is used?
4. What task do you perform today requiring little expertise on your part that would have required an expert a few decades ago?

Chapter 3

The Components
of a Knowledge System

T HIS CHAPTER DESCRIBES A PARTICULAR TYPE OF KNOWLEDGE SYSTEM CALLED a *production system*. It could also be called a *rule-based system,* or a *pattern matching inference system.* The components of the system, as well as its operation will be described. Finally, the chapter will review briefly some of the commercial products that are built using this model. In the next chapter alternative types of knowledge systems are reviewed.

THE PRODUCTION SYSTEM

A production system is considerably different from the classic von Neumann architecture of most computers. For the von Neumann architecture, a single memory is used for both the programs and data. A program is a sequence of procedural steps, stored in memory, that operates on the data to achieve a desired result. The program can even operate on itself as data, modifying itself as it executes. The production system, in contrast, has almost no procedural component and is mostly data-driven or descriptive. A production system consists of three key components: the rulebase, the working memory, and the inference engine. Three additional components are generally included as support tools and to provide a more intelligent interface with the user: a knowledge acquisition module, a natural language interface, and an explanatory interface (see Fig. 3-1).

The Rule Memory or Rulebase

If we examine how an automobile expert would approach the auto repair problem

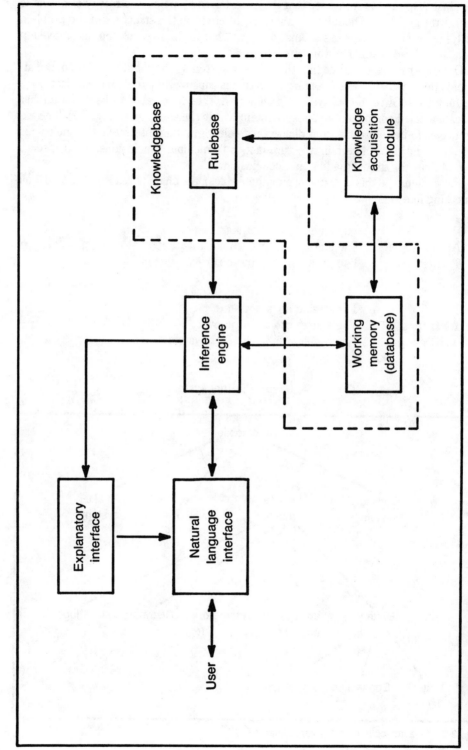

Fig. 3-1. The production-type knowledge system.

31

in the last chapter, you would see that the expert uses a particular strategy or heuristic to solve the problem. Though the expert might envision the structure of the problem poorly, he or she nonetheless seems to know what to do at each step and moves in a very organized manner toward a solution.

Once the expert identifies that the primary system (automobile) has failed, the attempt is then made to identify a subsystem that is causing the problem (electrical, cooling, fuel, etc.). Once the subsystem is identified, then he or she works down further to locate a failed component or subsubsystem within the subsystem (Fig. 3-2). The expert seems to be following an implicit set of rules, drawing intermediate conclusions when the conditions of certain rules are met. Intermediate conclusions, in turn, serve as conditions for drawing additional conclusions.

For example, in this case (using simplified rules), the chain of reasoning would look something like this:

IF   The engine does not start.
AND   The starter motor does not turn over.
THEN   The problem is in the electrical system.

IF   The engine does not start.
AND   The starter motor turns over.
THEN   The problem is in the fuel system.

IF   The problem is in the fuel system.

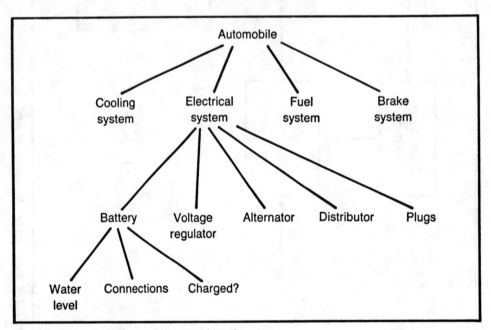

Fig. 3-2. The automobile repair system hierarchy.

```
IF    The engine does not start.
                                          ⎫
AND   The starter motor does not turn over. ⎬ Antecedent
                                          ⎭

THEN  There is a problem in the electrical system. ——— Consequence
```

Fig. 3-3. The production rule.

AND   The fuel gauge indicates there is no fuel.
CONCLUSION   The gas tank is empty.

IF   The problem is in the electrical system.
AND   The battery connections are not tight.
CONCLUSION   The battery connections are loose.

Our knowledge system, then, must have as one component a "rule memory" that consists of a number of situation-action rules, each of which is in IF-THEN form. These are called *production rules.* Each rule contains two parts. The first is called the *antecedent* or *premise,* and consists of clauses linked together by logical connectives such as AND and OR. The second part, the *consequent* or *conclusion,* consists of one or more clauses that represent a conclusion or an action to be taken (Fig. 3-3). The antecedent represents a *pattern,* and the rule is *triggered* if the facts in the working memory (see next section) match the antecedent. When the action is performed, the conclusion is added to the working memory and the rule is said to *fire.*

Each rule in this simple system consists of an *attribute* and *value.* In the first case, for example, we could say "does not start" is a value and "engine" is an attribute (see Fig. 3-4). Each rule consists of one or more attribute-value pairs and a conclusion.

This production model used for the rulebase is essentially the stimulus-response model that has been used in psychology and automaton theory before the advent of knowledge systems. Some scientists consider this model as the basis for animal behavior.

The Working Memory or Database

Another part of knowledge system is the *working memory or database.* This memory contains a set of facts that describe the current situation and contains all the attribute-

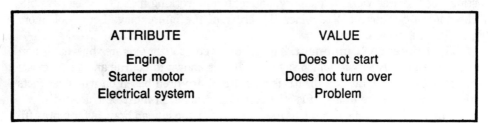

ATTRIBUTE	VALUE
Engine	Does not start
Starter motor	Does not turn over
Electrical system	Problem

Fig. 3-4. Attribute-value (A-V) pairs.

value relationships that have been established during the consultation. These change with time, becoming more and more extensive as additional rules fire.

When this example was started, only a few facts were in the working memory: The engine does not start and the starting motor does not turn over. Soon a second fact is added: The electrical system is at fault. Eventually, the final conclusion is added to the working memory. The working memory or database contains the dynamic part of the knowledgebase that changes with time and the environment. New facts are added to the working memory by inferring them from the existing facts and the rules. The knowledgebase consists of the rulebase and the working memory.

In a *monotonic* system, the facts (stored in the working memory) are static and are not changed during the course of problem solving. In a *nonmonotonic* system, the existing facts are modified or deleted from the working memory. A knowledge system that is used to plan future financial strategies for a company is a good example of a nonmonotonic system. Data is entered to the system that projects certain conclusions, after which you may wish to change the data to alter the conclusions. In such a system, you are changing the attribute values in the working memory. This, in turn, will undo certain conclusions that have already been reached and are a part of the working memory. As a result, there must be some way to retrace and undo decisions that are affected by the new attribute values.

The Inference Engine or Rule Interpreter

The *inference engine* or *rule interpreter* performs two tasks. First, it examines the existing facts in the working memory and the rules in the rulebase, adding new facts to the working memory (database) when possible. Second, it determines in which order the rules are scanned and fired. The inference engine conducts the consultation with the user, keeping the user informed about the conclusions it has reached and asks the user for information when it lacks sufficient data in the working memory to fire additional rules.

In some systems the inference engine reasons forward, using the facts in memory to eventually reach a conclusion. In other systems, the inference engine reasons backward, trying first one conclusion and then another until it can find the supporting facts for a particular conclusion from the working memory or user. In most knowledge systems, the inference engine is a relatively small program. Almost all of the computer memory space is used for the rules.

We could consider, then, that the inference engine consists of two components: inference and control. The inference component handles the first task, examining existing rules and the working memory, adding to the working memory when possible. The control component determines the order of the inferencing. Let's look more specifically at each of these.

The Inference Component. The inference component operates by what is normally called *modus ponens*, which says this: If A is known to be true and a rule exists that says "IF A, THEN B", then B is true. Rules are fired based on whatever facts are available. If a premise is true, the resulting conclusion must be true.

Although in principle this seems easy, in practice the human brain is far more efficient. Take, for instance, the simple fact:

Mary had a little lamb.

This could either imply a simple act of ownership or could imply a remarkable achievement. Here are two other facts that are interpreted in radically different fashion:

Fruit flies like a banana.
Time flies like an arrow.

The meaning of these facts become even more complex when used as part of productions by *modus ponens* to draw conclusions. For example, look at the following production:

IF	A white car is easy to see at night.
AND	Jack's car is white.
CONCLUSION	Jack's car is easy to see at night.

This rule is relatively easy for even a child to understand, but the conclusion cannot be reached by even the simplest of today's expert systems or any type of animal. Here is another example:

IF	Susan went to Silvia's Restaurant.
AND	Susan ordered a steak.
AND	Susan paid the cashier for a steak dinner.
CONCLUSION	Susan ate a steak dinner at Silvia's Restaurant.

Again, the conclusion is relatively easy for any human to grasp, but is beyond the ability of today's knowledge systems without additional rules. In summary, a human can draw a large number of conclusions using the very large knowledgebase of the human mind; artificial knowledge systems can only draw a relatively small number of conclusions from a given set of rules.

Second, the inference component must be able to deal with missing information. In our automotive repair example, the fact that the battery connections were loose may not be a part of the working memory when the consultation is started. The inference engine may prompt the user for information about the connections, but suppose the user does not know? The inference engine must be able to continue reasoning, eventually reaching a conclusion even with limited information. The conclusion may not be as certain, but the program should not stop (as a conventional program for a bank loan would) because certain input information is missing.

The Control Component. The control component of the inference engine determines the order in which the rules are scanned and whether facts can be changed during the consultation (monotonic versus nonmonotonic reasoning). The control component has four functions:

1. Matching—Matches the pattern of the rules against the pattern of the known facts.

2. Selection—Determines which is the most relevant rule to fire based on the currently known facts (conflict resolution).
3. Firing—When the pattern is matched, the rule is fired.
4. Action—The working memory is updated, and the conclusion added to the known facts in the working memory. An output action may be initiated (such as in a security system).

The control module operates in cycles. In each cycle the existing rules are scanned to see which ones have premises that match the known facts in the working memory. The control module also decides the order of the scanning. The rule is then fired, with the conclusion added to the working memory. The cycle is then repeated.

Only one rule can fire in each cycle. If more than one rule matches the facts, the control module must have some method of deciding which rule to fire. An illustration of this control cycle is shown in Fig. 3-5. Knowledge in the working memory or database is used to examine the rulebase, and the premises that match the rule are selected as the conflict set. The control strategy is used to resolve this conflict, resulting in a single execution set. This rule fires, which results in action: The conclusion is added to the working memory, the control strategy is changed, or other event activated (alarm sounded, procedure initiated, motor turned on, etc.).

New knowledge, then, can alter the control strategy. If a knowledge system is playing chess, for example, it might have an offensive strategy toward which it is moving as it makes each move. If you can make the proper moves against the computer, the computer must shift to a defense strategy (at least temporarily), and then perhaps return to a new offensive strategy at a later time. The changes in the control strategy are based on the conclusions reached after examining the board positions (working knowledge in the database) and rules of the game (static structural knowledge) and structural dynamic knowledge (heuristics).

There are really no procedures, then, that determine the path through the problem space to the problem solution and no real guarantee that any solution exists at all. It is as though the path through the problem space is controlled by hidden or virtual procedures. In some cases these are called *demons,* which are virtual or hidden procedures that lurk about the system and activate rules when they are asked to help—rather friendly, as demons go.

The demon concept came from "Maxwell's demon," used in thermodynamics to explain entropy, and Oliver Selfridge's early Pandemonium model of the human system, which viewed the operation of a biological system as a pattern-action demon model. At a more practical level, researchers refer to the control procedures as *nondeterministic,* i.e., the path through the problem space is data-dependent.

The design of the control section of the inference engine involves some decision as to how the rules will be searched for triggering. This will be discussed in the section in this chapter on control strategies. In frame-based systems (Chapter 4), control can be done using demons that can be a part of the frame slots; we will learn more about them when the frame systems are discussed.

The Knowledge Acquisition Module

The knowledge acquisition module is used to add new rules to the rulebase and

36

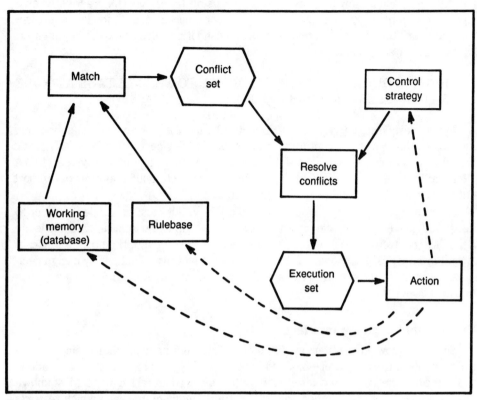

Fig. 3-5. The control cycle.

to modify existing rules. It must be able to save the rules in the rulebase in a form that can be used by the inference engine. In the simplest case, the knowledge acquisition module is no more than an editor or word processor for entering the rules to a file. In a more complex system, it contains additional control features to make sure that added or modified rules do not conflict with existing rules and are self-consistent.

For some applications, knowledge acquisition requires more than a single approach. An example of this is DETEKTR, an expert system development tool for electronic instrument troubleshooters, being developed by the knowledge engineering program at Tektronix.

The knowledge engineers at Tektronix distinguish three types of knowledge that require different approaches to knowledge acquisition.

operational knowledge—The knowledge an expert uses to actually accomplish some task.

supporting knowledge—Knowledge an expert may not have in his head, but may have ready access to.

parenthetical knowledge—Knowledge about the environment in which the task is performed.

In the prototype versions of DETEKTR that have been demonstrated so far (Fig. 3-6), the operational knowledge is acquired by using the INKA (INteractive Knowledge Acquisition) subsystem. INKA makes use of a specialized "knowledge acquisition grammar" that describes the form of troubleshooting rules an expert might enter. An example of such a rule is:

IF THE VOLTAGE AT NODE 4 IS EQUAL TO THE VOLTAGE AT NODE 5 THEN RESISTOR 2 HAS FAILED.

In troubleshooting electronic instruments, the most important type of supporting knowledge that must be captured consists of the device connections, schematic diagrams, and circuit board maps. DETEKTR contains a separate subsystem, PIKA (PIctorial Knowledge Acquisition) that makes it possible to build diagrams of this sort and extract the device connections from them.

Parenthetical knowledge is not captured directly, but must be studied in order to design and deliver an effective expert system. An example of parenthetical knowledge is the fact that troubleshooting technicians spend a great deal of time trying to locate parts. Parenthetical knowledge of this sort is used to motivate and justify design decisions, such as the inclusion of circuit board maps and schematic diagrams to make such locations easier to perform.

The Natural Language Interface

Since the knowledge system is computer-based, it normally functions using the natural symbols of the computer—bits and bytes. Some type of interface must be added so that the user can communicate with this system using a natural language. Most knowledge systems today use a rather primitive natural language interface which restricts the user to the symbols used in the actual knowledgebase. Eventually users will be able to converse with knowledge systems using complete sentences and natural languages—nouns, verbs, prepositions, adjectives, and adverbs.

Most simple knowledge systems (such as the production system in this book) use a simple dialog with the user that requires no more than a "no" or "yes" response (or perhaps a "why?") from the user. At a more complex level, the interface needs to be able to *parse* the input from the user. Parsing is the process of determining how the parts of a sentence fit together. Elaborate natural language interfaces, such as the user interface in the Infocom games, have complex and well-developed parsing algorithms that enable the user to use complete sentences in the dialog with the computer. The parsing algorithm determines the subject, verb, and other parts of the sentence.

The Explanatory Interface

Most experts and users would never trust a conclusion reached by any type of knowledge system unless they could query the system on how the decision was made. If you visit your doctor and he tells you that you have a certain disease, you would certainly want to know how the doctor reached this conclusion. You would probably ask to see the X-rays, blood tests, or whatever else the doctor used to reach the conclusion. You

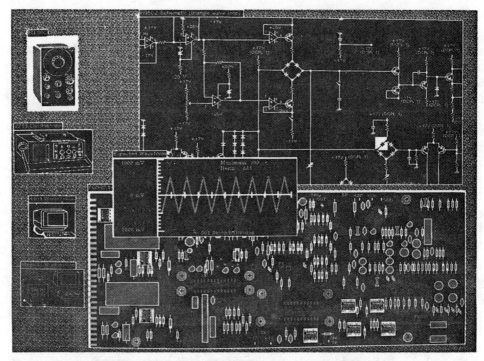

Fig. 3-6. Prototype version of Tektronix DETEKTR system (courtesy Tektronix).

would also want to know the process of reasoning that the doctor used to reach the conclusion from the test results. Using a knowledge system is no different.

As an example, your doctor may use a computer system that can analyze your blood chemistry and draw conclusions from the test results. The final conclusions reached for a patient in an analysis might be that a liver problem exists and there is also an iron malabsorption problem. The patient would still want to know *why* the computer reached this conclusion.

That component of the knowledge system that explains how the conclusion was reached is the explanatory interface. The interface should always be available at any point in the consultation. For example, if the knowledge system were asked how it reached the conclusion that a liver problem exists, it might respond:

It has been concluded that:

The albumin level is high, indicating dehydration or liver insufficiency.
The bilirubin is low, indicating liver disorder or fatigue.
The creatinine is high, indicating poor liver or kidney function unless the patient is an athlete.
The patient is not athletic.

Therefore:
There is considerable evidence of liver insufficiency.

In summary, then, the production or rule-based system operates in cycles. In each cycle, the productions (rules) in the knowledgebase are examined in an order determined by the control component of the inference engine. If a rule is found that matches the known facts in the working memory, it is fired and the conclusion added to the working memory. The cycle is then repeated. The four phases are called *selection, matching, conflict resolution,* and *action* (updating).

Each rule may be called a PDM or *pattern-directed module.* A PDM is a single and separate unit of the rulebase. This permits incremental program growth and debugging, since the addition or editing of a particular PDM does not affect other PDMs in the rulebase. Each PDM is normally assigned a number (such as *Rule 06*) that permits easy analysis of the firing of a chain of rules. A *rule-based system* (RBS) is composed of PDMs, each with a premise (antecedent) and conclusion (consequence). The inference engine may be called a *pattern-directed inference system* (PDIS). A production system is a rule-based system (RBS) with an inference engine containing the inference and control components.

CONTROL STRATEGIES

One important issue in the design of the control portion of the knowledge system is the decision of the search procedure, the order in which the rules are scanned for triggering. This involves a decision on the direction of the search and the search method. Control procedures are normally a part of the inference engine, and the knowledge engineer has only limited control over the procedure in most systems.

There are two search decisions that must be made in designing the control strategy:

1. What is the starting point? In starting a search through a problem space, the knowledge system must have some way of deciding a starting point. The starting point determines whether the search uses forward chaining or backward chaining.
2. How can the search be made more efficient? This involves developing heuristics to resolve conflicts when multiple paths exist and for eliminating paths that are not useful.

Backward and Forward Chaining

In a backward-chaining system, a conclusion is assumed and the inference engine works backward in an attempt to find the facts supporting that conclusion (Fig. 3-7). As soon as it finds a valid conclusion, it moves to a subgoal for that conclusion and then tries to prove this. This type of search is often called a *goal-driven* or *consequence-driven* search. Backward chaining is used when the goals are known and are relatively few in number.

In a forward-chaining system, the inference engine starts with the facts, and then works forward to find a conclusion that is supported by the facts (Fig. 3-7). As each new conclusion is reached, it is added to the working memory. Forward search strategies are often called *data-driven* or *antecedent-driven searches.*

Diagnostic systems are generally forward-driven, while planning systems work best when backward-driven. Some systems use a combination of the two, such as a backward

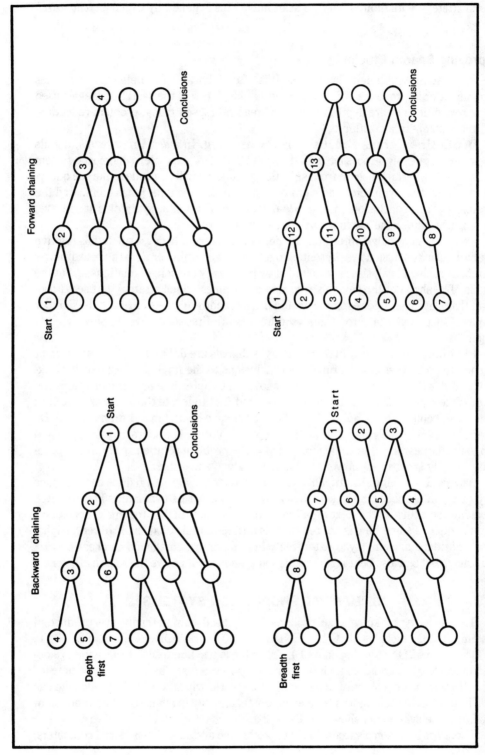

Fig. 3-7. Search strategy categories.

41

search strategy with limited forward searching. This is generally called a *cyclic search strategy*.

Improving Search Efficiency

In a system with hundreds of rules, it is often advisable to implement strategies to minimize or improve the efficiency of the search. A few of the search strategies used to improve efficiency are depth-first versus breadth-first searching, problem-reduction, and the alpha-beta algorithms.

Depth-first versus Breadth-first Searching. In a *depth-first search,* details are pursued as deeply as possible until the search fails. For example, a diagnostic system that suspects a certain disease from specified symptoms will continue to pursue querying for alternative symptoms and signs of this same disease until it has eliminated the possibility of this conclusion. In a *breadth-first search,* all possible symptoms at one level are scanned before the moving to the next detail level.

An expert generally appreciates the depth-first search, because all details relative to a particular conclusion are presented together. A generalist prefers the breadth-first search, as such an analysis is not bounded by previously conceived relationships of the details. The shape of the search space also determines which strategy to use: A program that plays chess, for example, would use a breadth-first search, since the number of moves that would have to be analyzed for a depth-first search would be very, very large.

Problem Reduction. In this strategy, subgoals are defined and then an attempt is made to prove these as intermediate conclusions to the final goal. An excellent example of this (the one used in XCON) is shown in Chapter 5. Another example is the automobile repair problem. In this we attempted first to locate the subsystem at fault (electrical, cooling, etc.), after which the search space was limited dramatically. By carefully defining the rules so that the problem solution is a hierarchy of goals and subgoals, the search path can be minimized in the problem solution space. If the problem is poorly structured, however, this is not always possible.

Alpha-Beta Algorithm. This search strategy attempts to reduce search space by cutting off branches in the search space that need not be evaluated. This involves checking the nodes at the next detail level to see if any further testing is necessary. (For example, if something is not red there is no need to ask what shade of red.) Alpha-beta algorithms are employed extensively in gaming systems (such as chess-playing programs), but can also be used in production systems to improve the search efficiency.

COMMERCIAL PRODUCTION SYSTEMS

The majority of knowledge systems being used commercially are production systems. The list includes MYCIN, DENDRAL, PROSPECTOR, PUFF, INTERNIST, XCON, and SACON (see Appendix E). All of these use hundreds of rules and are designed to operate on mini- or mainframe computer systems. The development time for each of these has been approximately 10 man-years, with the later systems (such as PUFF and XCON) taking less time as better technology is available. The function of each of these systems is shown in Table 3-1.

There has been some success in using production systems with personal computers,

Table 3-1. Overview of Selected Production Systems.

System	Developer	Purpose
DENDRAL	Stanford	Organic chemistry—mass spectometry
INTERNIST	University of Pittsburgh	Diagnosis—internal medicine
MYCIN	Stanford	Medical diagnosis--blood bacteremia and meningitis infections
PROSPECTOR	SRI International	Exploratory geology
PUFF	Stanford	Pulmonary disease diagnosis
XCON	DEC	Computer configuring

but most applications have been in relatively small domains and proprietary applications. Some examples of these were mentioned in Chapters 1 and 2. The most immediate application of knowledge system principles on the personal computer will be the use of knowledge system techniques and theories in the enhancement of many programs for applications that are currently dominated by procedural techniques. Word processors, spreadsheet programs, and database managers will evolve to include production systems, inference engines, and language interfaces as a natural part of their internal "intelligence."

USING TOOLS

One of the most remarkable aspects of production systems is that you can create a completely new knowledge system by simply changing the knowledgebase. MYCIN is perhaps one of the most formidable knowledge systems ever developed for diagnosing and treating meningitis and bacteremia infections. By changing the knowledgebase, it became PUFF, a knowledge system for diagnosing and treating pulmonary diseases. The part of the knowledge system that is constant between various applications is known as the *shell*, and consists of the inference engine, the explanatory and natural language interfaces, and the working memory. The shell for MYCIN is known as EMYCIN.

The shell is often sold independently as a tool, permitting the knowledge engineer to build a specialized rulebase and gain a full knowledge system with an expertise dependent only upon the size of the rulebase and the quality of the rules. This also reduces development time, since by using a shell the knowledge engineer can concentrate on the development of the knowledgebase. This does mean, however, that the engineer is limited to the control strategy of the shell. The better shells have enough flexibility to enable the engineer to choose from a variety of control structures.

The use of commercial shells dramatically reduces the time required to develop the knowledge system. Today, these tools are already permitting users to develop production systems for about 8 man-hours per rule. A short list of available personal computer tools for production systems is shown in Table 3-2. The history of these tools as applied to commercial systems is shown in Fig. 3-8. A more extensive list is in Appendix D. In Part II of this book you will find a listing for a shell (which can also be purchased on a disk from the publisher). Add a rulebase, and you have a complete knowledge system!

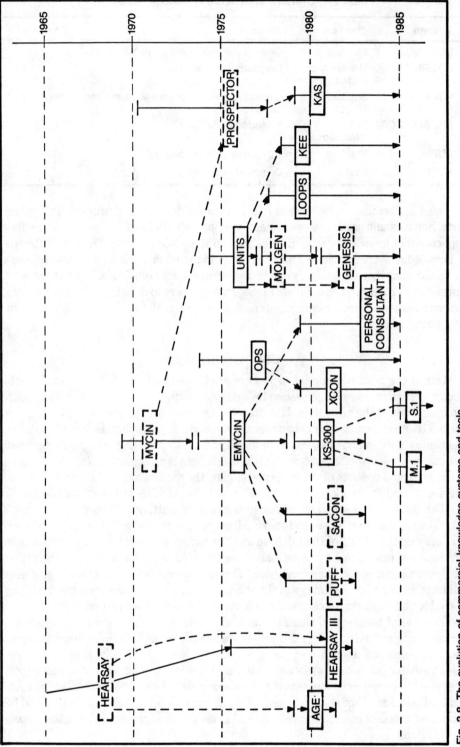

Fig. 3-8. The evolution of commercial knowledge systems and tools.

Shell	Manufacturer	Cost	Language
ES/P ADVISOR	Expert Systems International	$1,895	Prolog
INSIGHT	Level 5 Research	95	Pascal
M.1	Teknowledge	12,500	Prolog
Personal Consultant	Texas Instruments	3,000	IQLISP
SeRIES-PC	SRI International	5,000	IQLISP
KES	Software A&E	4,000	IQLISP
Expert-2	Mountain View Press	100	Forth

In selecting and purchasing knowledge system tools, the knowledge engineer must select carefully. The number of rules, the user interface desired, the type of application, and the control strategy are all important considerations. Since the control strategy is a part of the inference engine, the shell imposes the limits on this control. Cost is also an important consideration. If you are developing a knowledge system as a product that will be sold to many users, you will need to include the cost of the shell in the cost of the product for each user. Unlike a language compiler, in which the compiler cost can be amortized over the entire user base, the shell is more like an interpreter, i.e., each user will need his or her own copy. In addition, all of the better tools require training in order to use them effectively. The cost of this training should be considered as an integral part of any budget for developing a knowledge system.

COMPUTER LANGUAGES FOR KNOWLEDGE SYSTEMS

Knowledge systems can be written using almost any type of computer language, but the better systems are almost always written using a computer language that permits symbolic processing, such as LISP or Forth (see Chapter 6). Such languages are generally interpretive, which limits the speed of their application. There is a concerted effort today to develop adequate compilers for symbolic processing, which will enhance the use of knowledge systems dramatically.

At the next level (Fig. 3-9) are a variety of language tools, such as Prolog, that can be used specifically in the development of knowledge systems. Prolog, for example, is often written in LISP and is specifically useful for developing knowledge systems.

At the highest level are the shells. These are often written using LISP (or Prolog) and reflect the interpretive nature of these languages. The shells have less flexibility and cost more than a language, but save time in that the user need only concentrate on the development of the knowledgebase.

THE HUMAN BRAIN

One reason for the popularity of the production system as a model for knowledge

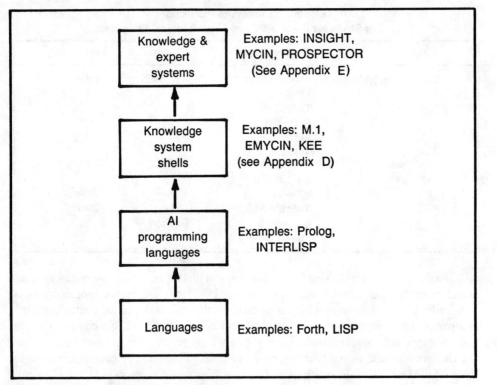

Knowledge & expert systems	Examples: INSIGHT, MYCIN, PROSPECTOR (See Appendix E)
Knowledge system shells	Examples: M.1, EMYCIN, KEE (see Appendix D)
AI programming languages	Examples: Prolog, INTERLISP
Languages	Examples: Forth, LISP

Fig. 3-9. Overview of knowledge system software.

systems is the parallel between it and the functional process of the human brain (and the expert) in solving problems. The long-term memory is similar to the knowledgebase, and the short-term memory to the working memory or database. Symbolic patterns are created in short-term memory using objects and object relationships. These are used to locate and fire productions in long-term memory, after which the conclusions are added to short-term memory.

Each collection of patterns (attribute-value pairs) in the working memory is a single chunk, and from four to seven chunks can be processed simultaneously in short-term memory. The brain, however, has one further capability—the ability to maintain a hierarchical relationship among the chunks as it solves a problem. As we shall see in the next chapter, this can be done in our knowledge system by using another form of knowledge representation known as a *frame-based* system.

One should be cautious, however, in trying to apply the analogy of the production system to the human brain too closely. The human expert is not merely following rules, but is using experience to recognize exceptions to the rules, as well as analogy, intuition, and induction. In addition, rulebases are always an abstraction of the knowledge of the expert. At the edge of a domain of knowledge the expertise of the expert degrades gracefully, whereas in a knowledge system there is an abrupt degradation. The expert also uses a dynamic knowledgebase, constantly forming new concepts, comparing these with existing concepts, learning, and reorganizing knowledge. Finally, the expert can always apply common sense to a problem, something lacking in even the best computers.

EXERCISES

1. What are some general strategies you could use to reduce the search space in a computer program that plays chess?
2. In designing a search strategy, should you first test a rule that is most likely to fail or least likely to fail? Why?
3. Compare the efficiency of a traditional computer program (using procedures, logic, and a decision tree) to solve problems, versus a knowledge system designed to solve the same type of problem. What are the advantages and disadvantages of the knowledge system? How would the size of the knowledgebase differ, and what happens in each, if the amount of knowledge used to make decisions doubles?
4. In what way do tools make the system design easier? In what ways do they make it harder?
5. How would you select a tool for a particular application? What criteria would you use?

Chapter 4
Representing Knowledge

I N THE PREVIOUS CHAPTER A KNOWLEDGE SYSTEM WAS DESCRIBED THAT USED a particular type of knowledge representation known as *productions* or *rules.* In this chapter some alternative methods of representing knowledge will be discussed and compared with the production system. To simplify the comparison, we will use a simple example and develop a portion of the knowledgebase for each type of representation. The example we will use is called "the animal game." This may seem a trivial example, but remember that replacing the rules with another set of rules and extending the number of rules and conclusions would make it possible to construct a system of any level of complexity for other types of problems.

All of the representation methods described have limitations. The longer-range quest for knowledge representation research is to find a general theory or method for representing any knowledge.

THE ANIMAL GAME

In the animal game, the user thinks of an animal and the computer tries to guess the animal that the user is thinking about. The knowledgebase for the animal game consists of knowledge about various types of animals stored in the computer, where it can be applied in a dialog between the user and the computer. A typical dialog is shown in Fig. 4-1. The computer asks the user a series of questions to which the user must reply, the answer to each being a simple "yes" or "no." From the user's answers, the computer is eventually able to guess the animal. At any point in the dialog, the user is also able to query with a "Why"; the computer then can reply with the chain

Fig. 4-1. Sample dialog for the animal game.

```
Is this true?
(FLIES)
Y/N? N

(HAS FEATHERS)
Y/N? N

(GIVES MILK)
Y/N? Y

(CHEWS CUD)
Y/N? Y

(HAS BLACK STRIPES)
Y/N? Y

Hypothesis (IS ZEBRA) is true.
```

of reasoning that indicates why the computer asked this particular question.

KNOWLEDGE REPRESENTATION WITH RULES

In the production or pattern-directed inference system discussed in the last chapter, we could represent the game knowledge by storing a set of rules in the rulebase. The rules are used to represent the relationships between certain antecedents and consequences. In our example, we will use 15 rules to identify any of seven different animals. In Fig. 4-2 is a list of the 15 rules, and a map of the network is shown in Fig. 4-3.

A working memory is also created that stores facts about the animal that are developed during the dialog. At the start, there is no data in the working memory about the animal. A conclusion is assumed, and the computer works backward to find a question to support that conclusion:

[(Assumed)	The animal is an albatross.]
(Asked)	**Does the animal fly?**

Notice from Figs. 4-1 and 4-3 that the computer works backward from the assumed conclusion to find the highest-level question that supports the conclusion, then uses forward chaining to work toward that conclusion beginning from that question. If the answer to the first question is "yes," for example, the following would be added to the working memory:

FLIES

The working memory stores the attribute-value pairs established as true in solving a particular problem. In this case the object (animal) is assumed to minimize the storage space. The knowledgebase rules in this type of system consist of attribute-value (A-V) pairs, with each part of the antecedent and consequence containing a single attribute and value:

```
        RULE 01     IF          The animal has hair.
                    THEN        The animal is a mammal.

        RULE 02     IF          The animal gives milk.
                    THEN        The animal is a mammal.

        RULE 03     IF          The animal has feathers.
                    THEN        The animal is a bird.

        RULE 04     IF          The animal flies.
                    AND         The animal lays eggs.
                    THEN        The animal is a bird.

        RULE 05     IF          The animal eats meat.
                    THEN        The animal is a carnivore.

        RULE 06     IF          The animal has pointed teeth.
                    AND         The animal has claws.
                    AND         The animal has forward eyes.
                    THEN        The animal is a carnivore.

        RULE 07     IF          The animal is a mammal.
                    AND         The animal has hoofs.
                    THEN        The animal is an ungulate.

        RULE 08     IF          The animal is a mammal.
                    AND         The animal chews cud.
                    THEN        The animal is an ungulate.

                    IF          The animal is a mammal.
                    AND         The animal is a carnivore.
                    AND         The animal has a tawny color.
                    AND         The animal has dark spots.
                    HYPOTHESIS  The animal is a cheetah.

        RULE 10     IF          The animal is a mammal.
                    AND         The animal is a carnivore.
                    AND         The animal has a tawny color.
                    AND         The animal has black stripes.
                    HYPOTHESIS  The animal is a tiger.

        RULE 11     IF          The animal is an ungulate.
                    AND         The animal has a long neck.
                    AND         The animal has long legs.
                    AND         The animal has dark spots.
                    HYPOTHESIS  The animal is a giraffe.

        RULE 12     IF          The animal is an ungulate.
                    AND         The animal has black stripes.
                    HYPOTHESIS  The animal is a zebra.

        RULE 13     IF          The animal is a bird.
                    AND         The animal does not fly.
                    AND         The animal has a long neck.
                    AND         The animal has long legs.
                    AND         The animal is black and white.
                    HYPOTHESIS  The animal is an ostrich.

        RULE 14     IF          The animal is a bird.
                    AND         The animal does not fly.
                    AND         The animal swims.
                    AND         The animal is black and white.
                    HYPOTHESIS  The animal is a penguin.

        RULE 15     IF          The animal is a bird.
                    AND         The animal flies well.
                    HYPOTHESIS  The animal is an albatross.
```

Fig. 4-2. Production rules for the animal game.

	Attribute	Value
IF	animal	flies
AND	animal	lays eggs
THEN	animal	bird

In some production systems each proposition may consist of an attribute, value, and object. In this case the antecedents and consequences consist of A-O-V triplets. For example, the MYCIN knowledgebase includes the following rule:

IF	The gram stain of the organism is gram negative.
AND	The morphology of the organism is a rod.
AND	The aerobicity of the organism is anaerobic.
THEN	There is suggestive evidence that the identity of the organism is Bacteroides.

In this case A-O-V triplets are used and can be represented with the following table:

	Attribute	Object	Value
IF	Gram Stain	Organism	Gram Negative
AND	Morphology	Organism	Rod
AND	Aerobicity	Organism	Anaerobic
THEN	Identity	Organism	Bacteroides

Notice that in this case all of the objects are identical. In a system in which all of the objects are identical, the object could be assumed and an A-V system used. In the case of MYCIN, the use of O-A-V triplets permits the system to include the patient or culture as the object. Most of the available production systems are the simpler A-V systems.

In knowledge systems there is a very clear distinction between an implication or hypothesis and a conclusion. An *implication* or *hypothesis* is tentative conclusion reached by deduction from the known facts that may or may not be true. A *conclusion* is a fact reached by deduction from known facts that is accepted as true.

For example, if the animal flies and lays eggs, we may *imply* or *hypothesize* that it is a penguin (see Fig. 4-3). This is tentative conclusion that needs further testing. We can *conclude,* however, that the animal is a bird. Assuming the hypothesis is true, we can then ask if it swims. If so, we can hypothesize the animal is a penguin. Finally, at some level, we can make the conclusion that the animal is, indeed, a penguin. Conclusions are added to the working memory or database. Hypotheses are not added to the database but are a part of the control strategy.

In many cases it may be necessary to deal with uncertain rules. For example, in the MYCIN rule just mentioned the conclusion has only a 70 percent certainty. Depending upon the system, it may be desired to assign certainties to the antecedent or consequence. The effect of uncertainty upon the knowledgebase and the inference engine will be discussed later in Chapter 10.

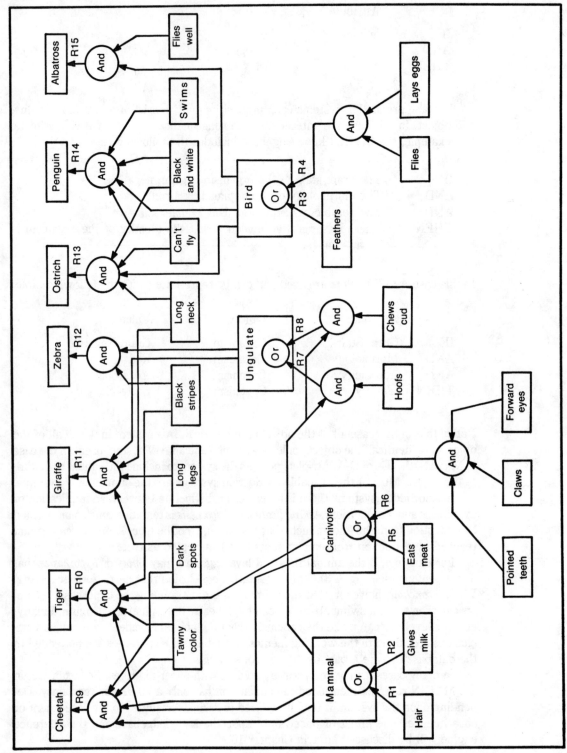

Fig. 4-3. Animal game network.

Production systems have the following advantages over other types of expert systems (see next chapter):

1. Modularity.
2. Uniformity (the primary components can be used as tools in other systems).
3. Naturalness—conclusions are reached in much the same way that an expert would reason.
4. Flexible hierarchy—the hierarchy is controlled only by the relationship of the rules. By changing the rules you can change the hierarchy.

There are also some disadvantages:

1. The operation is relatively inefficient. Much computer time is wasted in unnecessary cycles.
2. It is hard to follow the control of the problem solution.
3. The hierarchical relationships are difficult to visualize.

A production system is said to be *flat*. A relational database is also said to be flat because it is distinguished from a network system by the fact that hierarchies—the relationships between items in the database—are not stored in the database. In the same way, a production system is said to be flat because there is no way to represent a hierarchy of rules. The size of the knowledgebase grows linearly in size with the addition of new knowledge. This is in contrast with decision tree models used in procedural programming, in which the size of the knowledgebase grows logarithmically with the knowledge.

Most of the available commercial knowledge systems are production systems. A brief overview of these was included in the last chapter (see Fig. 3-1).

FRAME REPRESENTATIONS

It is not unusual for there to be several hundred rules in a production system. At this complexity it becomes very difficult for the knowledge engineer to control the rulebase and the relationship of the rules. Added rules may duplicate or contradict existing rules. Software tools may be used to check for duplication and contradiction, but something even more important begins to happen—the effectiveness of the system is destroyed because the knowledge engineer loses an awareness of the interaction among the different rules. The network map begins to look like an organization chart for the federal government. The hierarchical relationship between the rules is lost and not easily visible to the engineer.

The frame-based representation is an alternative knowledgebase representation that permits the hierarchical information about object relationships to be stored in the knowledgebase. A *frame* is a knowledge structure that is used to describe one or more values of attributes arranged in a *slot* or filler format. A typical system of frames for a knowledge system about birds is shown in Fig. 4-4. Each slot can contain a value for the attribute, a procedure for calculating the value (an algorithm), or one or more production rules for finding the value (heuristic).

A slot may also contain multiple values. For example, a *brother* slot in a patient

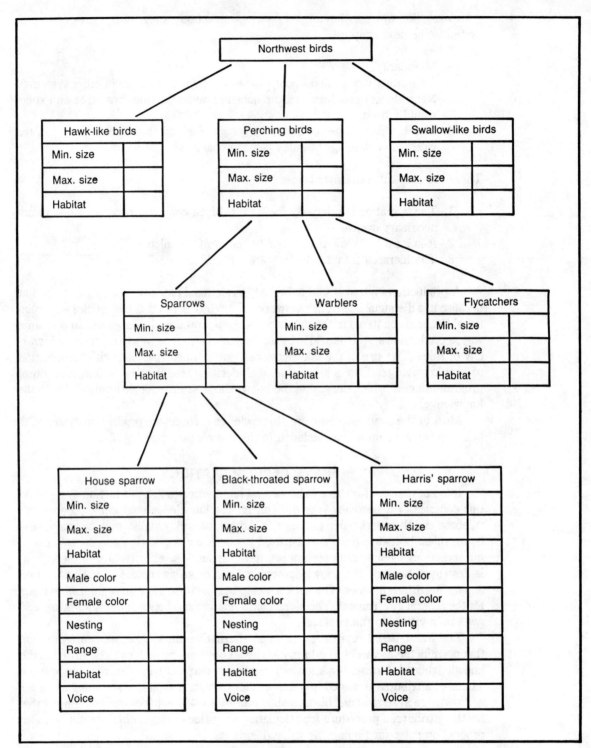

Fig. 4-4. Frame-based knowledge system structure.

frame may contain multiple names. Some slots, defined as *facets,* are used to constrain the values used for frame attributes. Facets may be used to control the maximum number of values entered for an attribute (such as the maximum number of *brother* entries permitted) or a minimum and maximum value permitted for an attribute.

Slots can be used to store values, procedures, or rules. When a slot needs to be evaluated, the procedure or rules are activated. We could say that the slot procedures and productions are controlled by demons (see Chapter 3), which are activated when needed. For example, a frame may have attribute slots for a person's birthday and age. The birthday slot contains a value. The age slot contains a procedure that can calculate the age from the birthdate and the present date. A procedure attached to a slot in this way is said to be an *attached procedure* (see Chapter 10). The procedure is activated whenever the present date is changed.

The frames are organized in a hierarchical relationship, with the highest level frame containing information that applies to all frames below it. Any frame related to a frame of higher order is said to *inherit* the characteristics of the higher-order frame. For example, an *African Elephant* frame may inherit the *Color* attribute of *Gray* from a higher-level *Elephant* frame. This higher-level attribute could be used as a default value for frames below it in the hierarchy, and could be overridden if a lower-level frame contains an attribute of a different value. For this reason the frame system can handle exceptions easily. For example, if the Asian elephant is brown, the *Asian Elephant* frame could have an attribute color of *Brown,* overriding the *Gray* color attribute of the *Elephant* frame (see Fig. 4-5).

In a given system, the frames can be static or dynamic. In a static system the frames cannot be changed or updated during the problem-solving process. In a dynamic system, it is possible to alter the frames.

Programming systems using frames are said to be object-oriented programs. Each

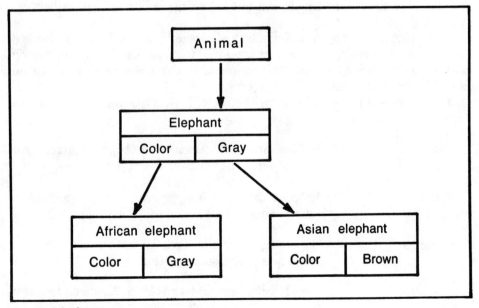

Fig. 4-5. Inheritance.

frame represents an object, and the slots contain data associated with the object. The slots, then, contain values that are associated with attributes. A frame is similar to a property list or, in a database, a record.

The frame-based system has an inherent advantage if the hierarchical relationship is relatively static and there are few exceptions to the relationships. In the frame system, knowledge relationships are stored as well as the knowledge. Attribute values are stored only once and at the highest level at which the attribute applies, reducing the memory storage required. A second advantage of the frame system is that the value of each slot can be evaluated using either procedures or heuristic methods. This enables the engineer to incorporate both procedural and heuristic methods in the design of the system.

The disadvantage of the frame system is the relatively higher complexity that must be a part of the inference engine design, as well as the difficulty of changing the knowledgebase hierarchy once the knowledgebase is designed. In addition, it is very difficult to handle exceptions. For example, in the animal game, how would an albino cheetah be represented?

Although only a few frame-based systems are available, a popular one is Intellicorp's KEE system. The system software is in the LISP language and requires special hardware. The software costs about $60,000, with the LISP hardware costing $50,000-$100,000. Total system cost is normally a minimum of $250,000.

SEMANTIC NETWORK REPRESENTATIONS

Semantic network representation is considered the most general representation scheme, and is perhaps the oldest in artificial intelligence. In a semantic network, abstract relationships between objects are represented using links and nodes. The objects are represented by *nodes*, and the relationships between the objects are represented by *links*. An albatross, for example, is a bird and a bird is a flier and has feathers (see Fig. 4-6).

Objects (represented by the nodes) are physical objects that can be seen or touched. They can also be events, acts, abstract categories (such as "carnivore"), or descriptors (such as "feathered" or "flier"). Descriptors, which are also nodes, represent additional information about a class of objects.

Links represent relationships between objects. Typical types of link relationships include:

Is-a	Indicates an object is a member of a larger class (taxonomic relationship). The albatross *is-a* bird.
Has-a	Indicates the object is a property of another node. A giraffe *has-a* long neck.
Caused-by	Used to represent causal relationships. A low albumin is *caused-by* a liver disfunction (Fig. 4-7).
Definitional	Used to define a value for an object. A patient, for example, may have *two* brothers (Fig. 4.8).

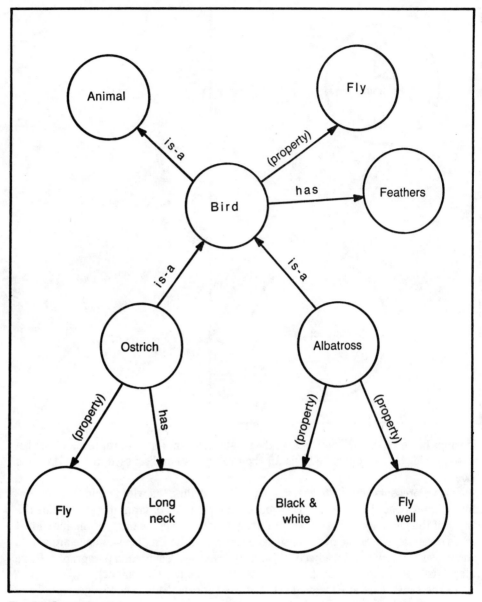

 Fig. 4-6. Semantic net.

As with the frame system, hierarchical relationships can be constructed and nodes can inherit properties of higher-order nodes. As a result, semantic network representations have some of the advantages and disadvantages of frame-based systems. The primary disadvantage is the difficulty of handling exceptions.

FIRST-ORDER LOGIC REPRESENTATIONS

A fourth form of knowledge representation is the use of logic propositions and rela-

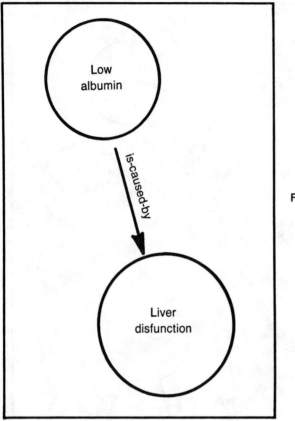

Fig. 4-7. Caused-by link.

tionships between them. This is one of the most important forms of representation discussed in this book, as it is the basis for the Prolog system discussed in Part II of this book.

This representation is a formal language for encoding knowledge and the relationship of knowledge. In the English language we have rules of grammar that define the *syntax* of the language. These rules are independent of the meaning of the individual words or semantics. Some of the basic components of the English language are words (nouns, verbs, prepositions, adjectives, and adverbs), sentences, and paragraphs. Basic rules exist about the relationships of these components in a sentence.

In the same way, any language that is used for encoding knowledge must have components and a syntax. The language must also have a way of expressing logical relationships. Two logics have been developed to express logical relationships: propositional logic and predicate logic or first-order logic. These have been around since before the advent of the computer. Before introducing logic, let us look for a moment at some basic logic concepts.

Logical Concepts

A *predicate* has a value of TRUE or FALSE and is used to represent relations. A *proposition* is an expression in which the predicate affirms or denies something about the subject. A *constant* represents an object in the domain. *Atomic formulas* are the sentences or propositions of logic.

An *interpretation* of a proposition is its truth for a given set of bindings for its variables. *Bindings* are substitutions of constants for variables. A proposition is *valid* if it is true for all interpretations. A proposition *logically follows* from the premises if it is true whenever the premises are true.

IF	The animal has feathers.
AND	The animal lays eggs.
THEN	The animal is a bird.

In the above proposition, for example, "The animal is a bird" logically follows from the other two propositions. The conclusion is true whenever the two premises are true. Rules of inference are *sound* if their conclusions logically follow from the premises. Rules of inference are *complete* if all propositions that logically follow from the premises can be inferred from the premises. A knowledgebase is complete if any proposition implied by the knowledgebase can be proved from the knowledgebase.

Prefix Predicate Calculus (Predicate Logic)

A common logic is *propositional logic*, which has no variables. Statements are either TRUE or FALSE and linked with operators such as AND, OR, and NOT which are known

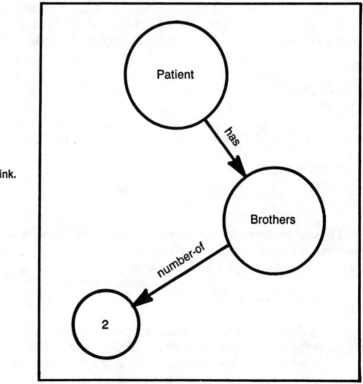

Fig. 4-8. Definitional link.

as *boolean operators*. Basic rules of propositional logic are used to combine logical values. For example, if X is TRUE and Y is FALSE, X AND Y is FALSE and X OR Y is TRUE. Variables can only have logic variables.

Logical operators are part of most programming languages including BASIC, C, and Pascal. Even propositional logic is not powerful enough to be very useful for symbolic processing. For symbolic processing, quantified variables are needed.

Prefix predicate calculus (PPC, a predicate logic) is an extension of propositional logic that permits the expression of symbolic relationships between objects through the use of variables.

The Syntax of Predicate Logic

The basic symbol unit (component) in PPC is the *atom*. There are three types of atoms: the constant symbol, the function symbol, and the relation symbol.

Constants represent real-world objects. Examples of object symbols include:

ALBATROSS
BIRD
UNGULATE
FEATHERS

A constant is composed of one or more alphabetic capitals, numerals, or nonalphabetic characters (excepting parentheses).

A *function symbol* operates on an object to return an object. A *function* is a function symbol followed by one or more terms. Examples of functions include:

+
COLOR
AGE

A *predicate symbol* defines relations between objects. Examples include:

BROTHER-OF
FATHER
IS-A

Propositions are expressed using these three types of atoms with parentheses and operators in a simple structure called a *term*. For example, we can express the truth that the albatross is a bird using the term:

(IS-A ALBATROSS BIRD)

Using these three types of atoms, we can construct three types of propositions: atomic propositions, logical propositions, and quantified propositions.

An *atomic proposition* consists of a predicate symbol and one or more terms. For example, the following are atomic propositions:

60

```
(IS-A CAT ABYSSINIAN)
(BROTHER-OF JACK JOHN)
```

Functions can also be expressed as relation symbols in such expressions:

```
( = ( + 4 2) 6 )
```

This is also an atomic proposition and is equivalent to:

```
(= (SUM 4 2) 6)
```

Logical propositions are statements of truth with logical operators. Logical operators include AND, OR, NOT, and IF:

```
(NOT (IS-A BEAR BIRD)
(IF (AND (FLIES) (LAYSEGGS) (BIRD))
```

Finally, a *quantified proposition* contains a quantifier of ALL or EXISTS with one or more variables and a proposition:

```
(ALL x (IF (ABYSSINIAN x) (CAT x)))
```

Formulas constructed using connectives and quantifiers (see Table 4-1) are called WFF (well-formed formulas). FOL provides many formal inference rules for combining formulas. As in a production system, we can use inference to create new WFFs from old structures. We can create new WFFs by applying rules of inference to a set of WFFs. For example, if the following predicates are true:

```
(ALL x (IF (CAT x) (HASPAWS x )))
(ALL x (IF (ABYSSINIAN x) (CAT x)))
```

we can infer that Abyssinian cats have paws:

```
(ALL x (IF (ABYSSINIAN x) (HASPAWS x )))
```

To prove a WFF, a knowledgebase of WFFs is assumed, as well as a set of rules of inference. Whenever the knowledgebase contains propositions matching the premises

CONNECTIVES		QUANTIFIERS	
$\wedge$	AND		
$\vee$	OR	$\exists$	THERE EXISTS
$\neg$	NOT	$\forall$	FOR ALL
$\rightarrow$	IMPLIES		
$\equiv$	EQUIVALENT		

Table 4-1. Propositional Calculus Operators.

that are known, it is permitted to add the conclusion to the knowledgebase. This rule of inference is known as *resolution*.

The question of syntactic legality is independent of truth. This is true of any language. Propositions may have correct syntax, but may not be valid.

Predicate calculus also includes a concept called *unification*. Unification permits us to match expressions. Two expressions are said to *unify* with each other if and only if there is a substitution for the variables in both expressions that, when applied, makes them identical. The substitution is called a *unifier* for the expressions. Assume the following statements are true:

```
(MOTHER-OF JANE MARY)
(MOTHER-OF MARY SUE)
```

This states that Jane is the mother of Mary, and Mary is the mother of Sue. From this we can infer than Jane is the grandmother of Sue. We can write a general expression that states this relationship with variables:

```
(ALL x y z (IF (AND (MOTHER x y)(MOTHER y z)) (GRANDMOTHER x z)))
```

BLACKBOARD SYSTEMS

In a *blackboard representation,* several independent knowledgebases are used with a single working memory. The knowledgebases may be of different types, permitting the user to store knowledge in whatever representation is appropriate for that knowledge and still use the combined representations to solve problems with a single inference engine and working memory. The HEARSAY knowledge system is an example of this type of representation.

REPRESENTATION BY EXAMPLE

Another method that is growing in popularity with users who have a minimum of knowledge engineering expertise is *representation by example*. In this type of system, the user describes several examples to the system of problems and the solution. From this, the system *compiles* a knowledgebase that can be used to solve additional problems. At any time during knowledgebase creation the user can display the knowledgebase as a matrix and see the "holes" in the matrix for which additional problem/solutions are needed.

The knowledge in such a system may still be stored as rules (or any other representation), but the user always sees the knowledgebase as a matrix of examples. The matrix is defined by the user, then compiled to whatever form is desired. If the knowledgebase is updated or edited, the user updates or edits the matrix.

The advantage of the example representation, of course, is ease of use: the user does not need to know anything about production rules, declarative languages, frames, or predicate calculus. The disadvantage is the loss of flexibility in the design of the system. The user is also isolated from seeing the structure of the relationship in the knowledge. It works fine if you have another problem similar to an existing problem, but what if you have a new type of problem in the same domain? The system cannot apply existing knowledge to the new problem.

One of the best examples of this type of system is Expert-Ease, a relatively inexpensive approach to knowledge system design that is also easy to use. A corporation, for example, could use this system to evaluate expense reports for salespeople to see if a trip is deductible under current corporate rules. The knowledgebase is created by entering examples of expense reports of trips that are permitted and trips that are not permitted. From this, Expert-Ease compiles the knowledgebase, which can then be used to evaluate other trip reports on a routine basis.

USING AN EXAMPLE

The animal game of this chapter can be used to create a knowledgebase that is shown in Appendix B. If you have the disk with the system, you can begin to use the game immediately by entering ANIMAL. If you do not have the disk, follow the directions of Appendix A and then Appendix B to load the system components. Once you have completed the loading, you can start the game by entering the word DIAGNOSE (see Fig 4-9). The map of the system was shown earlier as Fig. 4-3. The rules are shown as Fig. 4-2 and are in Screens 81 and 82 in Appendix B.

The system will ask a series of questions, and from this determine the animal that corresponds to the answers. From this example, you can notice several things about the design of the knowledgebase and the rules:

Fig. 4-9. Sample dialog generated by the DIAGNOSE modification of the animal game.

```
DIAGNOSE
HAS-FEATHERS
Is this true (Y/N)?Y

FLIES-WELL
Is this true (Y/N)?N

FLIES
Is this true (Y/N)?N

DOES-NOT-FLY
Is this true (Y/N)?Y

SWIMS
Is this true (Y/N)?Y

IS-BLACK-AND-WHITE
Is this true (Y/N)?Y

CONCLUSION:
(IS-PENGUIN)
ok
```

1. The questions to the user relate to observable facts or symptoms. The answers are saved in a working memory (a FACTS list), which is used to draw conclusions.
2. The facts are used to draw conclusions from the rules using backward chaining. The early conclusions are more general in nature (such as "It is a mammal"), and gradually the system works toward more specific conclusions.

EXERCISES

1. What form of knowledge represenation would be best for the following types of applications:

   a) Classification of biological entities (birds, flowers, etc.)
   b) A computer repair system.
   c) Medical diagnostic system.

2. How would you evaluate the complexity of a problem?
3. What influence does the type of system (diagnostic, planning, interpretation, etc.) have on the representation—or does it have any influence?
4. How would you evaluate the power of the knowledge in a knowledgebase? Can it be evaluated?
5. Give an example of metaknowledge in the automobile repair system example.
6. Convert the following propositions to sentences:

   (AGE JOHN 32)
   (NOT (MARITAL-STATUS MARY SINGLE))
   (ALL x (IF (APPLE x) (COLOR x RED)))

7. What type of proposition is each of the above?
8. Convert each of the following the predicate calculus:

   Bill is a horse.
   John is a dog.
   There exists a horse that can outrun any dog.
   Jane is the sister of Sue.

9. Design a frame-based representation of the organization chart of a small company. Give an example of inheritance in this representation.

Chapter 5

Introduction to Knowledge Engineering

O NE OF THE MAJOR PROBLEMS IN THE DESIGN OF ANY EXPERT SYSTEM IS THAT of converting the knowledge and problem-solving techniques of the expert to a knowledgebase that can be used effectively to solve problems in the domain of expertise.

An expert typically does not use methods that are procedural or linear in the solution of a problem. Analogy, intuition, and abstraction are important tools in the problem solution. Often, the expert cannot even describe how he or she reached a particular problem solution. At best, the expert can only describe the basic concepts, or heuristics, used in the problem solution. The knowledge engineer has the extremely complex job of converting these concepts to a precise, complete, and consistent system that can solve problems with the skill of the expert.

In this chapter we will look at the basic concepts of how the knowledgebase is constructed from the knowledge of the expert. This involves three steps:

1. Defining the domain.
2. Defining the representation and representational theory.
3. Acquiring the knowledge.

Although defining the three steps in this way may seem to imply that the knowledgebase design is a structured and linear process, in actuality the process is far more complex, less structured, and more cyclic than linear in nature.

This chapter is one of the most difficult in this book to understand—but also one of the most important. To clarify the concepts, let us examine the design of a knowledge system that can be used to help a doctor analyze blood chemistry and symptoms and provide knowledge that can be used to improve the health of his or her patients. We will occasionally use other examples along our journey to illustrate specific points, then apply this information to our medical example.

DEFINING THE DOMAIN

The first task of the knowledge engineer is to define the domain of the problem. The engineer is essentially creating the boundaries of the system and problem for solution. This involves five substeps:

1. Defining the goal (problem).
2. Identifying the objects in the domain.
3. Identifying the relationship of the objects.
4. Designing a representational theory.
5. Identifying the key problem areas.

The knowledge engineer must express the problem systematically. At the same time, the engineer must recognize that the problem is unstructured and may resist attempts at formalizing or applying systematic approaches. The primary decision in starting is that of defining how the representation, which is essentially a level of abstraction, will take place. This basic problem of knowledge representation is shown in Fig. 5-1. The knowledge system must use a knowledgebase that is created from some type of domain. The domain, in turn, is an abstraction of real-world entities.

Let us look at our medical example. In Fig. 5-2 is a simple diagram of the problem of health care. We are born with certain genetic characteristics. Various environmental factors act on the body: nutritional patterns, environment, stress, etc. These, in turn, produce signs. Eventually signs can be clustered to symptoms, and the symptom pat-

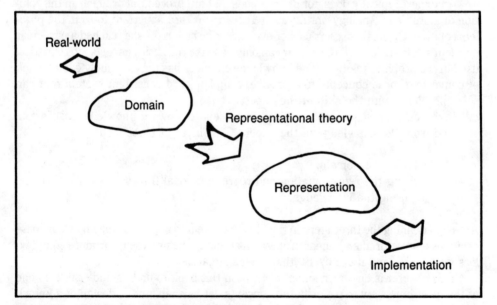

Fig. 5-1. Creating a representation from a domain.

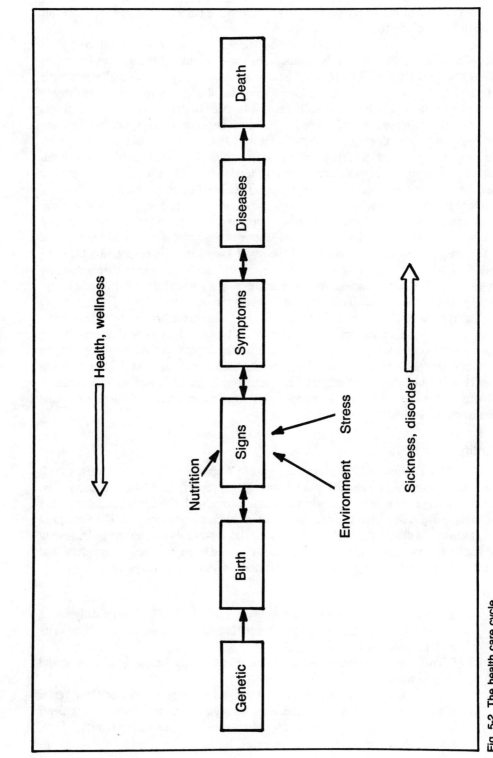

Fig. 5-2. The health care cycle.

terns lead to one or more disease patterns. The disease patterns can eventually result in death if not corrected.

Doctors all look at the *same* real-world problem, but each takes a different view and defines the domain differently. A diagnostic doctor looks at the system fairly late in the cycle. When you visit this doctor, he assumes something is wrong (that you have a complaint), and he or she works backward from this state to try to correct the disease pattern and restore health. A preventive specialist tries to detect signs and symptoms fairly early in the cycle, when the problem is much easier to correct, but has little expertise if a disease is already in evidence. Naturopaths, metabolic doctors, and predictive specialists all view the same system, yet see different domains (Fig. 5-3). Even diagnostic specialists (such as a dermatologist) tend to view disease patterns from their specialized domain. Defining the domain is a first level of abstraction.

Once the domain is defined, the knowledge engineer must design a formal method of representation for the domain. In order to create this representation, there must be a representational theory that can be used to create the representation of the domain. At the present time there is no general theory of knowledge representation that will work for all domains. The engineer must use a representational theory that is domain-dependent. When (and if) scientists can ever develop a general theory, this can be applied to new domains that have resisted representation.

The representation, then, is an abstraction of the domain, which is an abstraction of reality. The human mind can work with multiple types of domains and multiple types of representation, viewing the real-world entities in multiple ways, doing multiple types of abstractions and comparing knowledge across the boundaries of each of these using a variety of problem-solving methods. The computer, in contrast, is much more limited. It is often possible to use multiple representations on a computer, but current systems are always limited to a single domain.

Identifying the Problem

Now let us continue with the medical example. Suppose we wish to create a knowledge system to attempt an analysis of laboratory test reports for blood chemistry. The knowledge engineer must first begin a communication with the expert and design the knowledgebase. The expert must be an expert in the domain of interest. The first question is always to define the problem (goals) for the system. What, specifically, should the knowledge system accomplish? The goal definition must be precise, complete, and consistent. The following goals may be defined for our medical system:

1. Is the patient healthy (is the system working)? If not, what specifically needs correction in the patient? If there is more than one problem, what is the priority of the problems?
2. What changes are recommended in the diet and nutritional supplements, and what is the priority of each?
3. What further tests are recommended, and what is the priority on these tests?
4. What changes are recommended in the lifestyle or environment of the patient?
5. Does the patient need to be referred to a specialist in another domain? If so, what type of specialist?

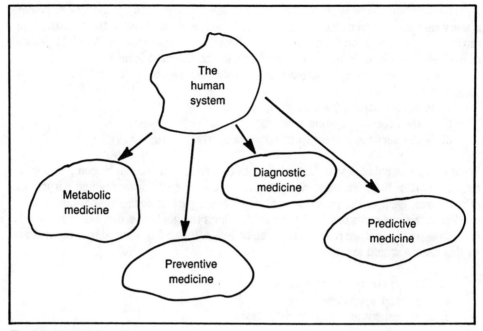

Fig. 5-3. Medical domains.

Can you think of other items that should be a part of the goals?

Once the system goal has been defined, the engineer begins work to describe subgoals. This helps in creating the hierarchy and modularizing the system. The subgoals should be defined in terms of the relationships of the knowledge. The basic strategy at this level is to break the problem down into two or more smaller problems, and then try to solve the smaller problems. The smaller problems, in the same way, could be broken down further.

As an example of identifying subgoals, let us look at the XCON knowledge system that is used by Digital Equipment Corporation to configure computers for customers. The primary task, that of configuring a VAX computer system, is broken down into six subtasks:

1. Check the purchase order for any gross errors.
2. Put the appropriate components in the CPU and expansion cabinets.
3. Put the boxes in the expansion cabinet and put the components in the cabinets.
4. Put the panels on the cabinets.
5. Lay out the floor plan for the system.
6. Complete the cabling.

The actions within each subtask are highly variable, depending upon what has happened to that point in previous tasks and the components involved. In XCON there are about 800 rules used in configuring a VAX system.

The system planning is done backward from the goals, defining the goals for the first hierarchical level and then for the next level below it. Each goal level represents a partial solution of the problem, one state in the domain state space. The engineer is working top-down from the abstract (a diffuse and abstract goal) to the specific. The further back the design proceeds, the more specific the design becomes. All of the design of one level should be completed before moving to the next level.

In our medical example here are a few subgoals we could define:

1. Is the circulatory system working?
2. Is the digestive system working?
3. Is the nervous system functioning properly?

What other subgoals can you think of? Notice that each of these can be compared with the first part of the first question in the five-question goal list mentioned earlier. In other words, each of the previous goal items are a part of each subgoal question.

From this, we can work backward establishing the goals at a more detailed level, continuing until facts are reached that can be evaluated and measured, our *input data*. In this case it would include:

1. Blood chemistry tests results.
2. Signs and symptoms.
3. Environment and genetic definition.

What other input data would be needed? How would each of these be obtained (testing, questionnaires, etc.)?

Identifying the Objects in the Domain

The next step is to identify the objects in the domain. In systems theory, this involves establishing the system boundary. Again, the objects must be defined precisely, completely, and consistently. What specific laboratory tests will be included? Will the patient history be included, if so, what data? What about other history information concerning relatives (such as any history of cancer and of what type)? Should any drugs and supplements of the patient be included in the analysis? Should the occupation or lifestyle of the patient be included? What about data on the patient's environment or eating habits? What about symptoms of the patient (headaches, fever blisters on the mouth, etc.)?

This establishes the boundaries for the input data, but what about the problem space itself? In this case we are selecting what subgoals to include and which to exclude at each level of the hierarchy. At the first level you would need to define, as much as possible, each subsystem to be included.

Identifying the Relationship of the Objects

The next step is to identify the relationship between the objects. A low LDH test, for example, may indicate an overactive pancreas. It could also mean other things. All of these relationships must be defined, as much as possible, within the limits of the knowledge that is available.

Expressing Knowledge in a Language

Finally, there must be some way of representing this domain in some type for formal language. This provides a method for encoding this knowledge in the knowledgebase. There must also be representational theory to get the knowledge of the domain into the formal language of the representation.

Identifying Key Problem Areas in the Application Domain

The key problems areas are generally determined by the type of knowledge system being designed (see Chapter 2). As the medical system is a diagnostic system, the following key problem areas can be defined:

1. Signals (test results and symptoms) can be masked by other signals.
2. Signals can be intermittent, varying with time or the environment.
3. Testing equipment can be faulty.
4. Some important signals are often unavailable or expensive to retrieve.
5. The relationship of the objects may not be fully understood.

These same key problem areas are true of any diagnostic knowledge system.

Creating the Representational Theory

The next step is to create and organize the objects and to define their relationships in the domain using the representational theory. This is particularly important in the design of frame-based representations and semantic nets, but is also important in the design of production systems. Some domains are *taxonomic* in form—that is, the relationships can be defined as IS-A relationships. An example are the biological domains used to represent birds or flowers.

All domains, however, are not taxonomic in form. Our medical example is not taxonomic. In some cases the design of a production system can be simplified if the productions can be classified so that they can be created and edited by groups or modules, as we did in the automobile repair example. In our medical example we could classify a group of productions as relating to the first subgoal: Is the circulatory system healthy? At the next goal level, we could classify a smaller group of productions as relating to it.

In defining the organization for a domain, the classification, hierarchy, and definition of the objects depends upon how the system is viewed by the expert and engineer. There are basically three types of hierarchical structures: functional, causal or behavioral, and structural (see Fig. 5-4). Let us diverge for a minute from the medical example and look at a computer system as viewed from each of these hierarchical structures. In working through this example, keep these facts in mind:

1. In the example, each type of hierarchy represents a different view of the same domain.
2. The domain itself may have a hierarchy. There are thus two hierarchies discussed here: a hierarchy that exists in the domain and a hierarchy of how the domain is viewed. This will be clearer as the example is explained.

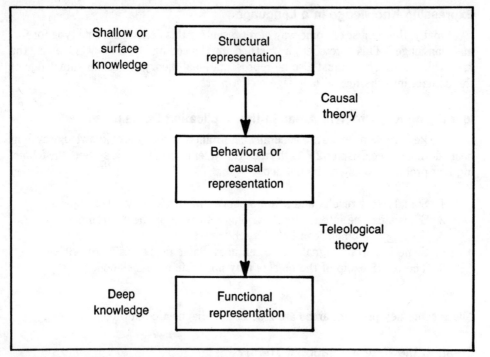

Fig. 5-4. Types of hierarchies and their relationships.

3. All domains do not have a hierarchy.
4. The concept of shallow and deep knowledge introduced in the example applies to any domain, and is a general concept that will be described in more detail after the examples.

Structural Hierarchy

In a structural representation of a computer, it is viewed as an assembly of physical components; at the highest level is the computer system itself. At the next level is a collection of assemblies, and the computer is viewed as a collection of assemblies. At the third level are the cards, and the system is viewed as a collection of electronic cards. At the fourth level are the circuit-board components.

If the computer (highest level) quits working, the assemblies are switched with other good assemblies until the defective assembly is found. The defective assembly is opened, and the cards are switched with good cards until the defective card is found. Finally, the circuit-board components are changed until the defective component is found. Notice that this strategy involves no knowledge of how the computer works or any knowledge of electronics. It is not even necessary to know the function of the box. The knowledge engineer calls such a representation *shallow knowledge*.

Behavioral or Causal Hierarchy

A second hierarchy would represent the system in terms of its behavior. The computer system is seen as a hierarchy of causes and effects. For example, at the highest level the output is displayed (or printed) whenever certain keys are pressed on the keyboard. If this fails, we could then look at the next level in this hierarchy. The printer, for example, has behavioral definition; when input data is applied to a connector, this data is printed. If this printer behavior fails, you could then examine the behavior at the next level using a voltmeter or an oscilloscope. There are other behavioral aspects of the printer that can give clues to the failure. Is the light on the front panel on? If this behavior fails, you might assume the power supply is not supplying power, the cord is failing to bring power to the printer (is it plugged in?), or the fuse is open.

If you use a diagnostic program, it can produce controlled causes, and the effects can be analyzed to determine what has gone wrong at the next level of the hierarchy. The program can then move down to the third level of the hierarchy and again test, producing an effect that can help you to determine the true problem. On an IBM PC XT system, a memory tester program might draw a picture of the memory board, indicating which chip on the board is defective in a visual diagram on the monitor. Now we have moved to a deeper level of knowledge, but this does not mean necessarily that this computer can do useful problem-solving work. Viewing the system from a behavioral hierarchy takes more knowledge than using the structural hierarchy, but is still rather shallow in terms of the true purpose of the computer as applied to most problem solutions.

Functional Hierarchy

At the third (and highest) level of abstraction, you can view the computer as a hierarchy of functional units. At the highest level the computer itself has a defined function, that of outputting certain information from input information using defined algorithms and (if you have a knowledge system) heuristics. At the next hierarchical level is another collection of functions: inputting data, processing data, storing data temporarily, storing and reading data in a more permanent fashion, and outputting data. If the primary function failed (no output data or incorrect output data), you could then move down the hierarchy and try to define the function at the next level that failed. Suppose, for example, the computer no longer stores data in a more permanent way, e.g., the floppy disk drive failed. The next step would be to locate the function at that level of the hierarchy that failed. You might, for example, touch the drive and conclude that the drive motor was not turning the disk.

We could now take these same hierarchical definitions and apply them to the medical analysis problem of the medical example of the previous section. At the structural level we could define a physical hierarchical level of organism, organs, tissues, cells, molecules, and genes. At the functional level is the total system, then the subsystems (muscle system, the neural system, circulatory system, etc.), to whatever level is desired. The structure of the knowledge system, then, is determined by how the objects, relationships, and hierarchies are defined. For our medical example we would use a behavioral hierarchy, since most of our attribute-value pairs will be chemistry values and symptoms. A *cause* is a necessary relationship between two behaviors, and we can represent causes in terms of behavior.

As you move from the shallow to the deep knowledge level in any domain, there must be an increasing amount of knowledge needed about the domain and how the parts relate to the whole. In moving from the structural to the behavioral level, you will need some type of causal theory of representation. To move from the behavioral to the functional level, you will need a teleological theory of representation (Fig. 5-4).

Deep Knowledge versus Shallow Knowledge

Since the primary purpose of the computer is a functional one, the knowledge at this level is the deepest knowledge for the user's domain. *Deep knowledge* is defined as the basic theories, facts, and axioms about a specific domain, and contrasts with the surface or shallow knowledge of the structural hierarchy or physical hierarchy. The definition of deep knowledge and shallow knowledge in a particular domain and problem solution depends on the problem. Deep knowledge in a domain refers to basic theories and facts in a particular domain. Shallow knowledge refers to basic heuristics and experiential judgments that are used when the basic theories and facts are not known.

Again remember that the human mind does not distinguish these hierarchies and deep/shallow knowledge so readily in solving a problem. The expert brings all resources available: Shallow (and deep, if available) knowledge is applied to the solution of a problem. In building a knowledgebase, in contrast, you must distinguish these hierarchies in defining the type of representation that will be used.

Another way to view the difference between deep and shallow knowledge is to imagine yourself as a knowledge engineer working with a doctor to implement a knowledge system to help the doctor make decisions. You work with many doctor/patient sessions (perhaps videotaping) to learn the correlation between the test results, the patient history, and various health problems. Suppose you don't worry about how the doctor reasons to a specific conclusion, you just code the information and the conclusions in production rules. This enables the knowledge system user to make the same decisions in an identical situation. Such a system, however, would be very dangerous to use and no patient would trust it. This is shallow knowledge, because the basic theories that the doctor learned in medical school and from experience are missing.

In the same way, you could watch an expert poker player, memorize the decisions the expert makes with a particular hand when particular cards are played, and then try to reproduce these decisions. Again, this is a very shallow knowledge. The deeper rules that the poker player used to make decisions are not there.

In implementing deep knowledge, the engineer must explore the deeper functional aspects of the knowledge in the domain. The basic theories that relate to decisions are all there. In some areas of the domain, the knowledge may be missing. In this case heuristics and more shallow representations must be used.

Representing versus Implementing Knowledge

The knowledge engineer defines the domain and creates the representation for the domain. A representational theory is used to get from the domain to the representation (see Fig. 5-1). The animal game knowledgebase was described in Chapter 4 using production rules. To implement this in Prolog, you will need to use another type of representation: predicate logic. This means converting the knowledgebase from one representation to another. The Prolog version is the *implementation*.

If you use any of the knowledge system tools, you may find the way you communicate the knowledge to the system (the knowledge representation) and the way the system stores and uses the knowledge (the implementation) is different. To use Expert-Ease, you describe the knowledge to the system as a matrix of examples of problem solutions. The program then compiles this to a rulebase that is used by the system to solve new problems. The implementation is often called the *architecture of the system*, to distinguish it from the representational theory.

ACQUIRING KNOWLEDGE

The final step is that of actually acquiring the knowledge and putting it into the knowledgebase. The problem should be broken down, as much as possible, into several small subproblems. The knowledge engineer needs to listen to the expert to determine where this partitioning can be done. The engineer also needs to determine the basic strategies used by the expert in approaching and solving the problem.

The initial language used by the expert is often specialized, limited to the domain of the problem, and often inadequate for the problem solution. The expert does not need to spend time learning the representational theory, the vocabulary of knowledge systems, or any aspects of the representation. That is the job of the knowledge engineer, and detracts from the expert's ability to solve problems in his or her domain.

The acquisition process is cyclic rather than linear, and is less structured than any part of the knowledgebase design. The engineer will first obtain as much knowledge as possible on a particular module or part of the system. This part of the knowledgebase is then tested, and both the expert and engineer can expect major limitations at this point. The knowledgebase is then modified, expanded, then tested again. This process continues, with the system gradually increasing in ability.

Here are some general design rules:

1. Select a task that is suitable for knowledge system design.
2. Specify the precise goal you are trying to accomplish.
3. Become as familiar as possible with the problem.
4. Identify subgoals, breaking the problem into small problems.
5. Identify key problem areas.
6. Find an expert who is familiar with the domain and will make the commitment to help you with the knowledgebase design.
7. Follow through with the expert on the solution of several example problems. Record the processes in detail.
8. Select the software that you will use for the system tools. This will be determined by the type of problem to be solved, the financial resources available, and the size of the problem domain. Select the hardware to support the software.
9. Build a prototype model using your example problems solved by the expert.
10. Begin the design of the knowledgebase. Define the objects, the relationships of the objects, the hierarchies, and taxonomy. Structure your knowledgebase as the expert would see it.
11. Use the cyclic method of adding knowledge, testing, then modifying, and adding again.
12. Design and purchase tools that will help with the design.

13. Document your design.
14. Work toward creating limited but accurate models at the beginning to gain the confidence of the expert, i.e, use modular design.

The knowledge engineer should avoid approaching the expert with an IF-THEN type of dialog. In this approach the engineer creates an example and asks the expert how the expert would solve that particular example. The result of this approach is a rather shallow knowledge. The better alternative is to try to build a prototype or model of the domain.

If you are approaching your first design, work with a problem that is well-bounded and can be clearly defined within the limit of the financial and technical resources available. It is better to underestimate your expectations to the expert than to overestimate what can be expected. If you are writing a proposal for a system design use examples of what has been done and do enough research to indicate the cost and time it took to accomplish these projects in the past. Build a prototype that is as accurate as possible within a small domain. This will gain the confidence of the expert. Then gradually expand the domain of the prototype.

EXERCISES

1. Assume the following application: the design of a knowledge system for automobile repair.

   a) What strategies would an expert use to acquire knowledge in this domain?

   b) What are the steps that the knowledge engineer would use in knowledge acquisition and the design of the system?

2. How is developing an expert system similar to writing a traditional computer program? How is it different?
3. How would you evaluate an expert system? Design an evaluation strategy for the automobile repair example. What would you measure? What cannot be measured?
4. Can you think of an example in which you would wish to use a shallow representation in a knowledge system? How does the issue of shallow versus deep knowledge systems relate to learning? Would a learning system start from a shallow representation? Discuss the relationship with a specific example.

PART II

BUILDING KNOWLEDGE SYSTEMS

K NOWLEDGE SYSTEM CONSTRUCTION IS AS MUCH A SKILL AS A SCIENCE AND is developed through practice. In Part II, the major emphasis will be on detailed development of knowledge-system concepts. The major parts of a knowledge system will be constructed in Forth, a readily available computing environment. Chapter 6 is a Forth tutorial, and the foundation for further software development. In Chapter 7, the core of AI programming—list processing—is introduced. Some of the more difficult AI programming techniques are explained in detail in Chapter 8. With this background, a knowledge system rule interpreter like the one in Prolog is constructed and explained in detail. Finally, Chapters 10 and 11 discuss other AI concepts not covered in building the Prolog system. Chapter-end exercises provide additional exposure to AI-style program construction.

DENNIS L. FEUCHT

Chapter 6

Forth: A Versatile Expert Systems Language

E XPERT SYSTEMS CAN BE WRITTEN IN ALMOST ANY COMPUTER LANGUAGE. Even old languages such as BASIC and Fortran could be used to construct rule interpreters and create knowledgebases. More recent languages such as C, Pascal, and Modula-2 would be more appropriate, but they also are not optimized for AI programming. None of these languages provides the data structures needed to represent knowledge easily or access, modify, or make logical inferences from them.

AI languages make the representation of facts and rules easier and more explicit, allowing the programmer to think in terms of the problem being solved rather than the coding details. Two languages in particular, Prolog and Smalltalk, provide much of the underlying capability to allow expression of the problem domain. One of the oldest languages, LISP, is continuing to gain usage even though it is almost as old as Fortran.

LISP is more general in its capabilities than Prolog or Smalltalk in that the commands of the language allow data manipulation at a lower level of abstraction. It is primarily a language for processing lists. Since lists are a general, powerful data structure useful for creating knowledgebases, LISP can be used to build many different kinds of representations as well as many different rule interpreters. Because of its versatility and history, LISP has been the dominant language used by the AI community in America.

The main language to be considered here—and at some length—is Forth, which emerged primarily as a real-time control language in the early seventies. It was popularized by the Forth Interest Group (FIG) in the lower San Francisco Bay area in the late seventies, when their public domain Forth (called Fig-Forth) was made available for numerous processors. General Electric has used Forth to write an expert diagnostician for their locomotives.

Forth was chosen for detailed explanation of the knowledge system implemented here because of its ready availability for essentially any small computer, its low price, and its similarity to AI languages such as LISP. In Chapter 7, a LISP-like extension to Forth in presented. An appendix contains a list of sources that supply Forth.

Later chapters present discussion of LISP, Prolog, and Smalltalk, focusing on the AI concepts of major interest in each of them. The Forth language will be described in detail because it will be used to implement and experiment with AI concepts. The following chapters will make extensive use of Forth. Forth is explained more fully in several books, which would be a recommended accompaniment to this introduction. A list is given in the appendix.

The main advantages of Forth for knowledge system development are its extreme extensibility, its interactive, interpretive environment, and its conceptual simplicity. Its main disadvantage is that it requires attention to programming details that other languages hide, especially having to do with parameter passing on a stack.

WORDS AND THE DICTIONARY

Forth is a highly interactive interpreted language. It consists of a *dictionary* that contains Forth *words*. These words represent procedures or data, and all of them can be executed. Associated with each word is a procedure which is invoked when the word is executed. At execution, this *run-time procedure* acts as an interpreter for the word, determining what action should be taken.

Forth is defined by a set of standard words. Some of these words can be used to create new words. They are known as *defining-words*. To write a program in Forth, one or more of the available defining-words are used to "define" new words. The most common defining-word, a colon (:), is used to define procedures. It is used in the form:

: name *definition* ;

The name of the word to be defined immediately follows the colon.

In Forth, the space (or blank) is the delimiter used to separate words. Since : is a word, it is followed by a blank to separate it from the name of the word to be defined. After the word name, the names of other previously defined words are given in the sequence in which they are to be executed. Finally, the definition is ended with a semicolon, which is also a word—the word that ends colon-definitions.

The : is not the only defining-word in Forth. Other standard ones are CODE, VARIABLE, and CONSTANT. CODE is used to write words in assembly language. Most Forth environments provide a Forth assembler for this purpose. CODE is used in the form:

CODE name *assembly-code* END-CODE

(Sometimes C; is used as a synonym for END-CODE.) This capability can be important for AI programming, since words that execute often (such as the rule interpreter) can run faster by being recoded as CODE words. Once the algorithmic aspect of a word has been worked out as a colon-definition (or "high-level" definition), it can then be rewritten in assembly language as a CODE word. This capability allows Forth to span an extremely wide range of abstraction, from assembly language up to problem-oriented word definitions.

The remaining standard defining-words are used to create variables and constants as data types. VARIABLE creates variables, and is used in the form:

VARIABLE name

where the name of the variable follows VARIABLE. VARIABLE allots a memory cell (usually 16 bits) where the value of the variable can be stored. When a variable is invoked, the run-time action will return a pointer to this location. This pointer can then be used to read or write (or, in Forth language, "fetch" or "store") the variable value.

Similarly, CONSTANT defines constants; they are "fetch-only" values and are defined as:

value **CONSTANT name**

where the value preceding CONSTANT is a number. When the defined constant is invoked, the run-time action will return the value of the constant. Thus, even data types "do" something when invoked, making Forth a completely procedural language; all words are best thought of as procedures.

PASSING DATA USING THE STACK

Constants and variables return either numbers or pointers to numbers when invoked. But where are they returned to? Forth has a data stack (or *parameter stack*) which is used by words to send data to each other. A stack is a common data structure in itself and was popularized by its use in Hewlett-Packard calculators. Numbers can be successively *pushed* onto a stack, and when they are *popped* from it, they come off in the order: last on, first off. For example, if the numbers 1 2 3 are pushed on the Forth data stack and then the stack is popped three times, the order of the numbers coming off the stack would be 3 2 1. To actually demonstrate this, the word in Forth for popping the top number off the data stack and printing it is simply a period (.). The result of typing:

1 2 3 . . .

(followed by a return) would be:

3 2 1 ok

The **ok** is the Forth prompt.

To indicate how a word will affect the stack, a notation commonly in use is to write the items on the stack left to right, with the rightmost item being on the top of the stack. Then, the effect a word has can be shown by indicating the state of the stack before the word is invoked followed by its state after the invocation. The two states are separated by a dash (−) or a right-pointing (− >). For example, . will remove the top item from the stack and print it as a number with stack activity:

(n − >)

where n is the number and the absence of n on the right side of the arrow indicates that it was removed from the stack. To further illustrate, the word for adding the top two numbers on the stack is +. It leaves the sum of n1 and n2 as n3:

(n1 n2 − > n3)

With this notation, stack activity can be kept track of as a sequence of words are being followed in reading Forth code.

HIERARCHICAL DECOMPOSITION AND MODULARITY

To some who have looked at Forth, the need to keep track of the stack is an arduous exercise. Although it allows a low-level view of what is going on, it also tends to distract the programmer from the problem to the details of coding. This is, perhaps, the major criticism of Forth. Because Forth can be extended by defining new words, however, low-level activities can be hidden by higher levels of abstraction. Languages that use local variables instead of a stack do this, of course, but their disadvantage is that they do not allow the programmer access to their inner workings. In contrast, Forth is transparent all the way down to its CODE words. That is, the words that implement Forth can also be used by the programmer. (Local variables can be implemented in Forth but will not be used here.) Explicit use will be made of the stack because it often provides insight into what a word does. This is especially true of recursive programming, where words call themselves and pass arguments to themselves via the stack.

Forth encourages *functional* programming. That is, each word acts as a function, receiving its arguments from the stack, performing a computation on them, and returning the result on the stack. By confining the affected data to the stack, no side effects on global data can occur. Each word can be treated as a self-contained module which has a well-defined and easily traced action in the overall program.

This modularity makes program diagnosis (or "debugging") much easier, since the overall program can be decomposed into individual modules which can be tested, one at a time. Decomposition reduces the complexity to manageable *levels* of abstraction. A set of such levels forms a *hierarchy*. Forth at its lowest level consists of the Forth *nucleus*, a small set of CODE words from which all the high-level Forth words are defined. Then, using these standard words which define Forth, an application can be built by defining a set of words that perform the application. This "layering" results in successively higher levels of abstraction from the raw machine code of the CODE words at the bottom. This abstraction hierarchy is illustrated in Fig. 6-1.

At the bottom level is Forth, which contains several levels in itself. At its bottom is the nucleus of machine-dependent CODE words. Next is the *device layer*. It contains the words used in Forth to interact with the keyboard, display, and disk. The third

Applications layer	Words written in Forth and compiled in the dictionary which perform a task for the user.
Compiler layer	Words which create new words in the dictionary (defining-words) or aid compilation of new words.
Interpreter layer	Words which support interpretation of the text from keyboard or disk.
Device layer	Words that allow access to I/O devices: • keyboard and display drivers • disk driver words
Nucleus layer	Words defined in machine code that control the execution of the fundamental operations of the virtual Forth machine. • run-time words for defining-words and compiling-words • inner interpreter (address interpreter)

(Forth-83 bracket spans Compiler layer through Nucleus layer)

Fig. 6-1. Forth is organized in levels, forming a hierarchy.

layer is the *interpreter layer,* which contains the words needed to implement the Forth interpreter that the user interacts with. This interpreter is also called the *outer interpreter.* Finally, the *compiler layer* contains control constructs and defining-words. This layer allows the creation of new words in the Forth dictionary. The required word set of Forth-83 is shown in Fig. 6-2. Some of the most common of these words will be described here. All the words are given functional definitions in the *Forth-83 Standard* (see appendix.)

FORTH ARITHMETIC

We have seen that Forth operates on arguments via a stack, and that + and . can act on stack items. The 16-bit integer number is standard for Forth on 8-bit machines; on 32-bit processors, however, this "cell" size is often 32 bits. As long as consistency of size is maintained throughout an implementation of Forth, the cell size should not affect the basic function of the Forth words themselves. This size, whatever it may be, is the size of a Forth single-precision number and machine addresses.

Forth defines both single- and double-precision numbers. Double-precision arithmetic is not needed for symbolic computing and will not be discussed further here; see the references for detail.

nucleus layer

!	2+	CMOVE>	MOD
*	2-	COUNT	NEGATE
*/	2/	D+	NOT
*/MOD	<	D<	OR
+	=	DEPTH	OVER
+!	>	DNEGATE	PICK
-	>R	DROP	R>
/	?DUP	DEXECUTE	R@
/MOD	@	EXIT	ROLL
0<	ABS	FILL	ROT
0=	AND	I	SWAP
0>	C!	J	U<
1+	C@	MAX	UM*
1-	CMOVE	MIN	UM/MOD
			XOR

device layer

BLOCK	KEY
BUFFER	SAVE-BUFFERS
CR	SPACE
EMIT	SPACES
EXPECT	TYPE
FLUSH	UPDATE

interpreter layer

#	<#	FIND	PAD
#>	>BODY	FORGET	QUIT
#S	>IN	FORTH	SIGN
#TIB	ABORT	FORTH-83	SPAN
'	BASE	HERE	TIB
(	BLK	HOLD	U.
-TRAILING	CONVERT	LOAD	WORD
.	DECIMAL		
.(	DEFINITIONS		

compiler layer

+LOOP	,	."	:
;	DO	LOOP	VOCABULARY
ABORT"	DOES>	REPEAT	WHILE
ALLOT	ELSE	STATE	[
BEGIN	IF	THEN	[']
COMPILE	IMMEDIATE	UNTIL	[COMPILE]
CONSTANT	LEAVE	VARIABLE	]
CREATE	LITERAL		

Fig. 6-2. The required word set of Forth-83.

84

Forth has the four basic arithmetic functions and some variations on them. Subtract is:

–	(n1 n2 –> n3)	Subtracts n2 from n1, leaving n3 on the stack.

Multiplication and division of numbers are accomplished by:

*	(n1 n2 –> n3)	Multiplies n1 and n2, leaving the least significant half of the product on the stack.
/	(n1 n2 –> n3)	Divides n1 by n2, leaving the quotient as n3.

To retain the remainder from a division, use:

/MOD	(n1 n2 –> r q)	Divides n1 by n2, leaving remainder, r, and quotient, q.

For quick multiplication or division by two (accomplished by shifting), 2* or 2/ are:

2*	(n1 –> n2)	The value of n2 is 2 times n1.
2/	(n1 –> n2)	The value of n2 is half n1. No rounding of the result occurs; it is truncated.

Also, we will often use words for incrementing and decrementing by one or two:

1+	(n1 – > n2)	Increments n1 by one.
2+	(n1 – > n2)	Increments n1 by two.
1–	(n1 – > n2)	Decrements n1 by one.
2–	(n1 – > n2)	Decrements n1 by two.

For example, to divide 60 by 11 and decrement the quotient:

60 11 / 1 –

results in 4. Since Forth numbers are signed integers, to negate a number:

NEGATE	(n1 –> n2)	The value of n2 = – n1

Besides these basic arithmetic functions, to find the minimum or maximum of two numbers, the words MIN and MAX are used:

MIN	(n1 n2 – > n3)	The value of n3 is the smaller of n1 and n2.
MAX	(n1 n2 – > n3)	The value of n3 is the larger of n1 and n2.

These words assume **n1** and **n2** to be signed numbers. To take the absolute value of a number:

ABS	(n1 – > n2)	The value of n2 is |n1|, the absolute value of n1.

Forth has more arithmetic words, but these are sufficient for implementing programs later in the book.

Internally, Forth arithmetic is done in binary (base-2), but Forth has the capability of inputing and displaying numbers in a base other than decimal. The base (or modulus) is defined by the value of a system variable called BASE. If BASE is 10, as it is initially, arithmetic is done in decimal. To change the base to 16 for hexadecimal arithmetic, use the word HEX. To change back to decimal, invoke DECIMAL. An example of this is:

    20 HEX . 14

where 14 in hexadecimal is 20 in decimal. A convention for indicating that the base of a number is hexadecimal is to precede it with a dollar sign ($). Thus, 20 is $14.

STACK MANIPULATION

It quickly becomes necessary to have words which move items around on the stack. For example, what if we want to divide 60 by 11 and keep the remainder instead of the quotient? /MOD returns the remainder as the second item on the stack. To remove the quotient, leaving the remainder on the top, the word DROP is used:

DROP (n1 ⟶)	Removes the top item from the stack.

To drop the top two items:

2DROP (n1 n2 – >)	Removes the top two items from the stack.

Sometimes we will need a copy of the top item:

DUP (n1 – > n1 n1)	Duplicates the top item on the stack.

For the top two items:

2DUP (n1 n2 – > n1 n2 n1 n2)	Duplicates the top two items on the stack.

Notice that **2DUP** is *not* (n1 – > n1 n1 n1). It duplicates the top *two* items, not the top item twice.

Sometimes, we will want a copy of the second stack item to work with:

OVER (n1 n2 – > n1 n2 n1)   Pushes a copy of the second stack item on the top of the stack.

Instead of making a copy, to actually get at the second item, the first and second items can be exchanged, or "swapped":

SWAP (n1 n2 – > n2 n1)   Exchanges the top two stack items.

Using these stack words, suppose that we wanted to keep the quotient from a division using /MOD. To get rid of the remainder, we could use DROP if it were on the top of the stack. To get it there, SWAP can be used:

60 11 /MOD SWAP DROP

The SWAP DROP combination drops the second item from the stack. It is a convenient combination, and some Forths define it as:

: NIP SWAP DROP ;

We will use it here, although it is not part of the Forth standard. In creating NIP, we have extended the set of words available for our use.

So far, words have been introduced for manipulating up to two items deep into the stack. All we will need is to go three items deep (although the words PICK and ROLL extend the depth indefinitely). To move the third item to the top of the stack:

ROT (n1 n2 n3 – > n2 n3 n1)   Rotates n1 to the top of the stack.

The inverse of ROT, which is – ROT, can be defined as:

– ROT (n1 n2 n3 – > n3 n1 n2)   Rotates the top item to the third place in the stack.

Finally, one conditional stack operation is sometimes useful:

?DUP (n1 – > [n1] n1)   Duplicates the top stack item only if it is not zero.

With these words, we can do all the stack manipulation needed to implement the AI programs to come.

ACCESSING DATA

To read and write (or fetch and store) memory, access words are needed. Forth lets you access memory addresses directly like PEEK and POKE do in BASIC. To access data words such as variables, fetch and store words are needed:

@ (addr – > n)
> Pronounced "fetch"; returns the number beginning at address **addr** to the stack.

! (n addr – >)
> Pronounced "store"; stores n in memory beginning at address **addr**.

In 8-bit machines, a Forth number is 16 bits and requires two memory locations to store. The order of the bytes (that is, whether the most significant byte of the number is stored at **addr** or **addr**+1) is machine-dependent.

Having memory access words, we can now handle variables. For example, to change the numeric I/O base to hexadecimal, we can now change the variable BASE:

16 BASE !

If we fetch **BASE** and print it:

BASE @

the result is 10 no matter what base we are in. (Why?)

Sometimes we will want to access a byte—one memory location—instead of a full 16-bit number. Text characters, in ASCII code, occupy a single byte. To access a character, we use:

C@ (addr – > n)
> Pronounced "c-fetch"; replaces the address **addr** with its contents. The MSB of the top item, **n**, is zero.

C! (n addr – >)
> Pronounced "c-store"; stores the LSB of **n** at address **addr**.

(MSB and LSB stand for most- and least-significant bytes.)

Besides these general access words are several specialized functions. To modify the value at an address:

+! (n addr – >)
> Pronounced "plus-store"; adds n to the contents of address **addr**.

The word +! performs a signed addition and can be used for stepping indices of loops. Two other words that are not part of the Forth standard, but are quite useful are:

ON (addr – >)   Stores a true flag at address **addr**.

OFF (addr – >)   Stores a **false** flag at address **addr**.

FLAGS, LOGICAL OPERATORS, AND NUMERICAL COMPARISONS

In Forth-83, flags are used to indicate yes/no or true/false outcomes of tests. A true flag is defined as -1 and a false flag as zero. The choice of -1 instead of 1 for true was made because all the bits of the number -1 are ones. (Forth uses two's complement arithmetic.) For a false flag the bits are all zero. With this choice, the Forth word NOT can change a true flag to a false flag and vice-versa. NOT is a Boolean operator; it performs a logical negation on the bits of a number.

NOT (n1 – > n2)   The value of **n2** is the logical bitwise complement of **n1**.

For any given bit in **n1**, if it is 0, then it will be changed to 1 in **n2**; a one will be changed to a zero. This bitwise activity is true of the other logical operators as well:

AND (n1 n2 – > n3)   The value of **n3** is the logical conjunction of **n1** and **n2**. A bit in **n3** will be 1 only if both corresponding bits in **n1** and **n2** are 1.

OR (n1 n2 – > n3)   The value of **n3** is the logical disjunction of **n1** and **n2**. A bit in **n3** will be 0 only if both corresponding bits in **n1** and **n2** are 0.

XOR (n1 n2 – > n3)   The value of **n3** is the bitwise exclusive-or of **n1** and **n2**. A bit in **n3** will be 1 only if the corresponding bits in **n1** and **n2** are of different value.

These logical operators are useful in combining flags. For example, if we want a flag which is true only if **flag1** and **flag2** are both true, we could combine these flags with AND to produce the desired flag.

We will want to place flags on the stack. Instead of using the numbers that define the flags, 0 and -1, it would make the code more readable to define TRUE and FALSE as constants whose values are those of the flags they represent.

Words which return flags are called *boolean operators* because quantities that can have only two possible values are boolean. Forth has some boolean operators that test numbers. The most common of these words is:

= (n1 n2 – > f)   Pronounced "equal"; if **n1** = **n2** then **f** is true.

Others are:

< (n1 n2 – > f)   Pronounced "less than"; if **n1** < **n2**, then **f** is true.

> (n1 n2 – > f)   Pronounced "greater than"; if **n1** > **n2** then **f** is true.

< > (n1 n2 – > f)   Pronounced "not equal"; if n1 does not equal n2, then f is true.

Operators which compare against zero are:

0 = (n1 – > f)   The value of f is true if n1 equals zero.

0< (n1 – > f)   The value of f is true if n1 < 0.

0> (n1 – > f)   The value of f is true if n1 > 0.

The flags produced by boolean operators and processed by logical operators are used by control words to direct the flow of word execution.

FORTH CONTROL CONSTRUCTS

So far, you have learned to do arithmetic, manipulate the stack, access data in memory, perform boolean tests, and logically combine their results. The words that perform these functions can be used to write procedures as colon-definitions. But to write nontrivial words, we will need *control words* which make decisions about what to execute next. Forth is based on *structured control* concepts. Forth words consist of modular fragments of code, where each module has controlled entry and exit points.

Figure 6-3 illustrates unstructured code, and Fig. 6-4 in comparison shows the control constructs of Forth, each acting as a module of code. Notice that each construct has only one entrance and one exit. (The only exceptions to this are in the use of LEAVE in do-loops, which we will not use, and in terminating execution due to errors. Forth has no GOTO.)

Figures 6-4A and 6-4B show the basic branching construct. The ELSE branch can be omitted. The Forth code reads:

IF A THEN or IF A ELSE B THEN

IF does the branching and has stack activity: (f – >). If the flag f is true, the IF branch, A, is executed. Otherwise, the ELSE branch, B, (or the code following THEN if there is no ELSE branch) is executed. When the code following IF reaches ELSE, it continues after THEN.

The BEGIN-UNTIL loop (Fig. 6-4C) tests a flag after executing sequence A of code. UNTIL does the test and takes a flag from the stack as IF does. If the flag is false it branches, just as IF branches to the ELSE code if its flag is false.

In Fig. 6-4D, WHILE also branches if its flag is false. For the BEGIN-WHILE loop, sequence A following BEGIN is executed. Then WHILE is encountered. WHILE takes a flag from the stack; if it is true, it executes sequence B, which ends with the word REPEAT. This word causes control to loop back to BEGIN. The Forth coding is:

BEGIN A WHILE B REPEAT

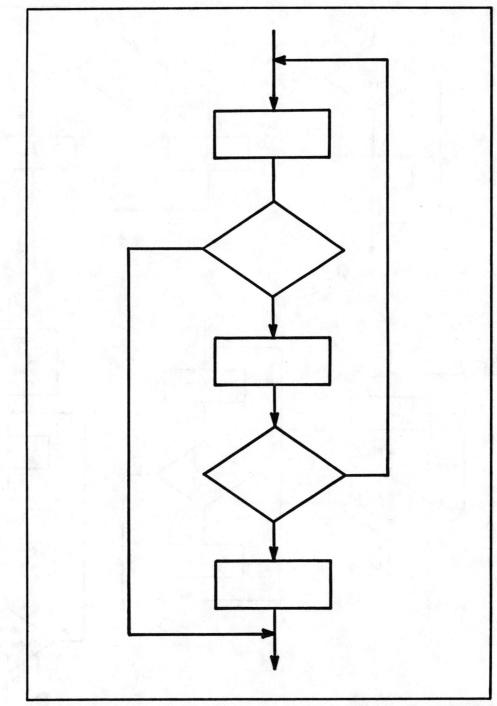

Fig. 6-3. An example of unstructured code. The boxes represent fragments of sequentially executed code. The loops formed by the decision points overlap, each branching into and out of the other's loops.

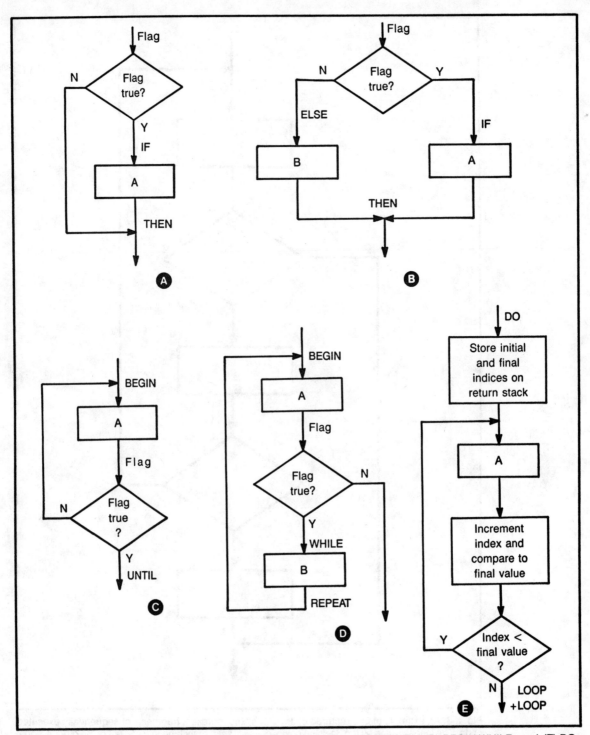

Fig. 6-4. Forth control constructs: (A) IF-THEN, (B) IF-ELSE-THEN, (C) BEGIN-UNTIL, (D) BEGIN-WHILE, and (E) DO-LOOP or DO-+LOOP.

For these control constructs, IF, UNTIL, and WHILE all branch if the flag is false. Because the action they take is similar, they share common run-time branching routines. When a control word is encountered in a Forth colon-definition (while compiling), it causes a branching routine to be compiled in the code which executes when the word being defined is later executed. When we examine what compiling-words do, the run-time details of control words will be explained.

Sometimes an iterative loop is needed for which the number of iterations is known ahead of its execution. In BASIC, this construct is FOR-NEXT, and in Forth it is DO-LOOP or DO − +LOOP, shown in Fig. 6-4E. DO takes two arguments from the stack:

DO (*limit index* − >)   Pushes index and limit on the return stack and removes them from the parameter stack. *Index* is the initial index value, and *limit* is 1 more than the final index value.

This description of DO introduces the other stack used by Forth, the *return stack*. It is called this because it is used mainly by Forth to keep track of where to return when it jumps to execute a word. This involves the Forth virtual machine, which will be discussed later. Do-loops also use it, since an entire loop must be within a Forth word. The use of the return stack by a do-loop is over by the time the word ends (at ;).

DO transfers the two index values from the parameter stack to the return stack. The index value is the initial value of the loop index, and *limit* is one count beyond the final index value. It is one beyond because LOOP increments the index first and then compares it to *limit*. If they are equal, it leaves the loop. LOOP increments the index by one.

If a different step size (including negative steps) is desired, +LOOP is used instead. Unlike LOOP, which does not affect the parameter stack, +LOOP takes the step size—the amount it should add to the index—off the stack. To access the value of the index within the loop, the word I is used to push the index value on the parameter stack.

With these control words, we can now begin to define sample Forth words. To print out the numbers from 1 to n, this use of a do-loop will do it:

(n − >)
: .#S 1+ 1 DO I . LOOP ;

First, it is always good practice to write the stack activity above the word. This is relevant when typing in word definitions as Forth source-code to be stored on disk. The name of the word being defined is .#S and it immediately follows the colon. The definition of .#S then contains the code which displays the numbers.

Since we are assuming that a number will be passed on the stack, 1+ sets the limit at one beyond the number (so that it is also printed). The initial number is one so the initial index value for the do-loop is set at one. Having done this in anticipation of DO, the stack now contains the two index values it needs. Within the do-loop, I pushes the index value on the stack and . prints it, removing it from the stack as well. LOOP completes the do-loop. If you have Forth available, try this word for **n** = 10. What you type is:

    10 .#S

and the response would be:

    1 2 3 4 5 6 7 8 9 10 ok

The same result could have been attained by using a control construct other than a do-loop. Here is the same word implemented using a BEGIN-UNTIL loop:

    (n – >)
    : .#S 1+ 1 BEGIN DUP . 1+ 2DUP = UNTIL 2DROP ;

The longer definition in this case shows that the do-loop is the better choice for this function. Within the loop, two numbers are used on the stack. The **2DUP** makes a copy of both the index and the limit for =, which consumes them and provides a flag to **UNTIL**. When the loop is exited, these indices are still on the stack; the **2DROP** removes them. To keep track of stack activity, the state of the stack can be written underneath each word, showing the result after the word has executed. More examples of these control words can be found on Screens 40 through 45 and 60 through 65 in Chapters 7 and 9, respectively, or in Appendix A.

A nonstandard but popular control construct is the CASE statement using the words CASE, OF, ENDOF, and ENDCASE. It is a generalization of the IF-THEN construct in that it allows for an indefinite number of branches. Each branch is enclosed by OF and ENDOF. An example of a CASE statement is:

    (n – >)
    CASE 1
        OF A ENDOF 2
        OF B ENDOF 3
        OF C ENDOF
        D
    ENDCASE

CASE takes an item on the stack, which often is a character, and compares it to what is pushed on the stack before an OF word. In this example, n is compared to 1. If they are equal, n is dropped from the stack and sequence A is executed. Then ENDOF causes execution to continue after ENDCASE. If n is not 1, then the next OF compares it to 2, etc. If none of the tests succeed, D is executed, with **n** still on the stack. Finally, ENDCASE drops n from the stack. A subtlety in writing D is that often n is used by D. In that case, D must leave something on the stack to be dropped by ENDCASE. CASE is used by READL on Screen 46 (Chapter 7/Appendix A).

THE RETURN STACK

We have seen that the return stack holds indices for do-loops. It can also be used under certain conditions as another stack. Handling data on the parameter stack occasionally becomes awkward, and if we could put items somewhere else for a while, our programming would be easier. Variables could be defined and data placed in them, but Forth enables the programmer to avoid creating variables only for temporary storage.

To access the return stack from the parameter stack, three words have been defined in Forth (other than index retrievers such as I):

>R (n – >)	Pronounced "to-r"; pops a number off the parameter stack and pushes it onto the return stack.
R> (– > n)	Pronounced "r-from"; pops a number off the return stack and pushes it onto the parameter stack.
R@ (– > n)	Pronounced "r-fetch"; pushes a copy of the top of the return stack onto the parameter stack.

The return stack operates in the same way as the parameter stack. The sequence of words:

```
1 2 3 >R >R >R R@ . R> . R> . R> .
```

produces:

```
1 1 2 3 ok
```

The 3 is first in and last out of the return stack.

The restriction in use of these words is in do-loops. Since LOOP and +LOOP use the return stack to manage indices, any use of these words within do-loops must return the stack to its original state before the looping word is encountered. A more subtle restriction is illustrated by the code:

```
. . . >R . . . DO . . . R> . . .
```

Here, an item is pushed to the return stack, to be retrieved within a do-loop. But the R> in the loop retrieves the index instead, since DO has pushed two items on the return stack. Thus, passing data into a do-loop using the return stack is restricted. It can be done by retrieving the third item of the return stack, but easier and less dangerous means usually can be found.

STRING HANDLING

A major aspect of computing is text processing. Computer programs are written in languages that are expressed as text. Source code is text that is handled by the Forth interpreter or compiler. Text consists of characters—ASCII characters for Forth—which are combined into sequences as *character strings.*

In Forth, strings occur in several ways; the names of Forth words in the dictionary are strings. A string is a data type structured as a sequence of one-byte characters preceded by a one-byte count of the number of characters in the string. This count is called the *string length.* The string "ABC" would be stored in memory as:

3 65 66 67

where the numbers 65 through 67 are the decimal ASCII codes for the letters A, B, and C, respectively.

Strings can be represented on the stack in two ways. The first is by a pointer (address) to the string. The second, and most common, is to leave a pointer to the first character along with the count. In stack notation this is:

(a u – >)

where **a** is the address and **u** the count. This will be standard stack notation here. If a pointer to a string is used, it will be indicated as a pointer by a ∧ preceding it. Thus, ∧a indicates a pointer to the count byte of a string.

A string pointer can be converted to a string (as represented on the stack) by the word COUNT:

COUNT (∧a – > a u) Converts a pointer to a string into a string representation on the stack.

COUNT fetches the count byte and increments ∧a by one. With a string on the stack, we can print it to the display with the word TYPE:

TYPE (a u – >) Displays a string on the output device.

Sometimes we will want to display a string literal. For example, suppose that we want to display the message "GOALS:" as shown on Screen 65 in the word TRACE. To do this, the word ." is used:

." (– >) Displays characters following the word as a character string up to a closing quote (").

Since ." is a Forth word, it must be followed by a blank. After one blank, the characters begin and continue until a double quote (") occurs. This quote mark ends the string.

Some Forth implementations allow the creation of strings with the Forth word ". It too must be followed by one space and ended with a double quote. This word will place the string in a temporary location, called the PAD, and will leave the string representation on the stack.

A word used for comments has already been in use. It is the left parenthesis, which allows comments until a right parenthesis is encountered. Any text following the left parenthesis, up to and including the right parenthesis, is skipped over. A nonstandard word, the backslash, ($\backslash$) is commonly used to make the rest of a line a comment for source code on disk. Its use can be seen on many of the source code screens throughout Part II.

Some characters are used so frequently that they have their own Forth word. A return (or "carriage return") is CR and a space or blank is BL. CR will output a return, while BL puts the blank character on the stack. SPACE, outputs a blank.

TEXT STREAMS

We have been assuming that text is output to the display and input from keyboard or disk. In Forth, text I/O is envisioned as streams of characters of indefinite length. These are called the *input stream* and *output stream*. As we saw earlier, just above the nucleus layer of Forth is the device layer. This layer contains the words which drive I/O devices. The input and output streams are channeled through two device words, KEY and EMIT. The input stream comes from KEY whether it is from the keyboard or not:

KEY (– > c)   Inputs a character from the input stream
                                and pushes it on the stack.

Similarly, all characters of the output stream go through EMIT:

EMIT (c – >)   Outputs a character from the stack.

These words are defined by a defining-word we have not yet seen called DEFER. It defines words that are *execution vectors*, i.e., words which can be set to execute another Forth word. For example, if the output stream is to go to the CRT display. EMIT can be set to execute (EMIT), the display driver. If the output stream is instead to be directed to the printer, EMIT can be set to, say, (PREMIT), a printer driver word. The details of DEFER will be discussed after Forth word structure is explained.

FORTH WORD STRUCTURE

The preceding description of Forth has paid little attention to the way in which words are actually compiled into memory. Forth implementation itself is not specified by a standard, since an optimal implementation depends on the processor and system on which it is to run. However, many Forth implementations are similar, and the implementation described here is very typical. Figure 6-5 shows the structural detail.

A word has four fields, as shown to the right of the memory. The base address of each of these fields has a name, as shown on the left. The first field is the *link field*. It is located at the *link-field address* (lfa). The link field contains a pointer linking a word to the previous word in the dictionary. This pointer is a link which is part of the list structure of the dictionary. The first word in the dictionary has a zero link field value indicating the end of the list.

Notice that the word WORD2 links back to the next field of WORD1, the *name field,* located by its *name-field address* (nfa). The name field is the most complex of the fields. Its first byte is broken into fields. The most-significant bit is always set to 1 to indicate an end of the name field. The last character in the name field will also have its MSB set to 1, and the other characters set to 0. This bit is used to traverse the name field. The next bit (bit 6) is set to 1 for compiling-words, which will be explained later. The lowest five bits are the count field, which contains the count of the characters in the name and acts as the count for a string. Thus, the name field is a modified string.

After the name field is the *code field* at the *code-field address* (cfa). This field contains a pointer to the word which will be run when WORD1 is executed. This run-time routine acts as an interpreter of the word; more on it later.

Finally, the last field is the parameter field or *body* of WORD1, and is at the *parameter-field address* (pfa). The body contains data or code defining the word. This is in a form called "threaded code," which also will be described with the Forth virtual machine.

Since each field of a word has a different use, we may at times need the address of a field. The default field in Forth-83 is the code field. To get the cfa of WORD1:

   ' WORD1

will return it, where ' (pronounced "tick")—a single quotation mark—pushes the cfa of WORD1 on the stack. The following words are used to get around within a word. Their stack activity explains their function:

    >BODY   (cfa – > pfa)
    >NAME   (cfa – > nfa)
    BODY>   (pfa – > cfa)
    NAME>   (nfa – > cfa)
    L>NAME (lfa – > nfa)

A word used to display the name-field string is .ID:

   .ID (nfa – >)   Outputs the name-field characters.

The Forth compiler uses the variable LAST to point to the nfa of the last word defined in the dictionary. It provides a pointer to the head of the dictionary list.

DICTIONARY MANAGEMENT

Forth has a few words for managing the dictionary itself. To list the dictionary words beginning with the most recently defined word (pointed to by LAST), use the word WORDS (or VLIST in some Forths). This is a nonstandard utility word that shows dictionary word order and is useful in seeing how far the compiler got in defining words.

In the normal course of word development, you may want to remove some definitions from the dictionary. All words can be removed back to and including a given word

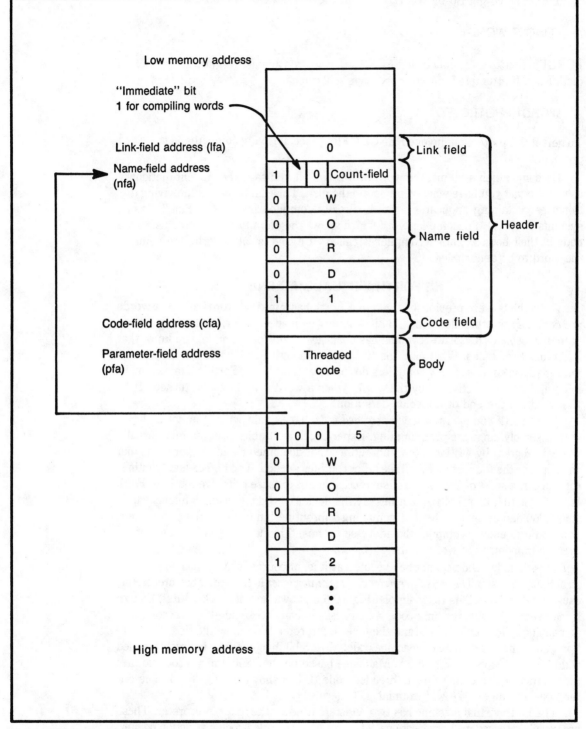

Fig. 6-5. Forth word and dictionary structure.

by FORGET. To get rid of WORD1 and all the words defined after it:

    FORGET WORD1

FORGET checks a variable called FENCE that guards against forgetting the boot-up dictionary. If attempted, an error message will appear:

    WORD1 PROTECTED

To defeat this protection, invoke FENCE OFF. Fence normally points to the last word protected.

On some Forth systems, the word SAVE will let you save the current dictionary as the one that you have when you boot up the disk. This can be useful for saving dictionaries containing applications words already compiled into them. Finally, some systems also have a decompiler word which shows the definitions of words using the code in their bodies. This decompiler is called SEE and is followed by the name of the word to be decompiled.

THE FORTH VIRTUAL MACHINE

A few hints were previously given that Forth has run-time words and that words are compiled as "threaded code." This will now be made clearer. As Forth has been unfolded, some of its software model has been revealed. For example, you know that Forth has two stacks. What else does it have? Although Forth could be compiled as pure machine code, as many compilers do for other languages, Forth contains a built-in compiler that is activated by the word : when a word is defined and turned off by the word ; at the end of the colon-definition.

Most Forth compilers produce *threaded code*. To explain what it is, let us begin with assembly language programming. Experienced assembler programmers usually write a program by writing a few subroutines that do some primitive operations that can serve as the foundation for all the other routines needed. The higher-level routines thus largely consist of a sequence of subroutine jumps to these primitive routines. Forth is similar in that its primitive routines are the nucleus words. For its high-level words (the colon-definitions), instead of compiling subroutine jump instructions to nucleus words, Forth merely compiles the addresses. Thus, threaded code is just a list of addresses in memory of words to be executed.

This threaded code cannot be executed as it is, of course, since it has no jump instructions. So a small *address interpreter* or *inner interpreter* is needed. This interpreter, usually called NEXT, is truly simple. Figure 6-6 shows how it works. First, though it may seem obvious, the only code which actually can be executed by the computer is machine code: CODE words and the inner interpreter. To follow the flow of execution, jumps must terminate on machine code. Most 8-bit machines use indirect threaded code (ITC) as shown in Fig. 6-6A. Machines based on the 68000 microprocessor are more efficient, executing direct threaded code (DTC) shown in Fig. 6-6B. The differences are minor. We will examine ITC here.

The Forth virtual machine has two registers used by the inner interpreter. These are usually reserved memory locations. The first is the threaded-code instruction pointer,

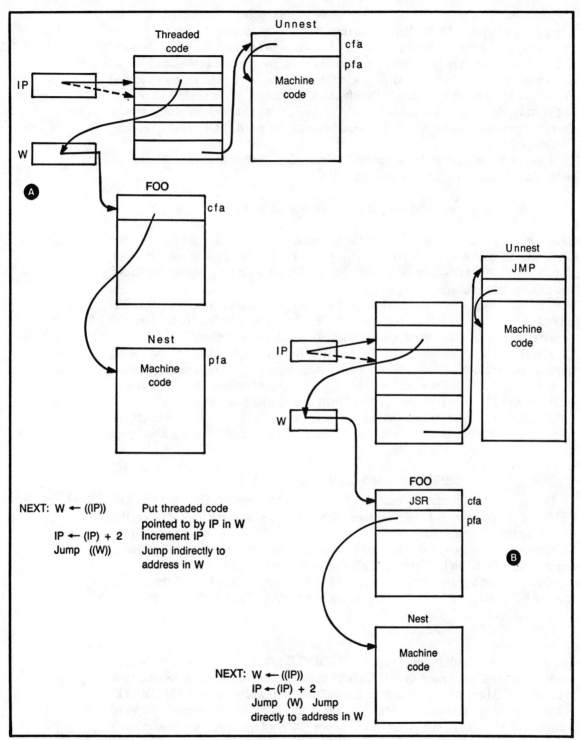

Fig. 6-6. The Forth inner interpreter: (A) for indirect-threaded code, and (B) direct-threaded code.

IP, which acts as a program counter. The other is a temporary working register, W. The inner interpreter, NEXT, interprets threaded code as follows. It first fetches the contents of the location pointed to by IP. This location will contain the cfa of the word to be executed. It is put in W and an indirect jump is made to the contents of W. To see where execution continues, W points to the cfa of the word to be executed (called FOO). The jump continues through the cfa to its contents. The cfa contains a pointer to the run-time word which will interpret the given word. For colon-defined words, the run-time word is called NEST; it is sometimes known as DO-COLON or (:) in older Forths.

Processor execution will continue with this word, so it must always be in machine code. This is worth stating as a general rule:

☐ *The cfa of a word must contain a pointer to machine code.*

NEST will push the contents of IP on the return stack and put the contents of W in IP, then increment it so that it points to the pfa of FOO. Since FOO is colon-defined, IP now points to the first threaded-code address of FOO. NEST then jumps to NEXT and FOO is interpreted.

The last threaded-code address interpreted by NEXT is the CODE word UNNEST. It pops the return stack into IP and calls NEXT. This causes the flow of the inner interpreter to return to the word which called the word just completed.

For DTC, NEXT jumps directly to the cfa of the word to be executed, so the cfa must contain a machine code jump to NEST. Consequently, DTC is more machine-dependent than ITC, but it hardly matters, since it is object code anyway. The source code for both ITC and DTC-interpreted Forth is essentially the same.

Besides the two stacks and the inner interpreter registers, the Forth virtual machine also has a reserved area of memory called N. It is a temporary working space used mainly by arithmetic words.

DEFINING- AND COMPILING-WORDS

Forth can either interpret or compile. The interpreter is usually the word INTER-PRET and the compiler is]. This may seem like a strange name for the compiler. But there is another Forth word, [, which causes the state of Forth to be changed to the interpret state. The two square brackets can then be used within colon-definitions to cause some code to be interpreted. This will prove useful later.

Whether Forth is interpreting or compiling depends on the value of the system variable STATE. If STATE is zero, Forth is interpreting. Thus, [can be defined as:

: [STATE OFF ; IMMEDIATE

The definition is trivial, but the word IMMEDIATE following the definition is new.

When a word is followed by IMMEDIATE, it is a *compiling-word*. Referring back to the name-field count byte, bit 6 in the last defined word will be set by IMMEDIATE. When the compiler encounters a word, it checks this bit; if set, it executes the word (immediately) instead of compiling its cfa. Since the word runs during compilation, it must be used to aid in the compilation itself. The word [is a compiling-word because it switches the state to interpret. It can only do this if it executes. If instead it were compiled as part of the definition, it would execute when the word being defined was executed (at its run-time). But then is too late The intent of [is to do something at compile-time. Thus, [is a *compiling-word*.

To show how [and] are used in colon-definitions, one more compiling word, LITERAL, needs explanation. When the compiler encounters a number in a definition, it runs LITERAL. It compiles a run-time word named (LIT) followed by the number itself. At run-time, (LIT) fetches the number from the location following it and points IP to the location following the one the number was in.

Now suppose that we wanted to compile the cfa of FOO in a colon-definition. We could do it by inserting:

    [' FOO] LITERAL

in the definition. When encountered, [switches to the interpreter, and then ' FOO returns the cfa of FOO. Then] changes the state back to compiling and LITERAL, a compiling-word, runs and compiles the cfa as a number. Since this kind of code happens so often, Forth-83 has a separate word which does the equivalent of the above code:

    ['] FOO

Notice that the brackets around ' in ['] suggest the equivalent code above.

What would happen if ' were used in a colon-definition? Since ' is not a compiling-word (although ['] is) it would be compiled into the word. When the word was executed, it would be executed and would look for the name of a word from the input stream and find its cfa in the dictionary. For example, consider the word:

    : FOO ' ;

FOO does the same as ' and must be followed by the name of a word. FOO WORD1, when executed, would run the ' within it which would take WORD1 from the input stream (following FOO) and return its cfa.

Other compiling-words are the control constructs. As we saw, IF, WHILE, and UNTIL branch if the flag on the stack is false and continue if it is not false (that is, not zero). These words, when executed during compilation, compile a run-time branching primitive called ?BRANCH followed by the branch address. When ?BRANCH runs, it pops the number (or flag) off the stack. If it is zero, it branches. Otherwise it moves IP to the threaded-code address following the branch address. This is shown in Fig. 6-7. For control words ELSE and REPEAT, BRANCH is compiled instead of ?BRANCH. It unconditionally branches to the address following it in the threaded code.

Compiling-words aid compilation. Defining-words are used to create new words. All of the words defined by a particular defining word have the same run-time action. For example, all colon-defined words will run NEST when executed. Variables, defined by VARIABLE, will run (VAR) and constants (CON). Their run-time activities have been explained. What has not been explained is how these words are compiled.

A very useful word for compiling new words is CREATE. It is followed by a name

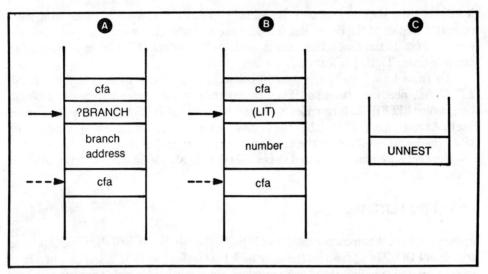

Fig. 6-7. Threaded-code compilations for (A) IF, WHILE, UNTIL (B) LITERAL, and (C) ;. IP is moved by the run-time word to the location of the dashed pointer.

and creates in the dictionary a name field for the name following it and also a cfa pointing to (VAR). If the word being created will not have the run-time action of a variable, the cfa must be changed later. CREATE also (first) builds a link field to link the header it creates into the dictionary. CREATE almost completely creates a variable. It falls short in providing storage for the variable value. That is, it does not produce a body, just a header. A variable needs one Forth cell as a body to store a number.

To allot memory, the word ALLOT takes a number and allots the memory:

ALLOT (n – >)   Allots n bytes in the dictionary.

ALLOT is a simple word. It is defined as:

: ALLOT DP +! ;

DP is another system variable of Forth. It points to the next available location which is just past the last byte of the dictionary. This address can, of course, be obtained by DP @, but this is done often enough to merit a standard Forth word:

HERE (– > addr)   Returns the address of the next available location past the dictionary.

Finally, the primitive dictionary building word , is defined as:

: , HERE ! 2 ALLOT ;

This definition is for Forths with 16-bit cells. Thus, to complete a defining-word for variables, we need only allot two bytes for the variable value. We could use 2 ALLOT,

104

but it also must be initialized to zero. In this case, it would be easier to "comma" in a zero:

```
: VARIABLE CREATE 0 , ;
```

What makes Forth more extensible than most other languages is not that you can define words in addition to those in the standard set, but that you can define new defining-words and also define their run-time activity. These defining-words are then used to define new words, just as : and VARIABLE are.

The time at which a defining-word is being compiled is a third time besides compile-time and run-time. It is called *define-time*. The word DOES> allows you to define the run-time activity for words defined by the new defining-word. To illustrate its use, let us define ARRAY, a word which creates arrays. First, at compile-time:

> ARRAY (n – >)   At compile-time, take the size of the array n, in number of cells.

Then, at run-time:

> ARRAY (n – > addr)   At run-time, arrays created by ARRAY will take an index off the stack and return a pointer to the array value.

The definition of ARRAY is:

```
: ARRAY CREATE 2* ALLOT DOES> SWAP 2* + ;
```

Suppose ARRAY is used as:

```
10 ARRAY A1
```

Then ARRAY will create a header named A1 and take the 10 from the stack, double it, and allot 20 bytes of memory in the body of A1. This finishes the compile-time activity for A1.

DOES> indicates that what follows is the run-time routine for arrays; it does several things. It redirects the cfa of A1 to point to what follows; it next compiles a machine-code jump to the run-time word of DOES>, (DOES>). This word causes the threaded code following JSR (DOES>) to be executed. The activity of DOES> is shown in Fig. 6-8. It is best described in terms of the three action times.

At define-time ARRAY is being defined (compiled). The compile-time part is compiled routinely and DOES> is encountered. It is a compiling-word and runs immediately. DOES>, a colon-defined word, compiles the cfa of (;CODE) into ARRAY, then a machine-code jump, JSR, and the pfa of (DOES>), a CODE word. Following DOES>, the run-time routine of ARRAY words is compiled as high-level (threaded) code.

At *compile-time*, now that ARRAY is defined, it is used to create an array, A1. Now it is run-time for ARRAY and compile-time for A1. The compile-time routine in AR-

RAY creates the header of A1 and allots array storage. Then (;CODE) is executed. It is a colon-defined word and it first pops the return stack. At this time, the top of the return stack now is a pointer into the threaded code of ARRAY. If it is removed, when the UNNEST in (;CODE) runs, the inner interpreter will continue to execute whatever word made the call to ARRAY. This is just a clever way of getting out of ARRAY without an UNNEST. This pointer popped from the return stack is pointing past (;CODE) in ARRAY and is the run-time address of ARRAY. The remaining words in (;CODE), after R>, store the rta in the cfa of A1 so that when A1 runs, it will execute starting at the rta.

At run-time for A1, NEXT will jump through the cfa of A1 to rta and execute the jump to (DOES>). It is a word similar to NEST in that it stores the contents of IP on the return stack, puts the contents of where W is pointing (which is rta) in IP, increments it by 3 to clear JSR (DOES>), puts the pfa of A1 on the parameter stack, and jumps to NEXT.

This is a somewhat complex procedure—about the most complex you will encounter in Forth. If this level of detail is not appealing, all you need to know about DOES> is that at run-time for the defined words, it leaves the pfa of the word being executed on the stack. Thus, the stack activity for DOES> at run-time is:

```
DOES>                          ( –> pfa)
```

ARRAY uses the pfa of A1 as a base address. It scales the index on the stack with 2* to get the offset into the array storage and then adds it to the pfa. The result is a pointer to the indexed array value.

To end this discussion, consider one more defining-word: DEFER. It has already been described earlier as a definer of execution vectors. It can be defined as:

```
: DEFER CREATE ['] NOOP , DOES> @ EXECUTE ;
```

DEFER first creates a header and then compiles, with comma, the cfa of NOOP, which is a word that does nothing:

```
: NOOP ;
```

Then we come to the run-time part of DEFER. DOES> returns the pfa of the DEFER-defined word, where NOOP was compiled. It fetches the cfa of NOOP from this location and executes NOOP with EXECUTE. EXECUTE is a Forth word which takes a cfa from the stack and runs the word. Since it is of no benefit to run NOOP only, the pfa of DEFER-words must be changed to point to an intended word. As we saw, EMIT points normally to (EMIT) the CRT driver word. To do this, invoke:

```
' (EMIT) ' EMIT >BODY !
```

or use a more convenient nonstandard word, IS:

```
' (EMIT) IS EMIT
```

106

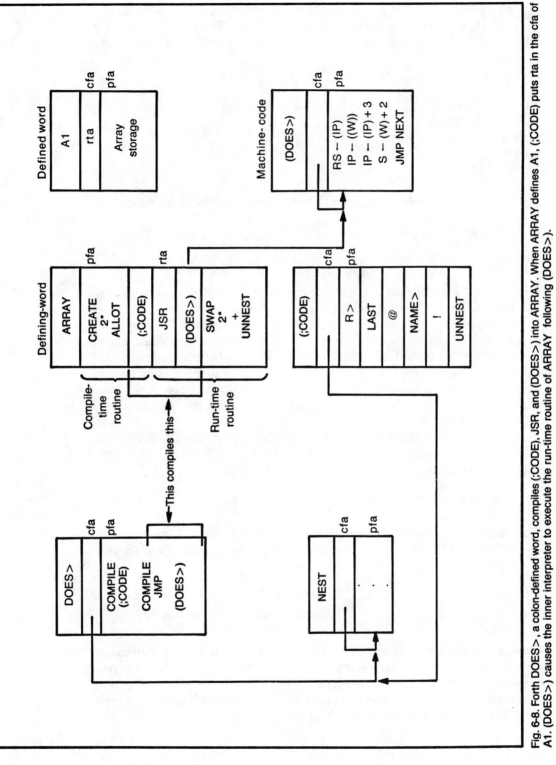

Fig. 6-8. Forth DOES>, a colon-defined word, compiles (;CODE), JSR, and (DOES>) into ARRAY. When ARRAY defines A1, (;CODE) puts rta in the cfa of A1. (DOES>) causes the inner interpreter to execute the run-time routine of ARRAY following (DOES>).

IS is a "state-smart" word and acts differently when compiling or interpreting. The word COMPILE takes the cfa in the next threaded code cell following it and compiles it in the dictionary. It is not a compiling-word since it acts during the run-time of the word it is in.

```
( cfa – > )
: IS STATE @
   IF COMPILE (IS)
   ELSE ' >BODY !
   THEN
; IMMEDIATE
```

IS must be a compiling-word to account for the compiling possibility; (IS) is defined as:

```
: (IS) R@ @ >BODY ! R> 2+ >R ;
```

DISK WORDS

Forth is more than a language; it is a computing environment, with its own management of the disk. The conceptual model of the disk it uses consists of 1024 (1K) byte blocks numbered from zero. Forth handles the disk as virtual memory. Within computer memory, 1K blocks of memory are established as block buffers. When a new block is brought in, an unused buffer is allocated to it. If all buffers are in use, the "oldest" (least recently used) block is written back onto disk to make room for the requested block. Flags are kept for each buffer to indicate whether the block has been updated. If no change has occurred to a block while in a buffer, the block need not be written back on the disk.

All buffers can be cleared and the data in them lost by invoking EMPTY-BUFFERS. To save onto the disk any updated blocks, invoke SAVE-BUFFERS. Before removing a disk, a useful word is:

```
: FLUSH SAVE-BUFFERS EMPTY-BUFFERS ;
```

Most important, to redirect the input stream to come from the disk are the words LOAD and THRU. LOAD "loads" one screen, while THRU brings in a range of screens.

LOAD (n – >)	Interprets block n.
THRU (b e – >)	Interprets blocks b through e.

To access source code on blocks, an editor is needed. Forth has no standard editor, so you will need to consult the documentation of the particular system available to you. Blocks are called *screens* when in the editor.

The appendix contains a glossary of Forth standard words and others used here. A list of sources of Forth literature also is provided.

EXERCISES

1. Define the following Forth words using standard words:

   a. ON and OFF
   b. 2DUP
   c. – ROT
   d. +!
   e. ?DUP
   f. COUNT

2. Explain the following words:

   a. (IS)
   b. ?CREATE on Screen 45 of the source-code listing (Appendix A).

Chapter 7

Introduction
to List Processing

D ATA CAN BE REPRESENTED IN COMPUTERS IN A VARIETY OF DIFFERENT FORMS
or *data structures*. In the last chapter, data structures used in Forth were the linked
list for the dictionary of words, stacks for passing parameters and holding return
pointers, and strings such as the character strings of the name fields of words. Of these
data structures, the list is particularly versatile. From it, other structures such as trees,
strings, or stacks, can be built. Such versatility is useful for representing knowledge
in complex forms in AI programs, many of which have been built out of lists. List-
oriented programming is characteristic of symbolic computing in general, and AI in
particular. It is one of the "tools" for building knowledge systems.

Forth list-processing words are presented here, patterned after the language LISP
(for "List processor"). LISP was invented by John McCarthy in the 1950s for research
in artificial intelligence. Although the language is old by computer standards, it has
not become as popular as some later languages such as Fortran or BASIC. This is not
because it is conceptually difficult but because it is best suited for symbolic rather than
numeric computing. Most computer applications continue to be largely numerically
oriented.

Numerical methods are commonly used to perform integration of functions or solve
equations. A program written in LISP called MACSYMA performs the same mathematical operations, but does so in the way taught in math courses. It identifies forms
of algebraic expressions and determines the rules of integration that can be applied
to those expressions. Only recently has symbolic computation begun to be used commercially. LISP machines are now being sold by several companies, and come with pro-

grams like MACSYMA. Chapter 9 presents another application, the topic of this book. A simple knowledge system is developed there, built upon list-processing words.

WHY EMULATE LISP?

LISP is a simple, elegant list-processing language, and was the natural choice to emulate. However, Forth has some advantages over LISP, and what is developed here is an attempt to combine the best of both languages by extending Forth in a LISP-like way. These list-processing words are *not* LISP written in Forth: the Forth interpreter has not been replaced by the EVAL-APPLY loop (which is what the LISP interpreter is called). But Forth and LISP are similar languages in several ways:

☐ Both are extensible in that new functions can be defined. However, LISP has no vocabulary concept; it is not possible to use the same function name in different contexts, as Forth allows. LISP also lacks define-time extensibility.

☐ Forth and LISP are both oriented to function calls. In passing arguments, Forth uses postfix ("reverse Polish") notation while LISP uses prefix (function name followed by arguments) notation. To avoid confusion, we will use the same order of arguments as LISP. Forth has a parameter stack for passing arguments to (words that are) functions. Use of this stack is explicit in Forth. However, LISP has a similar stack buried within it.

☐ Identifiers are variables in the Forth dictionary, which is a statically allocated list. The OBLIST of LISP is functionally similar.

☐ Forth and LISP are naturally recursive. Recursion is a programming technique (explained in Chapter 8, "Programming Techniques") which is characterized by a function calling itself while saving the state of the original. The stack allows this, since old parameters are pushed rather than modified by the new call to the same function.

☐ Forth and LISP have a simple syntax. This is partially a result of calling functions to carry out action.

☐ Forth and LISP are both small languages. A plain LISP will occupy about as much memory as a nonextended Forth.

☐ Both Forth and LISP are *language systems,* not just languages. They each contain operating system functions and can stand alone as a sufficient computing environment. Each comes with an enriched environment, with various extensions for aiding applications-level programming. Because of the extent of some LISP environments, LISP sometimes is erroneously considered to be a large language requiring megabytes of memory.

☐ Forth and LISP provide very interactive, interpretive environments and appeal to those with an AI style of programming, making it easy to experiment and "hack out" programs, bottom-up. While bottom-up programming is not wise for large, multiperson projects where the discipline of software-engineering-style programming is required, AI-style programs are comparatively short. In Forth or LISP, much can be done with little code, but that code must be thought out well. Also, the AI style is appropriate when exploring new ideas, since the overall (top-down) structure of the result cannot be thought out without knowing enough about the lower-level routines or the domain of the problem solved by the program being written.

Because the list-processing extension of Forth given here is so similar to LISP, books about LISP can be used to aid in programming. Recommended references are given in the appendix.

STATIC VERSUS DYNAMIC MEMORY MANAGEMENT

Forth words consist of a sequence of threaded-code addresses which point to other words. Once compiled, they stay where they are put. Thus, data structures such as constants, variables, strings, and arrays are defined and allotted a fixed amount of space in memory. For many applications, this *static* allocation of memory for data is adequate. However, for some applications, *dynamic* memory allocation is needed; that is, the memory space allotted to a given data structure is not fixed at compile-time. It can change while the program is running.

If we consider how this might be done for data structures found in Forth, such as arrays, complex schemes for managing memory can quickly result. The items of data in an array are fixed in memory location and accessed by index number. To rearrange the order of the items or have an indeterminate number of items assigned to an array would be difficult; to make room for more items, everything in memory above the array would have to be moved up and the pointers to this relocated code updated. This clearly is not feasible. Lists make dynamic management of memory conceptually simpler and computationally more efficient.

WHAT IS A LIST?

In LISP, a list consists of a set of connected *CONS-cells* or *dotted pairs*. These cells are the elemental structures of which lists are composed. A CONS-cell is a data type which consists of two main components, and can be represented graphically as shown in Fig. 7-1.

The component on the left is the *head* or *first* (or CAR), and the one on the right is the *tail* or *rest* (or CDR). The obscure names CAR and CDR (pronounced "coulder") remain only for historical reasons; they were the names of registers in the computer used to develop LISP. Both head and tail are pointers. The head points to a list item, and the tail points to the next CONS-cell in the list. We can construct a list with three items, as in Fig. 7-2.

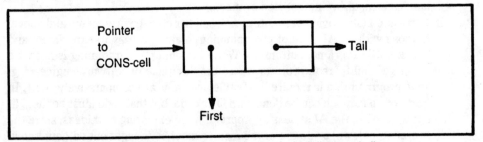

Fig. 7-1. A CONS-cell, the elemental data structure out of which lists are built.

112

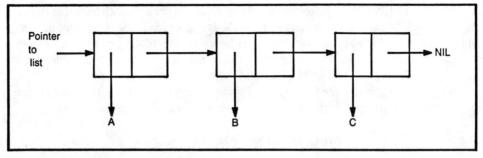

Fig. 7-2. A list of three items: (A B C).

The pointer to the list is itself just an address. Lists can be represented on the Forth parameter stack as a pointer to the first CONS-cell (or *head*) of the list. (This is even simpler than Forth string representation on the stack, which requires two stack items: string starting address and length.) The list shown in Fig. 7-2 has three items pointed to by the heads of the cells. In order of traversal of the list, they are A, B, and C. The tail of the last cell points to NIL, which indicates the end of the list. Here, NIL is a Forth variable.

An alternative (and more convenient) notation for lists is *parenthesis notation*. A list is simply enclosed in parentheses. The list shown in Fig. 7-2 is:

(A B C)

The implementation of LISP-like words in Forth is given on Screens 40 through 49, discussed and shown in this chapter and also shown in Appendix A, the source-code listing. In this implementation, lists are constructed somewhat differently than has been described. The use of CONS-cells results in a general, dynamic list-handling structure. To avoid dynamic memory management, lists have been created as Forth variables for which memory has been allotted. The list identified by a variable name contains the list itself in the body of the variable. The pfa of the variable contains a pointer into the allotted memory to the head of the list.

```
        40
0 \ LISP LIST-BUILDING WORDS IN FORTH-83
1
2 VARIABLE NIL NIL NIL ! \ THE EMPTY LIST
3
4 ( #ITEMS -> ) \ #ITEMS = MAXIMUM NUMBER OF ITEMS THIS LIST
5
6 : NEWLIST CREATE HERE 2+ , NIL , 2* ALLOT ;
7
8 ( @LIST -> @FIRST) \ @FIRST IS A POINTER TO FIRST ITEM OF LIST
9 : FIRST @ ;
10
11 ( @LIST | NIL -> FLAG) \ FLAG = TRUE IF LIST IS EMPTY
12 : NULL @ NIL = ;
13
14 ( @LIST -> @TAIL) \ @TAIL IS A POINTER TO THE TAIL OF THE LIST
15 : TAIL DUP NULL IF @ ELSE 2- THEN ;
```

Screen 40. List-building words: NEWLIST, FIRST, NULL, and TAIL.

The word NEWLIST is a defining-word that creates a variable with the name following NEWLIST. It also takes a number from the stack which is the maximum number of items the list will be able to hold. This number is used to allot memory space following the variable. The resulting word has the run-time activity of a variable, since CREATE in NEWLIST will build a cfa pointing to the run-time procedure of variables. NEWLIST also initializes the new list to be empty. A Forth variable with allotted memory is called an *extended variable*. Lists are extended variables here.

PRIMITIVE LIST OPERATIONS

To return the pointer to the first item of a list (the head of the list), the word FIRST is invoked. It will return the head of the first CONS-cell of the list, where ^LIST is a pointer to the list (and is on the stack). For example, the head of the list of Fig. 7-2 is A. To return the tail of the first CONS-cell of a list, invoke TAIL. (In LISP, the words CAR and CDR are still commonly used for FIRST and TAIL, respectively.) TAIL returns a pointer to the rest of the list:

(B C)

If we invoke TAIL again, (C) results—and again produces NIL. Thus, beginning with the original list:

TAIL TAIL TAIL

returns NIL. FIRST and TAIL let us get into lists. Each time we apply TAIL, we move one item down the list. Applying FIRST will return the pointer to the item at that location in the list. For example, if we want to retrieve the pointer to the second item,

TAIL FIRST

will return a pointer to B.

In LISP, some combinations of CAR and CDR are provided as a single operation:

CAAR	is	CAR CAR	or	FIRST FIRST
CDDR	is	CDR CDR	or	TAIL TAIL
CADR	is	CDR CAR	or	TAIL FIRST
CDAR	is	CAR CDR	or	FIRST TAIL

CADR returns the second item of the list, while CDAR returns a pointer to the second item of the head of the original list. For example the CADR of ((A B) C D) is C and the CDAR is (B).

CONS is used to build lists. In LISP, CONS will be given two arguments, ^ITEM and I, a list-id. It will get a free cell and set its head to ^ITEM and tail to I. In this implementation, CONS-cells are not used; instead, the heads of the list cells are organized in a reversed array, as shown in Fig. 7-3. The pfa of the list variable points to the head of the list, which is at the highest address. Pointers to items in the list (the heads of CONS-cells) are ordered in decreasing memory addresses until the last (and

```
         41
0 \ LISP LIST-BUILDING WORDS IN FORTH-83
1
2 ( I -> ) \ SET LIST TO NIL (EMPTY LIST)
3 : EMPTY DUP 2+ DUP ROT ! NIL SWAP ! ;
4
5   ( I @LIST -> ) \ SETS LIST-ID I TO POINT TO @LIST
6 : SET DUP NIL = IF DROP EMPTY ELSE SWAP ! THEN ;
7
8   ( @ITEM I -> ) \ ADDS @ITEM TO THE HEAD OF LIST-ID I
9 : CONS 2 OVER +! @ ! ;
10
11  \ RECURSION WORD
12 : RECURSE LAST @ NAME> , ; IMMEDIATE
13
14
15
```

Screen 41. List-building words: SET, CONS, and RECURSE.

initial) cell after the pfa. It terminates the list by containing a pointer to NIL. The list (A B C) is shown in Fig. 7-3.

Because CONS-cells are not used, CONS must always act on a list as a variable in memory; it cannot get free cells (which could be anywhere in memory), as LISP can. In LISP, CONS returns a pointer to the head of the resulting list. The CONS on Screen 41 does not return a pointer, since it must operate upon a list already in place in memory. Consequently, the list-id on the stack, I, is a list variable in the Forth dictionary.

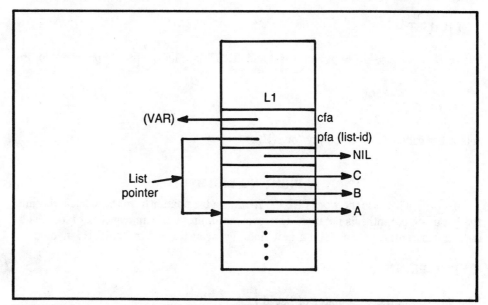

Fig. 7-3. Dictionary structure of a list created by NEWLIST. The pointer to the head of the list is stored at the pfa, while at pfa + 2 is a pointer to NIL, marking the end of the list (A B C).

Since these lists (defined by NEWLIST) have a fixed allotment of memory, they have a predetermined maximum length—a fixed maximum number of items. CONS adds a new item to the list by moving the list pointer (at the pfa) ahead one item and storing the pointer ^ITEM there. To delete an item from the head of the list, the list pointer need only be moved in the opposite direction, toward the pfa.

To build the list (A B C) onto the list named I1, invoke:

C I1 CONS B I1 CONS A I1 CONS

LIST IDENTIFIERS AND LIST POINTERS

Lists are identified by their Forth dictionary names. When these names are invoked they act as variables, returning a pointer on the Forth stack to the pfa of the list-word. These are *list identifiers* or *list-id* for short. The pointer stored at the pfa of a list-id points to the head of the list named by the list-id. This pointer is the *list pointer*. Since the pfa of a list-id word is at a known location with respect to the fields which comprise the word, it can be used to represent a list as a Forth word. On the other hand, given a list pointer it is not possible to know where the pfa of the corresponding list-id is. To act upon lists however, a list pointer is needed, and the words FIRST and TAIL must be passed a list pointer. This pointer will be called "the list" when on the stack.

Given a list-id, the list pointer can—and often must be—produced by fetching it with @. The list pointer of a list-id called I1 is returned by invoking:

I1 @

To set a list-id to point to a list, the word SET is used. Its stack notation is:

(I1 ^LIST – >)

where I1 is the list-id (its pfa address) and ^LIST is a list pointer. For example, invoking

I1 NIL SET

sets a list called I1 to be empty (or NIL).

PRINTING LISTS

To print a list, use the word PRINT. It takes a list pointer from the stack and prints the list using parenthesis notation. However, to improve the appearance of long lists, each left parenthesis begins on a new line. To print the list of list-id I1, invoke:

I1 @ PRINT

The @ returns the list pointer of list-id I1.

```
        42
 0  \ LISP LIST-BUILDING WORDS IN FORTH-83
 1
 2    ( NIL S1 S2 . . . SN I -> ) \ BUILDS LIST AT I
 3  : LIST >R
 4      BEGIN DUP NULL NOT
 5      WHILE R@ CONS
 6      REPEAT R> 2DROP
 7  ;
 8
 9    ( @LIST I -> ) \ RECURSIVE WORD FOR 2APPEND
10  : 2APPEND OVER NULL
11      IF 2DROP
12      ELSE OVER TAIL OVER RECURSE
13          SWAP FIRST SWAP CONS
14      THEN
15  ;


        43
 0  \ LISP LIST-BUILDING WORDS IN FORTH-83
 1
 2    ( @ -> FLAG) \ FLAG = TRUE IF @ IS PFA OF VARIABLE
 3  : ATOM? BODY> @ ['] NIL @ = ;
 4
 5    ( @LIST -> )
 6  : PRINTL CR ." ("
 7      BEGIN DUP FIRST DUP ATOM?
 8          IF DUP NULL NOT
 9              IF BODY> >NAME .ID ELSE DROP THEN
10          ELSE RECURSE
11          THEN TAIL DUP NULL
12      UNTIL 8 ( BACKSPACE) EMIT ." ) " DROP
13  ;
14
15


        44
 0  \ LISP LIST-BUILDING WORDS IN FORTH-83
 1
 2    ( @LIST -> )
 3  : PRINT DUP @ NULL
 4      IF DROP CR ." NIL"
 5      ELSE DUP ATOM?
 6          IF BODY> >NAME .ID
 7          ELSE PRINTL
 8          THEN
 9      THEN
10  ;
11
12
13
14
15
```

Screens 42, 43, 44. List-building words: LIST, 2APPEND, ATOM?, PRINTL, and PRINT.

LIST INPUT

CONS is the primitive list-building operation, but does not offer a convenient way of building lists for the user. The word LIST is somewhat better. It takes items from the stack and builds them into a list. To mark the start of the list on the stack, a NIL is used. Its stack activity is:

(NIL S1 S2 . . . SN I1 – >)

where S1 through SN are the list items and I1 is the list-id. The resulting list is:

(S1 S2 . . . SN)

in I1. Invoking

I1 @ PRINT

allows the list to be seen.

```
       45
0  \ LISP LIST-BUILDING WORDS IN FORTH-83
1
2  ( -> C) \ RETURN NEXT CHARACTER FROM INPUT STREAM
3  : READCH
4    BEGIN SOURCE >IN @ /STRING
5      IF C@ 1 >IN +! TRUE
6      ELSE DROP ['] SOURCE >BODY @ ['] (SOURCE) =
7         IF QUERY ELSE 1 BLK +! 0 >IN ! THEN FALSE
8      THEN
9    UNTIL
10 ;
11
12 ( ->CFA) \ IF WORD IS NOT IN DICTIONARY, CREATE IT AS VARIABLE
13 : ?CREATE >IN @ DEFINED
14   IF NIP ELSE DROP >IN ! HERE VARIABLE 4 + NAME> THEN
15 ;

       46
0  \ LISP LIST-BUILDING WORDS IN FORTH-83
1
2  ( I -> )
3  : READL >R
4    BEGIN READCH
5      CASE BL
6        OF FALSE ENDOF ASCII (
7        OF NIL FALSE ENDOF ASCII )
8        OF R@ LIST TRUE ENDOF ASCII @
9        OF @ FALSE ENDOF
10       -1 >IN +! ?CREATE EXECUTE FALSE ROT
11     ENDCASE
12   UNTIL R> DROP
13 ;
14
15
```

Screens 45, 46. List-building words: READCH, ?CREATE, and READL.

118

The items of a list are pointers to the pfa of Forth variables. The words S1 through SN must first exist before LIST can be invoked.

The easiest way to input a list is to use READL. It is a small input interpreter, producing lists from (,), @, atoms, and list-id. READL calls READCH which returns the next character in the input stream. It takes in lists in parenthesis notation directly. To type in a list, invoke

I READL

where I is a list-id. Then type the list in parenthesis notation. A left parenthesis, (, begins the list, which is ended by a right parenthesis,).

Only one level of list structure can be entered directly. A list such as:

(A (B C) D)

could not be entered because of the list within this list. For this implementation, every list must be defined with NEWLIST. If (B C) is defined as I1, then the above list could be input to list I2 by invoking:

I2 READL (A I1 @ D)

Notice both the @ following I1 and the blank after every item name, including the last one, D. The Forth parser is used to scan words and requires the blank as a delimiter. The @ is used to input the list pointer of I1, rather than the list-id. If I2 were printed, the result would be as shown above, but if

I2 READL (A I1 D)

```
                 50
  0  \ SOME LISTS
  1
  2  20  NEWLIST  I1
  3  20  NEWLIST  I2
  4  20  NEWLIST  I3
  5
  6  VARIABLE  S1
  7  VARIABLE  S2
  8  VARIABLE  S3
  9
 10  I1  READL  (S1 S2 S3 )
 11  I2  READL  (S1 I1 @ S2 S3 )
 12  I3  READL  (S3 )
 13
 14
 15
```

Screen 50. Some lists.

were invoked instead, then I2 @ PRINT would display:

(A I1 D)

LIST-PROCESSING DATA TYPES

In previous examples of lists, the heads pointed to other lists or items such as A, B, C, or NIL. These items are called *atoms*. In our Forth "LISP" an atom is represented on the stack as the pfa of a variable. List identifiers are a kind of atom. Atoms are either list-id or variables pointed to from the heads of lists. In LISP, atoms are data types much like constants and variables are in Forth. They are the items pointed to from lists and are not lists themselves.

The Forth word ATOM? on Screen 41 identifies pointers as atoms if they are the pfas of variables. Since list identifiers are extended Forth variables, they too are atoms. List pointers, however, are not; they represent lists rather than atoms since they point to actual list structure. An *S-expression* (which is short for "symbolic expression") is an atom or a list, and is represented here in stack notation by S. The taxonomy of list data types is shown in Fig. 7-4.

Invoking a variable in Forth returns a pointer to its value, and not the value itself. This pointer is designated by I in the stack notation when the variable is a list identifier. Pointers to lists are denoted by L or ^LIST and are themselves pointed to by list-id. To get the pointer to a list, @ is needed.

WHAT IS NIL?

NIL is the only atom which is also considered to be a list—the empty list. NIL is the same as ( ) in parenthesis notation. NIL also points to itself; NIL @ returns NIL. By definition, the head and tail of NIL are NIL.

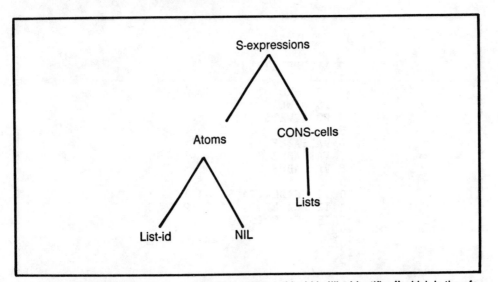

Fig. 7-4. A taxonomy of the data types of LISP used here. List-id is "list-identifier," which is the pfa of a Forth variable naming a list.

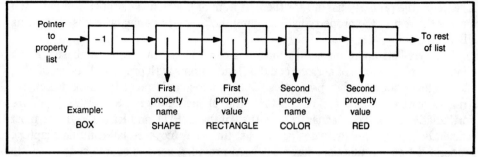

Fig. 7-5. Structure of a property-list with two properties of BOX.

A *proper list* contains a NIL tail in its last cell. This is necessary for many list-handling words, since NIL is the terminator they seek. Lists not ending in NIL (such as circular lists) can be constructed, but can lead to nonterminating procedures. NEWLIST installs NIL into new, empty lists.

PROPERTY-LISTS

Atoms can point to lists called *property-lists*. A property-list is distinguished from a normal list by having a head of −1 (or some special value). Property-lists are constructed such that property-names and values are alternately placed on the list. For list L, the head of L is −1; the second item is the first property, and the third is its value, as shown in Fig. 7-5. Words that operate on property-lists are the basic database access functions. One word, GET, has stack action:

(I P − > V)

where V is the value of the property P and is an S-expression. P is a property-name and is an atom. To return the value of the COLOR property of the atom BOX, invoke:

BOX COLOR GET

It returns a pointer to the value of COLOR. Then by invoking PRINT, RED is printed.
PUT or its synonym PUTPROP puts a property and its value on a property-list:

I V P PUT

will put property P with value V on the property-list of atom I. If property P is already on the list, its value will be replaced by V. PUT returns V. To remove a property, invoke:

I P REMPROP

which also returns a Forth true flag if the property was removed and a false flag if no such property was on the list. Finally, GETL is used in the form:

I L GETL

121

It searches the property-list of I for the first item of L which is a property of I. It then returns the rest of the property-list including the property name; otherwise it returns NIL.

Property-lists and their access functions can be used to create databases. For a phone directory, names of persons could be made atoms with property-lists containing address and phone-number properties. Their values could point to atoms which are strings (for street addresses) or constants (for phone numbers). SAVEing the entire Forth dictionary will consequently save the database. PUT and REMPROP are most efficiently implemented with destructive list functions (covered later in this chapter). Property-list access functions have not been provided here as source-code.

ASSOCIATION-LISTS

Property-lists are a kind of database structure. *Association-lists* or *A-lists* have a different structure in which property-value pairs are placed in the two halves of the CONS-cell within the A-list. (The head and tail of CONS-cells are sometimes referred to as "dotted pairs.") For example, an A-list with two properties, COLOR and SHAPE is shown in Fig. 7-6.

This list structure is not:

((SHAPE RECTANGLE) (COLOR RED))

as shown in Fig. 7-7. A-lists make more efficient use of CONS-cells than nested lists since they use fewer NILs. As a result, they are not proper lists.

ASSOC and ASSOC# access A-lists. ASSOC searches the list L for a property-value pair whose property-name is the same as X; the expression

X L ASSOC

then returns the pair with X. If no pair is found, NIL is returned. ASSOC# functions

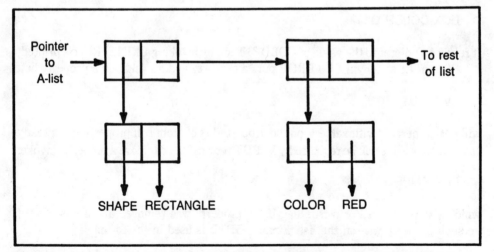

Fig. 7-6. Association-list or A-list structure with the same data as the property-list of Fig. 7-5.

122

```
              51
   0  \ LISP LIST-BUILDING WORDS IN FORTH-83
   1
   2  ( S L1 -> L2)
   3  : ASSOC DUP NULL
   4    IF NIP
   5    ELSE 2DUP FIRST FIRST =
   6        IF FIRST NIP
   7        ELSE TAIL RECURSE
   8        THEN
   9    THEN
  10  ;
  11
  12
  13
  14
  15
```

Screen 51. ASSOC, a list-building word.

similarly but uses EQUAL instead of EQ in comparing the heads of the pairs. The A-list access function ASSOC is provided in the source code on Screen 51.

EQUAL VERSUS EQ

EQ in LISP is the same as = in Forth. If two pointers on the stack are numerically equal, EQ or = returns a true flag. However, two lists may be constructed with identical list structure yet be different lists. Are these lists equal? Their pointers are not EQ, yet the lists themselves are constructed identically. Upon PRINTing, they would appear the same.

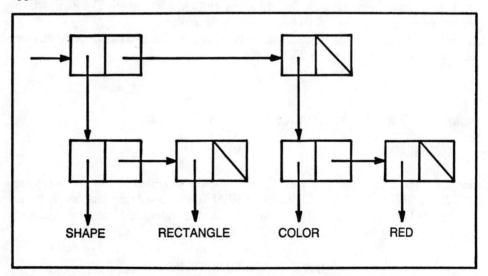

Fig. 7-7. A proper nested list containing the data of the A-list of Fig. 7-6. Notice the more efficient structure of the A-list. The backslash in the tail of a CONS-cell is NIL.

To find out whether two different lists have the same list structure, the word EQUAL is used. For atoms, EQ and EQUAL act the same, since atom identifiers (not their property-lists) have no list structure; they exist at some memory location indicated by a pointer (a pfa). To summarize the difference, EQ returns true for the same list pointers and EQUAL returns true for the same list structure. Thus, EQUAL does more than EQ since it has to compare the list structures as well. The EQUAL algorithm is shown in Fig. 8-4 and will be explained later in this chapter.

The difference between EQ and EQUAL leads to variations between some words. ASSOC and ASSOC# are similar except ASSOC# uses EQUAL where ASSOC uses EQ in its list searching. MEMB uses EQ while MEMBER uses EQUAL.

Another comparison function besides EQ and EQUAL is NULL. It returns a true flag if NIL is on the stack. Since several LISP functions return NIL if they fail in some way, this is a handy function. For example, if REMPROP cannot find the given property to remove on a list, it returns NIL. NIL acts in many cases like a false flag, and NULL is used to return a Forth flag from such a result. Since the control structures are Forth structures, Forth flags are needed by words like IF, WHILE, and UNTIL.

NIL contains the value NIL so that either NIL as a list or NIL as list-id will be recognized as NIL. NULL actually fetches the value pointed to by the pointer on the stack in comparing it to NIL, since if it is NIL, it will also point to NIL. That is, NIL @ is also NIL.

DESTRUCTIVE LIST OPERATIONS

List construction is performed by calling CONS. In LISP, some functions use CONS to create another list which is the processed result of the original list. A list function often could be performed on the existing list, by changing pointers in its CONS cells; this saves time and memory. For example, REVERSE reverses lists, doing so by creating another list (using CONS) which is the reverse of the original list. Unless the original list must be retained, it would be more efficient to use DREVERSE, which redirects the tails in the original list to reverse it in-place.

Several destructive list functions are found in LISP. The two basic operations for destructive list functions are RPLACA and RPLACD.

X Y RPLACA

replaces the head of X with Y and returns the modified list.

X Y RPLACD

similarly replaces the tail of X with Y, returning the modified X. Similar words are NCONC, DREVERSE, DREMOVE, and ATTACH, discussed next chapter. Because destructive list functions are often the most difficult to understand, they are explained while considering implementation details in Chapter 8.

OTHER LIST FUNCTIONS

Sometimes it is desirable to "merge" several lists into one list. The *APPEND construct does this for two lists; APPEND does it for more. Suppose lists L1 and L2 are:

L1: (A B)
L2: (C D)

Then

L1 L2 *APPEND

returns:

(A B C D)

For more than two lists, APPEND is used. *APPEND returns a pointer to the resulting list. Since lists are manipulated in place here, no result need be returned. This function is called 2APPEND and is given on Screen 42. To append list L1 onto L2 so that L1 is before L2, invoke:

L1 L2 2APPEND

The stack activity for 2APPEND is:

(^LIST I – >)

We have seen that TAIL and FIRST get us around in lists. For long lists, it becomes tedious to invoke a long chain of TAILs to get into the list. Instead, to get to the Nth item of list L, invoke:

L N NTH

which returns a pointer to the rest of the list with the Nth item as the head.

L LAST

returns the last item, but for atoms, returns the atom.
REVERSE (the nondestructive one) reverses the list on the stack, and:

S L REMOVE

removes all occurrences of S using EQUAL to compare S with list structure. S can be either a list itself within L (that is, a *sublist*), or it can be an atom; it is an S-expression.

L LENGTH

will return the number of items in the list. This is a count of only the top-level list items. If some items in the list are sublists, they are counted as one item.

```
        47
 0 \ LISP LIST-BUILDING WORDS IN FORTH-83
 1
 2 UNNEST
 3
 4   ( @LIST -> @LAST) \ RETURNS POINTER TO LAST ITEM OF @LIST
 5 : LAST DUP TAIL NULL NOT
 6     IF TAIL RECURSE
 7     THEN
 8 ;
 9
10 \ ITERATIVE LAST
11 : LAST
12     BEGIN DUP TAIL NULL NOT
13     WHILE TAIL
14     REPEAT
15 ;

        48
 0 \ LISP LIST-BUILDING WORDS IN FORTH-83
 1
 2   ( @LIST -> N) \ RETURNS NUMBER OF ITEMS OF LIST
 3 : LENGTH DUP NULL
 4     IF DROP 0
 5     ELSE TAIL RECURSE 1+
 6     THEN
 7 ;
 8
 9 UNNEST
10 \ ITERATIVE LENGTH
11 : LENGTH 0
12     BEGIN OVER NULL NOT
13     WHILE 1+ SWAP TAIL SWAP
14     REPEAT NIP
15


        52
 0 \ LISP LIST-BUILDING WORDS IN FORTH-83
 1
 2   ( L1 N -> L2)
 3 : NTH DUP 1 <
 4     IF 2DROP NIL
 5     ELSE
 6         BEGIN 1- DUP
 7         WHILE SWAP TAIL SWAP
 8         REPEAT DROP
 9     THEN
10 ;
11
12
13
14
15
```

Screens 47, 48, 52. List-building words: LAST, LENGTH, and NTH.

As we have seen, LIST puts S-expressions together into lists. It takes an arbitrary number of arguments and must begin with a NIL.

NIL A B C D I1 LIST

is the same as:

D I1 CONS C I1 CONS B I1 CONS A I1 CONS

2APPEND differs from LIST in that it puts existing lists together as a single list, while LIST creates a list out of S-expressions.

To determine whether a list, L1, is an item of list L2, invoke:

L1 L2 MEMB

(MEMQ is a synonym in LISP for MEMB.) MEMB returns the rest of L2, beginning with the first item EQ to L1. Otherwise it returns NIL. MEMBER is similar to MEMB but it uses EQUAL instead of EQ when comparing items of L2 with L1. (See the section "EQUAL versus EQ.")

Finally,

S1 S2 S3 SUBST

substitutes S-expression S1 for all occurrences of S2 in S-expression S3 and then returns S3. It uses EQUAL to compare S3 list items with S2. Atoms are returned unaffected.

SUBST, REMOVE, and REVERSE are not implemented here but are found in LISP.

```
      49
 0 \ LISP LIST-BUILDING WORDS IN FORTH-83
 1
 2   ( ITEM @LIST -> @TAIL)\ IF ITEM IS IN LIST, @TAIL IS REST OF
 3                         \ LIST BEGINNING WITH ITEM; ELSE NIL
 4 : MEMB SWAP OVER NULL
 5     IF 2DROP NIL
 6     ELSE OVER FIRST OVER =
 7         IF DROP
 8         ELSE SWAP TAIL RECURSE
 9         THEN
10     THEN
11 ;
12
13
14
15
```

Screen 49. MEMB, a list-building word.

127

EXERCISES

1. For the list:

   (A B (C D (E F (G) H) I)

   determine the result of the following list operations:

   a. TAIL
   b. TAIL FIRST
   c. FIRST FIRST
   d. TAIL TAIL FIRST TAIL
   e. TAIL TAIL TAIL FIRST
   f. TAIL TAIL FIRST TAIL TAIL FIRST
   g. TAIL TAIL FIRST TAIL TAIL FIRST TAIL TAIL FIRST
   h. TAIL TAIL TAIL FIRST

2. Explain why TAIL (Screen 40) does not unconditionally decrement ^LIST. What might happen if it did?
3. Draw a diagram similar to Fig. 7-3 for the list in Exercise 1, giving names to the sublists.
4. Given these three lists:

   L1: (S1 (S2 S3) S4)
   L2: NIL
   L3: (S2 S3)

   for each list determine the result of each of the following:

   a. S1 Ln MEMB PRINT
   b. Ln LENGTH
   c. Ln ATOM?
   d. L3 @ MEMB
   e. L3 MEMB

5. Write REVERSE, a word which reverses the items of a list.
6. Write FLATTEN. It takes items of sublists and puts them into the top-level list. For example:

   (A (B C) (D (E F) G)→(A B C D E F G)

7. Write the property-list access functions GETPROP and PUTPROP.

Chapter 8
Programming Techniques

I N LISP DATA AND INSTRUCTIONS ARE BOTH IN THE FORM OF LISTS AND ARE interchangeable. Here, however, lists can only be used as data (in a direct sense) because the Forth interpreter does not interpret lists; it interprets threaded code. The flow of control of a program is handled by the same words Forth normally uses. Forth actually has a richer variety of control words than LISP. The common CASE statement of Forth is similar to the COND function of LISP. However, LISP lacks the structured constructs of Forth: IF-ELSE-THEN, BEGIN-UNTIL, and BEGIN-WHILE-REPEAT. The last two constructs are *iteration primitives* of Forth. They cause a sequence of code to be repeatedly executed by looping backward.

RECURSION

While Forth is well-suited for recursion, the technique is not often used. List-based programming is an exception. *Recursion* occurs when a word calls itself. If the parameters used by the word are kept on the stack, they will be left unmodified when control returns to the original calling routine. Recursion can be thought of as calling a *copy* of the original word. This may happen several times, each time with the stack pushed deeper with the parameters of previous (calling) copies.

Eventually some condition must terminate the successive calling of copies. Consider, as an example, the word LAST:

```
: LAST DUP TAIL NULL NOT
       IF TAIL RECURSE
```

THEN

LAST takes a list pointer and performs the termination test: it checks the tail of the list to determine whether it is empty. If it is NIL, it exits. If it is not, it takes the tail of the list and calls LAST again. The word RECURSE is used to do this because, when LAST is being defined, the search for LAST will not include the word under definition.

To illustrate graphically how recursion works, suppose that LAST is called with a pointer on the stack to the list:

   (A B)

The sequence of word executions is shown by the arrows in Fig. 8-1.

Notice the two lines of LAST. The top line is the original function call, with (A B) on the stack. Since the tail of (A B) is (B), and not empty, the IF branch is taken. Then TAIL of (A B) returns (B) on the stack and RECURSE is encountered. It calls LAST again, as traced by the arrow to the second line. Once again, LAST begins execution, this time with (B) on the stack. The tail of (B) is NIL, so the IF branch is skipped to THEN and ;, which exits that copy of LAST and returns to the one on the top line—the one that called it. It continues where it left off after RECURSE. Then it too simply exits and (B), the last item of (A B), is left on the top of the stack.

If the list had been longer, the sequence of lists on the stack at each call of LAST would look like this:

   (A B C D)
    (B C D)
     (C D)
      (D)

Since the tail of the input list is returned each time LAST recurses, the list is successively trimmed of heads until only the last item remains. This kind of recursion is called *tail recursion*, because the word successively recurses on the tail of the list. Other words involving tail recursion are LENGTH and MEMB. In the case of MEMB two parameters are being passed, but ITEM remains the same while the tail of ^LIST is passed when MEMB is called recursively.

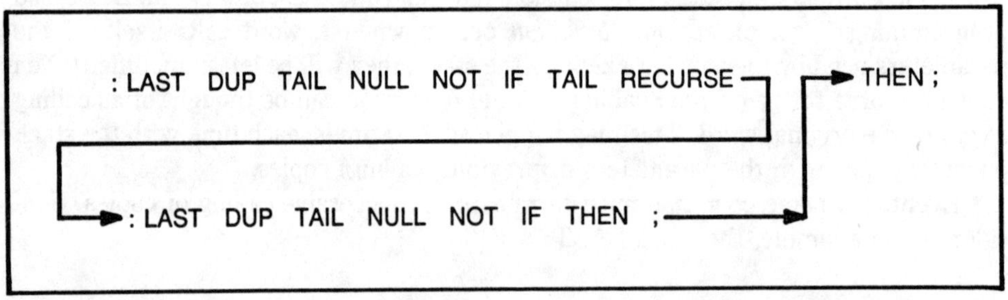

Fig. 8-1. Control flow for LAST, a recursive word. RECURSE calls a copy of LAST (second row), which terminates recursion.

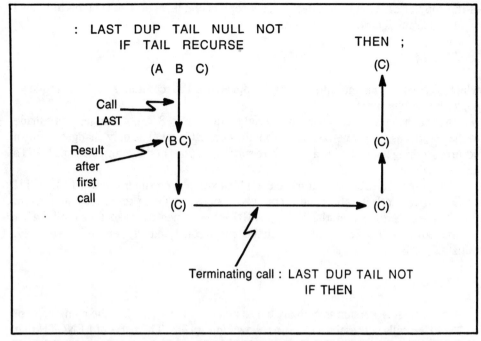

: LAST DUP TAIL NULL NOT
    IF TAIL RECURSE   THEN ;

Terminating call : LAST DUP TAIL NOT
                        IF THEN

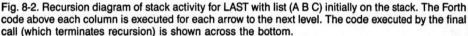

Fig. 8-2. Recursion diagram of stack activity for LAST with list (A B C) initially on the stack. The Forth code above each column is executed for each arrow to the next level. The code executed by the final call (which terminates recursion) is shown across the bottom.

Recursion is usually confusing at first. However, it is as "natural" as iteration. The confusion often occurs over the fact that the same function is being called. Keeping track of individual copies is the key to minimizing confusion. If necessary, name each new call (to LAST, say) by a different name, like LAST1, LAST2, etc. Remember that control will go through each copy twice, first when it is called, and second when it finishes after returning from its own recursive call. In LAST, the check by NULL and the TAIL in IF-THEN are executed. Then RECURSE calls LAST again. When control flow returns, it takes up where it left off. The IF-THEN construct is exited, and then LAST itself is exited.

The key to keeping track of what is happening between recursive calls is to note the stack activity. A graphic way of doing this, for LAST, is shown in Fig. 8-2. Starting at the upper left, the state of the list on the stack is shown as (A B C). Each successive call of LAST takes us down one level on the left side. The first call of LAST will leave (B C) on the stack when it recurses.

When the second copy recurses, (C) will be on the stack. Notice that control is repeatedly going through only the first part of LAST—the part from the beginning of the word to RECURSE. As it recurses, the same action is repeated. The list is being "pared down," one item at a time. What stops this *recursive descent* is the terminating condition: If the tail of the list passed to LAST is NIL, recursion stops.

When (C) is passed to LAST a third time, the tail of (C) is NIL, the empty list, and the recursion path through IF-THEN is avoided. This third call of LAST—the bottom one of Fig. 8-2—returns. When it does, it returns to what follows the RECURSE

131

of the copy of LAST which called it. This copy is one level up from the bottom level in the diagram. There it encounters

THEN ;

which also exits. This multiple exiting of copies of LAST continues until the top-level copy exits a final time.

During the recursive ascent on the right side of Fig. 8-2, no changes were made to the list. It was simply passed back from the deepest level. The only changes in Forth occurring during the recursive ascent were successive pops of the return stack as LASTs exited.

For a second and somewhat more complex example, consider the word LENGTH on Screen 48. Both iterative and recursive versions are given there for comparison. For the iterative algorithm, the BEGIN-WHILE loop repeatedly executes until the list is pared down to NIL. Each time through the loop, a count, initially zero, is incremented. the stack at BEGIN is:

(list count)

The recursive version is similar, but instead of looping within the same copy of LENGTH, it calls successive copies, as shown in Fig. 8-3. The parts of LENGTH that

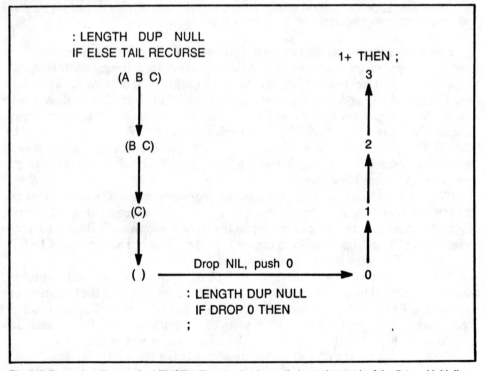

Fig. 8-3. Recursion diagram for LENGTH. The terminating call clears the stack of the list and initializes the count to zero.

are executed while descending and ascending are shown above each column. During descent, the beginning of LENGTH is executed until it reaches RECURSE. The effect of this is to pare down the list with TAIL. Each successive call of LENGTH passes a list that is shorter by one item. At the bottom, the terminating condition is true; the list is empty.

In this last call of LENGTH, shown across the bottom, the control flow is different since the IF rather than the ELSE branch is taken. This branch drops the empty list and places the initial count value of zero on the stack instead. Now this copy of LENGTH returns to the calling copy one level above it in Fig. 8-3. Since control returns to the code following RECURSE, it increments the number on the stack and returns. The number of increments equals the number of levels. Since each level is due to a recursive call in which one item was removed from the list while descending, the number of increments on the way back up will be the same as the number of calls. And this is equal to the number of items on the original list.

Another kind of recursion is *double recursion*. For this kind, RECURSE is called twice. Usually, one call passes the head of a list and the second passes the tail. An example of this is in EQUAL. The EQUAL algorithm is shown in Fig. 8-4 and source code is given on Screen 53. The stack notation is:

$$(\text{S1 S2} -> \text{F})$$

S1 and S2, if atoms, are compared and a flag returned without recursing. If they are lists, both heads and tails of S1 and S2 must be equal. The first recursion is on the head of each S-expression. This recursion continues until atoms are reached in the case that the heads are themselves lists to be compared. Then the original EQUAL recurses on the tails of each list. The flags from the two recursions are ANDed, since both must be true for the list structures to be equal. The overall action, then, is that the heads are recursively compared; then the process is repeated by recursing on the tails.

The final example of recursion, of course, is harder than the previous two. Figure 8-5 shows a recursion diagram, similar to those of the first two examples, for 2APPEND. It is somewhat more complex because more than one item on the stack is being affected on each recursion. 2APPEND, shown on Screen 42, takes a list (^LIST) and "connects" it to the front of another list with list-id I. The basic idea of the algorithm is to pare down ^LIST, passing a stack copy of LIST2 along with it; these copies will be needed during ascent. When ^LIST becomes NIL, the terminating call of 2APPEND drops the empty ^LIST and the accompanying I and returns, as shown at the bottom of Fig. 8-5.

On the ascent, the part of 2APPEND following RECURSE acts on the stack. The head of each version of ^LIST is CONSed onto I. This has the effect of successively CONSing one item at a time from the original ^LIST onto I, starting at the tail-end of ^LIST.

These three examples present recursion at the detailed level of the individual function calls. Once this is understood, a more abstract understanding is possible. Instead of following a recursion diagram to see what will happen, some deeper insight is needed to write recursive procedures. 2APPEND can illustrate this more abstract way of thinking. Since copies of a word are called when recursing, those copies must do exactly

133

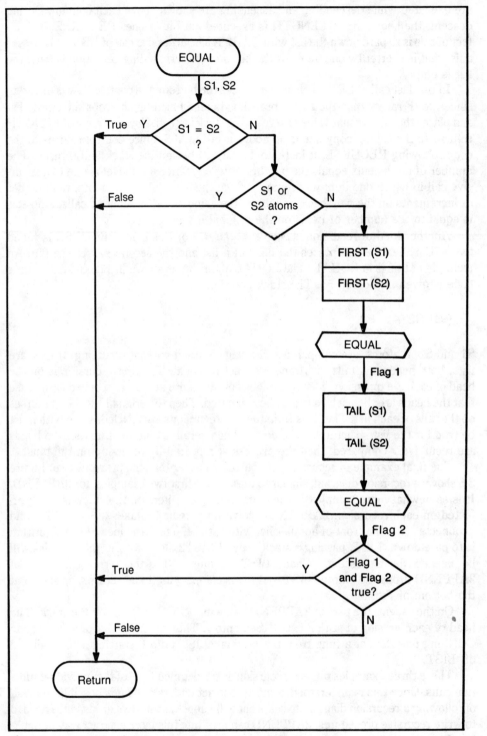

Fig. 8-4. The EQUAL algorithm, an example of double recursion.

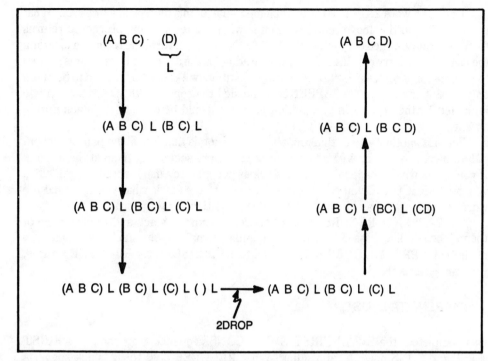

Fig. 8-5. Recursion diagram for 2APPEND. Two items (both lists) are passed each recursive call. Lists (A B C) and (D) are appended, resulting in (A B C D). List (D) is abbreviated L.

the same function as the word itself does when called for the first time.

2APPEND can be described in functional notation as:

2APPEND(X, Y)

It takes two arguments, X and Y, and appends X to Y. To do this, 2APPEND can be carried out by appending the tail of ^LIST to I, or:

2APPEND(TAIL ^LIST, I)

Then, append the head of ^LIST to this result:

2APPEND(FIRST ^LIST, 2APPEND(TAIL ^LIST, I))

Notice that 2APPEND is recursive since it contains itself as one of its arguments. The second argument of 2APPEND can be expanded:

2APPEND(FIRST ^LIST, 2APPEND(FIRST TAIL ^LIST, I), I)

The 2APPEND inside the above expression can in turn be expanded. These successive expansions can go on until some terminating condition is reached.

135

The Forth word 2APPEND is an implementation of this functional expression. What is not explicit in the above representation is what the terminating procedure returns to the innermost nested copy of 2APPEND. At the bottom level of the recursion diagram, the last call will carry out this set-up in preparation for the ascent. It does what is needed to prepare for ascent, since the terminating condition will cause this branch to be taken only once. For example, in 2APPEND we needed to drop from the stack the top two items left by the descent in preparation for what would be done to the stack during ascent.

Perhaps another way of thinking about recursion is that it is like a pair of sequential iterative procedures with a terminating procedure separating them at the bottom. If you follow what is happening on the stack as you go through a recursive word, when you get to RECURSE you can assume it will do to the stack what you designed the word to do overall (as indicated by the stack notation for the word).

For 2APPEND, RECURSE takes two items from the stack and returns none of them. The two lists passed to it at the beginning remain on the stack, and copies are made by OVER TAIL OVER to be passed to RECURSE. After RECURSE returns, you can assume that

2APPEND(TAIL ^LIST, I)

was completed, the SWAP FIRST SWAP CONS sequence then computes FIRST ^LIST and CONS does the appending. What RECURSE does to the stack suggests what the terminating procedure must do. In this case, at least, two items must be dropped. No other activity is called for; consequently, the IF branch contains a 2DROP. In the previous example of LENGTH, what was needed for a termination procedure can again be seen by looking at the stack activity around RECURSE. A list must be dropped and a number pushed onto the stack. Thus, the IF branch of LENGTH does that; it DROPs the list pointer and places a zero, the initial number, on the stack.

Double recursion can be handled in the same way as tail recursion, which was used in the examples given above. The usual pattern is to check for a terminating condition, then take the head and tail of a list, recurse on each of them, and then combine the result in some way. For EQUAL (Fig. 8-4), the terminator was a check for atoms and the flags returned by the two recursive calls were ANDed.

By studying these examples of recursion in careful detail and working out some others on your own, this concept should become as understandable as iteration. The LISP words on Screens 40 through 49 (Chapter 7 or the source code listing) offer several examples of recursively implemented words.

GARBAGE COLLECTION

An important part of a general LISP implementation involves the underlying activity of managing *list-space*, the region of memory that is allotted to lists. In our implementation, list-space is statically allotted (at compile-time). No run-time management occurs. Although this implementation is somewhat simplified, because management of list-space is an important factor in LISP and AI languages in general, it will be discussed here.

Because CONS-cells are used by CONS to build lists and are also removed from lists, some scheme is required to keep track of which cells are free to be used by CONS and which are in use already. Various schemes for managing list-space—which is a dynamic memory allocation problem—have been devised. The main problem is one of reclaiming unused CONS-cells. This activity is known as *garbage collection*. Most LISPs use a scheme known as *mark and sweep*. Another scheme, described in more detail here, is called *reference counting*.

To explain the difference, we should look first at two undesirable memory effects. They are *dangling references* and *garbage;* the first, dangling references, is the most serious. It occurs when a cell is assumed to be free when it actually is still in use. If other cells which are part of active (in-use) lists point to a cell which becomes free, that cell may be reused by CONS and made part of a new list. Of course, this leaves the pointers from the active cells "dangling," since what they point to is indeterminate. It thus is necessary never to allow an active CONS-cell to appear free. The second effect is the opposite one—to assume a cell is still active when it actually is free. In this case, the cell is "garbage" since it cannot be reused; there is no way to know that it is actually free.

Marking and sweeping avoids these two maladies by letting all of free memory be used up. Then the garbage collector runs. It goes through the lists pointed to by all the identifiers, since these are the active lists, marks a "garbage collection bit" in each active cell to indicate that the cell should not be made free, and then goes through all of list-space collecting the unmarked cells into a free-list—from which free cells can again be obtained by CONS. The problem that the mark and sweep scheme poses for real-time programs is that garbage collection takes a long time to complete since the task is enormous. On large machines, the pause due to the garbage collector may take seconds. Woe be it to any control loops depending on continual updating!

Reference counting avoids long pauses for list-space cleanup. Its disadvantages are that for destructive list operations, the programmer must consider cell memory management explicitly, and that each CONS-cell must contain extra storage for a reference count. This is a count of the number of active pointers pointing to the cell. Each time a pointer is removed, the reference count for the cell pointed to is decremented (by RC−) and whenever an active pointer is directed toward the cell, its reference count is incremented (by RC+). A reference count of zero indicates a free cell. When nondestructive list operations process lists, they build processed copies of the original lists using CONS. The reference counts of the cells of these lists are not incremented because they have not been assigned to an identifier and are, by definition, not active.

RC+ and RC− are used to manage reference counts. They differ only in that RC+ increments counts while RC− decrements them. They traverse the entire structure of a list, modifying the reference counts in every CONS-cell of the list.

Since CONS-cells must be saved only when they are part of a list pointed to by list-id, the word SET (or SETQ in LISP) can handle most of the reference count updating. SET invokes RC+ on a list when it is to be pointed to by a list-id. It also uses RC− on the list which that same list-id previously pointed to. Thus, cell management is handled simply by SET.

Recent implementations of garbage collectors are more sophisticated than the two schemes described here, and are usually combinations of them. Modern AI languages also have other kinds of data structures than CONS-cells for storing arrays, character strings, and numbers efficiently.

IMPLEMENTATION OF DESTRUCTIVE LIST FUNCTIONS

The destructive list functions of LISP modify existing list structure rather than create modified copies of lists. Some of the most common of these functions will be described here.

RPLACA invokes RC− on the given list, then calls RPLACA*, which does the list modification. It replaces the head of the list with the given S-expression. RPLACD replaces the tail instead. The other destructive list words use RPLACA* and RPLACD* because each word calls RC− to take care of reference counts. RPLACA* and RPLACD* are used as primitive list modifiers because they do not affect reference counts as RPLACA and RPLACD do.

DREVERSE iterates through the given list, L1, replacing the tails of cells with a pointer to the previous cell, as in Fig. 8-6. The tail of the first item of L1 is set to NIL to end the new list. L is the pointer returned, pointing to the head of the reverse list.

*NCONC (and also NCONC) "concatenates" L2 to L1 by replacing the NIL in the tail of the last item in L1 with a pointer to L2. ATTACH takes an S-expression, S, and a list, L, as arguments. If S is an atom, it will CONS S to L. If S is a list, in a manner similar to *NCONC, it points the tail of S to L. S becomes the first part of the new list.

Finally, DREMOVE uses DREMOVE1 which, like DREMOVE, takes S and L as arguments and removes any cells from L with heads EQ to S. The action of DREMOVE1 is shown in Fig. 8-7. The tail of the cell pointing to the one whose head is EQ to S is modified to "point around" this cell to the next one, thus removing the middle one. DREMOVE checks the head of the first cell of L for S. If it is not EQ, it calls DREMOVE1, which moves down L, bypassing cells with heads EQ to S by modifying tail pointers. However, if the first item of L must be removed, it replaces the head and tail of the first cell with the contents of the second one. This effectively bypasses the second cell, since the tail of the first cell now points to the third cell, as the second

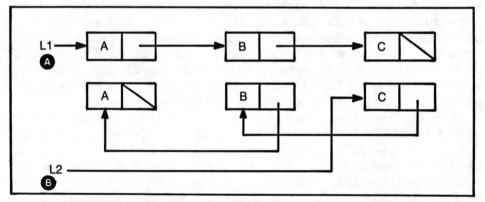

Fig. 8-6. A DREVERSED list, L2. The tails of the CONS-cells are replaced by pointers to the previous cell (B) in the original list, L1 (A).

138

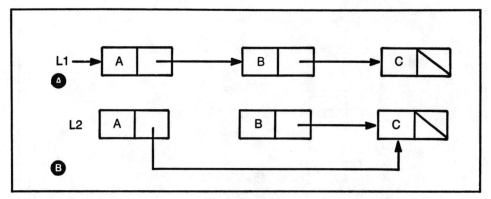

Fig. 8-7. DREMOVE1 is used to remove list item, B, from (A) list L1, resulting in (B) list L2.

cell did before being taken out of the list. After this, DREMOVE1 can be called on the list. DREMOVE is demonstrated graphically in Fig. 8-8.

Destructive list functions must be handled with care. Three reasons are:

1. Since lists are rearranged, if a list was pointed to by a list-id, it may not point to the head of the list after the destructive function. For example, DREVERSE will return a pointer to the head of the reversed list, but a list-id which pointed to the original list now points to the last item in the new list. After destructive functions are invoked, any list-id pointing to them must be repointed.
2. Because list items are reordered, keeping track of which CONS-cells are no longer used is no longer done automatically. Some dynamic list allocation must be done.
3. It is easy to form improper lists with destructive list words. Circular lists often occur inadvertently. Usually they are found when a PRINT is performed on one of them. The print-out is endless, requiring a hardware reset or other system abort.

DESTRUCTIVE LIST FUNCTIONS AND REFERENCE COUNTING

Destructive words complicate memory management because they change the structure of a list rather than return a copy. If a list-id is pointing to a list which is DREVERSEd or DREMOVEd, it is unclear what should be done to the reference counts.

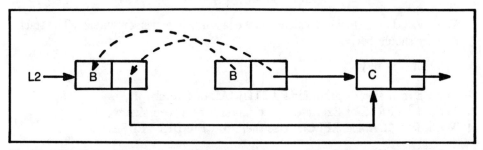

Fig. 8-8. DREMOVE algorithm. If the first CONS-cell of list L1 of Fig. 8-7 must be removed, then replace the head and tail of the first cell with the contents of the second one. Otherwise, call DREMOVE1.

```
                 54
     0 \ RECURSION EXAMPLE: FACTORIAL
     1
     2 ( N M -> )
     3 : *FACTORIAL OVER 0=
     4     IF NIP
     5     ELSE OVER * SWAP 1- SWAP RECURSE
     6     THEN
     7 ;
     8
     9 ( M -> M!)
    10 : FACTORIAL 1 *FACTORIAL ;
    11
    12
    13
    14
    15
```

Screen 54. Defining FACTORIAL and *FACTORIAL, which are recursive words.

It is not clear whether cells of the old list are still in the modified one (for DREMOVE) or whether new cells have been added somewhere in the new list's structure (as with RPLACA or RPLACD).

Fortunately, there is a simple way to deal with this problem. Before modifying a list, destructive words decrement the reference counts in the list using RC−. Then any cells lost from the list will not become garbage. The list modification is then carried out.

Afterwards, two points must be considered. Any list-id for the modified list is now invalid, since it still points to the cell which *was* the head of the list, but may be no longer. The list-id must consequently be reassigned to the resulting list. RC+ is performed first on the new list and then Forth functions store the list pointer in the list-id variable. A final consideration, and the most subtle, is to determine the effects on other lists which contain sublists in common with the "destructed" list. It is best to avoid this situation altogether by performing destructive list functions only on words which share no common sublists with other words.

EXERCISES

1. Write FACTORIAL, which calculates the factorial of n, using recursion. The stack activity should be:

    (n -> n!)

2. Draw a recursion diagram for FACTORIAL of Exercise 1.
3. Write REVERSE of Exercise 5 in Chapter 7 as a recursive word.
4. Write RPLACA and RPLCD. Use them to write DREVERSE.

Chapter 9

A Prolog
Knowledge System

C OMPUTER PROGRAMS THAT INTERPRET PRODUCTIONS OR RULES AND CONTAIN expert knowledge are called *expert* or *knowledge-based systems*, or just *knowledge systems*. In this chapter, a rule interpreter is developed using several of the programming techniques described in Chapter 8. Furthermore, it is a simplification of the rule interpreter in Prolog, the leading logic programming language.

LOGIC PROGRAMMING IN PROLOG

In the 1970s, the logic programming language *Prolog* emerged from France and Scotland. It has been chosen for the Japanese fifth-generation computer project. Prolog (which stands for "PROgramming LOGic") is a simple yet powerful language that is *relational* or *declarative* rather than *functional*. A function is a kind of procedure which takes arguments passed to it, processes them, and returns a result. Forth is a functional language.

A relational language program consists of statements which describe the relationships among the things represented. In Prolog this is done in predicate logic. Predicates are used to state facts, and are true or false. The predicate

    mammal (goat).

states: "A goat is a mammal." This statement declares a fact instead of prescribing a procedure.

A Prolog program is a list of *clauses,* which are facts or rules. Rules are written in the form:

head :- goal$_1$, goal$_2$, ... , goal$_n$.

The *head* of the clause is the conclusion of the rule, while the *goals,* separated by commas, are the premises or conditions. The :- symbol can be read "if." The goals to the right of the "if" symbol, taken together, are called the *body.* The rule can thus be read: "If goal$_1$ and goal$_2$ and...and goal$_n$ are true, then head is true".

The data types of Prolog are called *terms,* after terms in logic. Figure 9-1 shows that Prolog terms are constants, variables, or structures. Constants are either atoms or integer numbers. Atoms begin with a lowercase letter or are enclosed in single quotes. Variables are designated by names with uppercase first letters.

Structures consist of two parts, a *functor,* which is an atom, and *components,* which are terms enclosed in parentheses and separated by commas. Structures can be used as logical predicates, such as:

father (X,'Bill').

This is read: "X is the father of Bill" and is a predicate because it is either true or false. "Bill" is enclosed in single quotes to indicate that it is an atom. Without the quotes it would otherwise be interpreted as a variable, as X is. X and Bill are components of the structure.

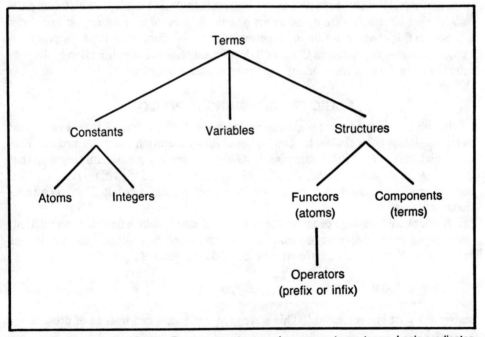

Fig. 9-1. The data types of Prolog. Functors are atoms and components are terms. Logic predicates and arithmetic operations are structures. Operators such as :- can be used in infix notation.

A functor is an *operator* if it can be used either in prefix or infix notation. For example, the "if" symbol (:-) can be used as:

:- (a,b,c).

or, in infix notation:

a :- b,c.

Not all functors are operators, but those which are naturally understood as operators (such as :- or +) are defined as such.

Facts, as well as the heads and goals of rules are all terms. Besides terms, Prolog also has lists. (Note that both rules and lists have "heads" but they are not necessarily the same.) In Prolog, lists are enclosed in square brackets. For example,

[a,b,c]

is a list of three items, with "a" as head and the list [b,c] as tail. The empty list is []. In the list

[H|T]

the vertical bar is used to separate head and tail.

Prolog has some predefined predicates, such as "if" (:-). Here are some others:

true
fail
var(X)   Returns true if X is a variable
atomic(X)   Returns true if X is a constant

Comments are included in source code by enclosing them in matched slash-asterisk pairs, thus:

/* ... */

Prolog has one procedure for all programs. This procedure must, of course, be very powerful and general if Prolog is to be used for a range of applications. It is a search procedure combined with a rule of inference known as *resolution*. Instead of having several inference rules, by which new facts can be deduced from existing clauses, this one rule suffices, eliminating complications such as choosing which rule to apply each step in the reasoning process.

The rules supplied by the programmer as clauses are not inference rules of Prolog but are logical implications and are equivalent to:

$$\text{head} \lor \neg \text{goal}_1 \lor \neg \text{goal}_2 \lor \ldots \lor \neg \text{goal}_n$$

where $\lor$ is logical OR (disjunction), $\land$ is logical AND (conjunction), and $\neg$ is logical NOT (negation). The logical relationship of Prolog clauses is conjunctive. That is, they are all true together, or ANDed together.

Now consider the two clauses:

```
goal, head :- goal
```

The first clause is a fact and the second a rule which can be expressed logically as ˥goal ∨ head. Since clauses are conjunctively combined, these clauses are equivalent to the logical expression:

```
goal ∧( ¬goal ∨ head)
```

Since goal ∧¬ goal cancel, the resulting expression is goal ∧ head. Resolution is the inference rule which combines two expressions, a fact and rule for which the goal(s) match to produce a new fact—the head of the rule; "goal" remains a clause but "head" is now added.

Both facts and rules are clauses and have the same form, since a fact is a rule without goals:

```
fact :-
```

Facts are rules which are unconditionally satisfied, having no goals. Also, negations of facts can be expressed as:

```
:- fact
```

This is equivalent to ¬fact because of the definition of logical implication.

Before describing the search procedure of Prolog, a simple example of a Prolog program is in order. An example in Chapter 8 illustrated recursion in the word 2APPEND. This function can be expressed in Prolog as a logical predicate (a Prolog structure):

```
append(L1,L2,L3)
```

which means: "Append L1 onto L2 with L3 being the appended list". For example, for (A B) as L1 and (C D) as L2, L3 would be (A B C D): In Prolog, append can be expressed as:

```
append ([],L2,L2).

append ([H|L1],L2,[H|L3]) :- append(L1,L2,L3).
```

The first clause is like the terminating condition of 2APPEND. It declares that if [] (or NIL) is appended to L2, the result is L2. The second clause contains append in both head and goal, suggesting recursion. If L1 is appended to L2 to form L3, then a list with head H and tail L1, when appended to L2, results in a list with head H and tail L3.

144

To illustrate **append** in action, **(a b)** will be appended to **(c d)**. The successive substitutions into the head of the rule are:

H	L1	L2	[H	L3]
a	(b)	(c d)	[a | L3]
b	()	(c d)	[a | [b | L3]]

The empty L1 of the last line triggers the terminating condition for **append**. The rule now does not match, but the fact:

> append([], L2, L2).

matches. The substitutions are:

[]	L2	[H | L3]
()	(c d)	[a | [b | (c d)]]

In this last match, L2 is substituted for L3, resulting in the appended list:

> [a | [b | (c d)]] → [a b c d]

Notice that while **[H|L1]** matches with **(a b)**, the third argument in the head of the rule, **[H|L3]**, builds a list instead. The inverse action is due to the substitution of L3 from the goal into L3 of the head. This causes the previous substitution of, say, **[a|L3]** for L3 to be substituted for the present L3 in **[b|L3]**, resulting in:

> [a | [b | L3]]

For the last iteration, L2 is substituted for L3, and the list is complete.

A PROLOG INTERPRETER

Repeated application of facts to rules, resulting in new facts, is called *forward chaining*. In *backward chaining*, conclusions (heads of rules) are searched for one that matches the goal. If one is found, then its goals in turn must be proved. Prolog uses backward chaining.

The search algorithm used in Prolog is depth-first search, and is shown in flowchart form in Fig. 9-2. It uses three lists. The first is CLAUSES, which contains the clauses. The second is the GOALS list; it contains the goals to be satisfied. Third, the SOLVED list holds the backtracking points and keeps a trail of clauses used to satisfy the goals. If successful, SOLVED contains the solution path for reaching the goals. It is a kind of trace of how the search procedure found the solution.

In Fig. 9-2, SEARCH first checks the GOALS list. If it is empty, no more goals remain to be proven, and it has succeeded. Otherwise, it removes the first goal from GOALS, and scans down the CLAUSES list for a matching clause. If one is found, a pointer (into CLAUSES) to this clause is added to the SOLVED list along with the goal itself. This pointer marks how far down the CLAUSES list SEARCH got to before a match was found. The goals of this matched clause are then tried; if one fails, the pointer is moved to the next matching clause in CLAUSES and its goals put on the GOALS list. This failure recovery is called *backtracking*. The new pointer replaces the previous one on SOLVED. Each time backtracking occurs, this pointer is moved further down the CLAUSES list. If the pointer is moved to the end of CLAUSES, no clause has been found which proves the goal, and SEARCH fails.

To explain the search procedure by an example, a list of clauses and a goal are needed. Clauses will be expressed in the form that is used in the implementation, shown on Screens 60 through 65. A small knowledgebase is given on Screen 70 for this example. The CLAUSES list is set to be, in order:

1. (GIVES-MILK)
2. (HAS-HAIR)
3. (HAS-HORNS)
4. (MAMMAL GIVES-MILK HAS-HAIR)
5. (GOAT IS-BILLY)
6. (GOAT MAMMAL HAS-HORNS)

Clauses 1, 2, 3, and 5 are facts; clauses 4 and 6 are rules. The GOALS list is set to be (GOAT). Thus, SEARCH will try to prove GOAT using the assertions in the CLAUSES list. The SOLVED list is initially set to be empty.

As shown in Fig. 9-2, SEARCH first examines GOALS, which is not empty. It then removes GOAT from GOALS, leaving it empty. It now finds the first clause with a head matching GOAT (clause 5) and puts GOAT and a pointer to 5 on the SOLVED list. Since a clause (clause 5) was found matching GOAT, the body of this rule is added to the GOALS list. It now contains:

(IS-BILLY)

SEARCH iterates. It removes this goal from GOALS and looks for a clause matching IS-BILLY. Since none exist, the search fails, and the backtracking branch is taken.

At this point, GOALS is empty, and the previous goal (GOAT) is retrieved from the SOLVED list along with the pointer to clause 5. The goal-pointer pair is removed from SOLVED and the goal search is taken up again starting after clause 5. The next clause in CLAUSES (clause 6) matches GOAT. It is a new backtracking point, and GOAT and clause 6 are placed on the SOLVED list. The goals of clause 6 are added to GOALS. Backtracking is now complete, and since a clause matching GOAT was found (clause 6),SEARCH does not fail, but once again iterates. This procedure continues as described above until all the goals are satisfied or until backtracking runs out of clauses in CLAUSES. If SEARCH succeeds, the SOLVED list contains a "trace" of the path through search-space. It shows how the goal was proven true. If SEARCH fails, the SOLVED list will contain a partial solution, showing how far SEARCH got before it failed.

To demonstrate the rule interpreter in action, some words have been written to make it more observable. By loading Screen 70, the knowledgebase described above will be compiled into the Forth dictionary and lists built. By invoking the word TRACE

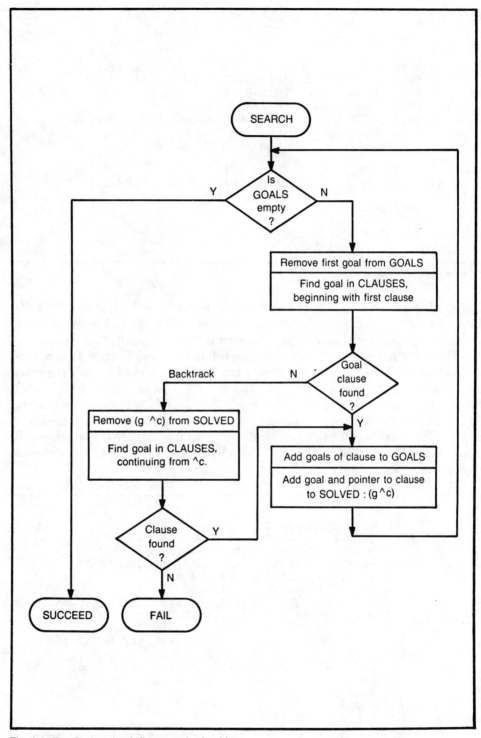

Fig. 9-2. The Prolog depth-first search algorithm.

```
      70
 0 \ KNOWLEDGEBASE
 1
 2 : MARKER ;
 3 RULE: GIVES-MILK  (GIVES-MILK )
 4 RULE: HAS-HAIR    (HAS-HAIR )
 5 RULE: HAS-HORNS   (HAS-HORNS )
 6 RULE: MAMMAL      (MAMMAL GIVES-MILK HAS-HAIR )
 7 RULE: GOAT1       (GOAT IS-BILLY )
 8 RULE: GOAT2       (GOAT MAMMAL HAS-HORNS )
 9
10 CLAUSES NIL SET CLAUSES READL
11 (GIVES-MILK @ HAS-HAIR @ HAS-HORNS @ MAMMAL @ GOAT1 @ GOAT2 @ )
12
13 SOLVED NIL SET
14 GOALS NIL SET
15 NIL GOAT GOALS LIST
```

Screen 70. A knowledgebase.

and starting and stopping it by pressing a keyboard key, the GOALS and SOLVED
lists will be displayed at each inference, i.e., each loop in SEARCH. Figure 9-3 shows
the flow of TRACE, with a blank line between each GOALS-SOLVED frame.

The first frame printed is the initial state before the first inference. In each suc-
ceeding frame, GOALS has deleted from it any failed goal and added to it the goals
from a newly matched clause. This clause also appears as the first one in the SOLVED
list. For the first inference in Fig. 9-3, the goal IS-BILLY fails. In the second frame,
IS-BILLY is removed from GOALS and the goals of the first clause in SOLVED is
added. This clause in SOLVED was found during backtracking. In the last frame all
goals have been solved, since GOALS is NIL; the SOLVED list shows the sequence
of inferences used to prove GOAT from CLAUSES.

```
        71
 0 \ KNOWLEDGEBASE
 1 : MARKER ;
 2 RULE: GIVES-MILK  (GIVES-MILK )
 3 RULE: HAS-HAIR1   (HAS-HAIR IS-GRUFFY )
 4 RULE: HAS-HAIR2   (HAS-HAIR )
 5 RULE: HAS-HORNS   (HAS-HORNS )
 6 RULE: MAMMAL      (MAMMAL GIVES-MILK HAS-HAIR )
 7 RULE: GOAT1       (GOAT IS-BILLY )
 8 RULE: GOAT2       (GOAT IS-GRUFFY )
 9 RULE: GOAT3       (GOAT MAMMAL HAS-HORNS )
10 CLAUSES NIL SET CLAUSES READL
11 (GIVES-MILK @ HAS-HAIR1 @ HAS-HAIR2 @ HAS-HORNS @
12   MAMMAL @ GOAT1 @ GOAT2 @ GOAT3 @ )
13 SOLVED NIL SET
14 GOALS NIL SET
15 NIL GOAT GOALS LIST
```

Screen 71. Additional development of the knowledgebase.

```
                    GOALS:
                    (GOAT)
                    SOLVED:
                    NIL

                    GOALS:
                    (IS-BILLY)
                    SOLVED:
                    (GOAT IS-BILLY)

                    GOALS:
                    (MAMMAL HAS-HORNS)
                    SOLVED:
                    (GOAT MAMMAL HAS-HORNS)

                    GOALS:
                    (GIVES-MILK HAS-HAIR HAS-HORNS)
                    SOLVED:
                    (MAMMAL GIVES-MILK HAS-HAIR)
                    (GOAT MAMMAL HAS-HORNS)

                    GOALS:
                    (HAS-HAIR HAS-HORNS)
                    SOLVED:
                    (GIVES-MILK)
                    (MAMMAL GIVES-MILK HAS-HAIR)
                    (GOAT MAMMAL HAS-HORNS)

                    GOALS:
                    (HAS-HORNS)
                    SOLVED:
                    (HAS-HAIR)
                    (GIVES-MILK)
                    (MAMMAL GIVES-MILK HAS-HAIR)
                    (GOAT MAMMAL HAS-HORNS)

                    GOALS:
                    NIL
                    SOLVED:
                    (HAS-HORNS)
                    (HAS-HAIR)
                    (GIVES-MILK)
                    (MAMMAL GIVES-MILK HAS-HAIR)
                    (GOAT MAMMAL HAS-HORNS)
                    SUCCEED
```

Fig. 9-3. A trace of SEARCH.

On Screen 71 is given a slightly extended knowledgebase that lists clauses in an order so that backtracking occurs twice for GOAT and once for HAS-HAIR. Since neither IS-BILLY nor IS-GRUFFY can be proven, and IS-GRUFFY occurs twice as a goal, three backtrackings occur.

IMPLEMENTATION OF SEARCH

The Forth implementation of SEARCH is shown on Screens 60 through 63 and the entire "package" goes through Screen 65. It is built on the LISP words of Chapter

7 and runs the programs of Screens 70 and 71. Having described the search algorithm itself, the implementation details will now be examined.

On Screen 63, the word SEARCH consists of a simple loop that iterates (SEARCH) on Screen 62. (SEARCH) does the work and passes a succeed/fail flag to SEARCH, from which it determines when to terminate. (SEARCH) first checks the GOALS list with NULL. If it is not empty, it gets a goal from GOALS with GET-GOAL. Then it gets a pointer to the head of the CLAUSES list to start the search for the goal from the beginning.

The word FIND-CLAUSE? takes the goal and pointer into CLAUSES and tries to find a clause with a head matching the goal. If it succeeds, it also places the goal and a pointer to the matching clause on the SOLVED list. It returns a flag which is true if a match was found.

For a matching clause, the IF branch in (SEARCH) is taken. It calls ADD-GOALS, which puts the goals of the matching clause (the pointer to which is on the SOLVED list). If no match was found, backtracking is required; the ELSE branch is taken and BACKTRACK is called. Both of these branches leave flags on the stack. The top of the stack will contain a flag for UNTIL in SEARCH. If it is false, search continues. If it is true, the search terminates and leaves a second flag indicating success or failure.

For the outermost IF-ELSE-THEN construct in (SEARCH), the ELSE branch is taken if GOALS is empty, and two true flags are left on the stack—the first to terminate and the second to indicate success. BACKTRACK is followed by an IF-THEN that does flag manipulation. BACKTRACK passes a flag that is true if it successfully backtracked. In this case, SEARCH should not terminate, and a false flag is left. If backtracking failed, a false flag is returned, and a false-true stack order of flags is returned.

FIND-CLAUSE? and BACKTRACK are given on Screen 61. Both (SEARCH) and BACKTRACK use FIND-CLAUSE?, which in turn uses FIND-CLAUSE on Screen 60 to do the actual search for a matching clause. FIND-CLAUSE takes a goal and pointer into CLAUSES and proceeds through the clauses, looking for one with a head

```
         62
 0 \ PROLOG RULE INTERPRETER
 1
 2  ( -> FLAG TRUE | FALSE) \ FLAG = TRUE => SUCCEED
 3  : (SEARCH)
 4      GOALS @ NULL NOT
 5      IF GET-GOAL CLAUSES @ FIND-CLAUSE?
 6         IF ADD-GOALS FALSE
 7         ELSE BACKTRACK
 8            IF FALSE ELSE FALSE TRUE THEN
 9         THEN
10      ELSE TRUE DUP
11      THEN
12  ;
13
14
15
```

Screen 62. A Prolog rule interpreter: (SEARCH).

150

matching goal. When found, it returns both the goal and a pointer to the matching clause. Since CLAUSES is a list of clauses, each of which is itself a list, then a pointer into CLAUSES will point to a list such as:

((GOAT IS-BILLY) (GOAT MAMMAL HAS-HORNS))

as it will for frame two of Fig. 9-4.

To retrieve the head of the first clause of this TAILed CLAUSES list, two invocations of FIRST are needed; the first one returns the first clause and the second the head of the clause. In FIND-CLAUSE this pointer to a clause head is then compared (using =) to the goal. Since the name of the goal will be the same Forth variable, the pointers to this variable will be the same, and = can be used to compare them. (In a full Prolog, = is replaced by UNIFY, explained later in this chapter.) If no match occurs and the list is not depleted of elements, the tail of the clause pointer will move

```
          60
  0  \ PROLOG RULE INTERPRETER
  1
  2  20   NEWLIST GOALS
  3  20   NEWLIST SOLVED
  4  200 NEWLIST CLAUSES
  5
  6  ( -> GOAL)
  7  : GET-GOAL GOALS @ DUP FIRST SWAP TAIL GOALS SWAP SET ;
  8
  9  ( GOAL @CLAUSES1 -> GOAL @CLAUSES2)
 10  : FIND-CLAUSE
 11     BEGIN 2DUP FIRST FIRST DUP >R = R> NULL OR NOT
 12     WHILE TAIL
 13     REPEAT
 14  ;
 15


          61
  0  \ PROLOG RULE INTERPRETER
  1
  2  ( GOAL @ CLAUSE -> FLAG) \ FIND MATCHING CLAUSE AND PUT ON SOLV
  3                           \ FLAG IS TRUE IF CLAUSE IS FOUND
  4  : FIND-CLAUSE? FIND-CLAUSE DUP NULL DUP >R
  5     IF 2DROP
  6     ELSE SOLVED CONS SOLVED CONS
  7     THEN R> NOT
  8  ;
  9  : ADD-GOALS SOLVED @ TAIL FIRST FIRST TAIL GOALS 2APPEND ;
 10
 11  ( -> FLAG) \ FLAG = FALSE IF SOLVED LIST EMPTY
 12  : BACKTRACK SOLVED @ DUP FIRST SWAP TAIL FIRST TAIL
 13     SOLVED DUP @ TAIL TAIL SET FIND-CLAUSE? DUP
 14     IF ADD-GOALS THEN
 15  ;
```

Screens 60, 61. A Prolog rule interpreter: GET-GOAL, FIND-CLAUSE, FIND-CLAUSE?, and BACKTRACK.

```
GOALS:
(GOAT)
SOLVED:
NIL

GOALS:
(IS-BILLY)
SOLVED:
(GOAT IS-BILLY)

GOALS:
(IS-GRUFFY)
SOLVED:
(GOAT IS-GRUFFY)

GOALS:
(MAMMAL HAS-HORNS)
SOLVED:
(GOAT MAMMAL HAS-HORNS)

GOALS:
(GIVES-MILK HAS-HAIR HAS-HORNS)
SOLVED:
(MAMMAL GIVES-MILK HAS-HAIR)
(GOAT MAMMAL HAS-HORNS)

GOALS:
(HAS-HAIR HAS-HORNS)
SOLVED:
(GIVES-MILK)
(MAMMAL GIVES-MILK HAS-HAIR)
(GOAT MAMMAL HAS-HORNS)

GOALS:
(IS-GRUFFY HAS-HORNS)
SOLVED:
(HAS-HAIR IS-GRUFFY)
(GIVES-MILK)
(MAMMAL GIVES-MILK HAS-HAIR)
(GOAT MAMMAL HAS-HORNS)

GOALS:
(HAS-HORNS)
SOLVED:
(HAS-HAIR)
(GIVES-MILK)
(MAMMAL GIVES-MILK HAS-HAIR)
(GOAT MAMMAL HAS-HORNS)

GOALS:
NIL
SOLVED:
(HAS-HORNS)
(HAS-HAIR)
(GIVES-MILK)
(MAMMAL GIVES-MILK HAS-HAIR)
(GOAT MAMMAL HAS-HORNS)
SUCCEED
```

Fig. 9-4. Another trace of SEARCH showing backtracking in the first two frames.

it to the next clause and the comparison repeated. When FIND-CLAUSE finishes, it returns the pointer. If no match was found, the pointer will point to an empty clause list.

FIND-CLAUSE? tests whether the returned list (pointer) is NIL (using NULL) and keeps a copy of this flag on the return stack (using >R). If the search failed, it clears the stack and passes back the flag. If a match was found, however, both the goal and the clause pointer are CONSed onto the SOLVED list. Thus, the structure of the SOLVED list is:

(goal$_1$ clause-pointer$_1$ goal$_2$ clause-pointer$_2$ ... goal$_n$ clause-pointer$_n$)

Figure 9-4 shows only the first clause of the remaining CLAUSE list pointed to by the clause-pointer.

BACKTRACK first retrieves from the SOLVED list the goal and clause pointer (which marks the backtrack point in CLAUSES) and then sets SOLVED to the tail of the tail of itself. That is, it moves down the list by two items, thus dropping the goal and clause pointer just retrieved. BACKTRACK then calls FIND-CLAUSE to resume the search for the goal, starting at the clause pointer. If it succeeds, it adds the new goals of the matched clause to GOALS by calling ADD-GOALS. If no match was found, SEARCH fails. BACKTRACK returns a flag indicating success or failure.

Two minor words of SEARCH remain to be explained. ADD-GOALS takes the goals from the list pointed to by the first clause pointer and appends them to GOALS. Getting to the goals, starting with the SOLVED list, is nontrivial. A sequence of FIRST and TAIL words does it. SOLVED @ TAIL moves past the first goal on SOLVED, returning the rest of the list. Then FIRST returns the list of clauses—the TAILed CLAUSES list. Another FIRST returns the first clause of this list, and the final TAIL moves past its head. What remains is a list containing the goals of the first clause.

GET-GOAL retrieves the first item from the GOALS list and then removes it from GOALS by setting GOALS to the tail of itself. Besides these words, the three lists needed are defined on Screen 60 and allotted a small amount of memory.

Besides SEARCH itself, some user interface and debugging words are added on Screens 63 through 65. In Prolog, a query about a goal can be stated as:

?- goal

A similar word given here is passed a goal list instead. To prove GOAT, invoke:

?- (GOAT)

The word ?- uses READL to obtain the goal list which is placed in GOALS. Also, ?- empties SOLVED for new search. The answer to a query will be either SUCCEED or FAIL. If you want to see a trace of the search, the word TRACE, as described earlier, can be installed in ?- by changing the execution vector INFER to point to TRACE:

' TRACE IS INFER

Initially, INFER is set to SEARCH which does not show a trace.

TRACE is given on Screen 65. It is similar to SEARCH except that it displays

```
        63
 0  \ PROLOG RULE INTERPRETER
 1
 2  ( -> FLAG) \ FLAG = TRUE => SUCCEED
 3  : SEARCH
 4      BEGIN (SEARCH)
 5      UNTIL
 6  ;
 7
 8  DEFER INFER ' SEARCH IS INFER
 9
10  : ?- SOLVED NIL SET GOALS DUP NIL SET READL INFER CR
11      ['] INFER >BODY @ ['] SEARCH = \ IS INFER SEARCH ?
12      IF
13          IF ." SUCCEED" ELSE ." FAIL" THEN
14      THEN
15  ;


        64
 0  \ PROLOG RULE INTERPRETER
 1
 2  \ MAXIMUM GOALS/RULE = 4
 3  : RULE: CREATE HERE DUP 2+ , NIL , 10 ALLOT READL ;
 4
 5  : .KB CLAUSES @ PRINT ;
 6  : .GOALS GOALS @ PRINT ;
 7
 8  : HOW? SOLVED @ DUP NULL
 9      IF PRINT
10      ELSE
11          BEGIN DUP NULL NOT
12          WHILE DUP TAIL FIRST FIRST PRINT TAIL TAIL
13          REPEAT DROP
14      THEN
15  ;


        65
 0  \ PROLOG RULE INTERPRETER
 1  : NUF? KEY?
 2          IF KEY DROP KEY 13 =
 3              ELSE FALSE
 4          THEN
 5  ;
 6
 7  \ TRACE SEARCH
 8  : TRACE
 9      BEGIN CR ." GOALS:" GOALS @ PRINT
10          CR ." SOLVED:" HOW? CR (SEARCH) DUP >R
11          IF
12              IF ." SUCCEED" ELSE ." FAIL" CR THEN
13          THEN R> NUF? OR
14      UNTIL
15  ;
```

Screens 63, 64, 65. A Prolog rule interpreter: SEARCH, ?-, RULE:, .KB, .GOALS, HOW?, NUF?, and TRACE.

the GOALS and SOLVED lists frames each iteration. The word NUF? lets the trace be started and stopped from the keyboard. When tracing, if any key is pressed, tracing will pause until any key except Return is pressed. If Return is pressed while pausing, TRACE terminates.

TRACE uses the word HOW? which prints the first clause in the clause list on SOLVED. The word .KB makes it easy to print CLAUSES and .GOALS GOALS. To easily create clauses, RULE: is used, as shown on Screens 70 and 71. It is used in the form:

RULE: clause-name list

where "list" is read in by READL within RULE:. To minimize names, a clause with a unique head can be named the same as the head. (See for example, MAMMAL or GIVES-MILK on Screen 70.) RULE: can take up to four goals as implemented since 10 bytes are allotted by it: two for the head and eight for the goals.

DEDUCTION TREES

The *deduction tree* makes it easier to follow search control flow. In Fig. 9-5, a deduction tree for the trace of Fig. 9-3 is shown. It graphically illustrates the sequence of inferences as nodes, numbered as they appear in the order of the trace frames. The goals of a rule lead to matching clauses, linked by branches to the rule. The tree structure is characteristic of search algorithms in general. The levels in the tree represent chaining of the rule interpreter.

Starting at the top, the goal GOAT is given. A search for a matching clause produces, at the next level, the rule at 2. Since it fails, backtracking to the top level occurs

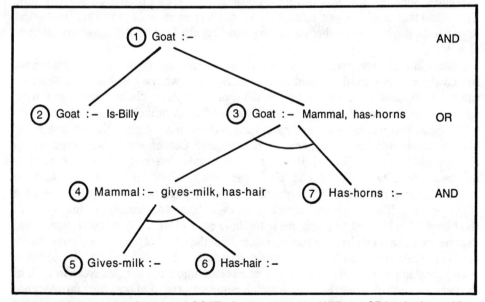

Fig. 9-5. A deduction tree for the goal GOAT, showing alternating AND and OR levels of branching. The numbers indicate the order of use of clauses.

and a search for another clause is carried out, resulting in 3. The rule at 3 establishes MAMMAL and HAS-HORNS as goals, leading to a lower level of search. Notice that the logical relationship between the nodes alternates between levels. At the top level, if more goals had been given, *all* of them would have to succeed for the search to succeed. Each goal can be considered a sub-problem for which all the sub-problems must be solved to solve the overall problem. Consequently, the logical relationship among the goals at the top level is conjunctive.

At the next level down, however, the branches represent alternative clauses, only one of which must succeed for the search to succeed. Either the inference at node 2 *or* node 3 must succeed. The logical relationship of nodes at this level is disjunctive. At the next level, both goals MAMMAL and HAS-HORNS must succeed; this level has conjunctively related branches. The curve connecting branches indicates that they are conjunctively related. The deduction tree thus graphically shows both the state-space path of the search and, in a different sense, the reduction of the problem of solving the top-level goal into subproblems.

BREADTH-FIRST AND HEURISTIC SEARCH

In depth-first search, as we have seen, the deduction tree is traversed downward until success or failure occurs. Only then does search come back up the tree and, if it failed, try a different branch downward again—hence the name "depth-first" search. The Prolog search algorithm is depth-first because new goals are added to the front of the GOALS list. What would happen if they were added at the end of the list instead? Instead of moving downward through the levels, all the alternative clauses would be tried first. The result is that control flow would scan across each level, moving to the next lower level only after trying all the nodes on that level. In other words, the alternative solutions would be developed concurrently rather than tried one at a time. This could take much longer, of course, but it also has some advantages. Depth-first search can go very deep before failing. In breadth-first search, backtracking is eliminated.

Early in AI history, search was one of the main topics of interest. At that time, search algorithms were developed that select a path down the tree based on heuristic rules. These rules depend upon the domain. For example, in chess many alternatives usually exist for a given board position. The number of branches from a given node in the deduction tree is large, and each path is deep to a solution (that is, a winning board position) because of the many moves in a game. Consequently, depth-first search alone would be very inefficient. Breadth-first search is able to explore all the possible moves to one or two moves ahead. Even then, not all possibilities may be able to be explored in an acceptable time. A means of choosing potentially good paths down the tree is needed. Rules such as: "prefer moves which increase control of the center of the board" can be used to eliminate potentially poor moves. These rules come from experience and are empirical in nature, rather than the result of a comprehensive theory of chess. They are called heuristic rules or just *heuristics*. They can be used to guide search, making it more efficient. The *uniform-cost* algorithm assigns costs to each of the branches and chooses the branch which minimizes the total cost thus far. Another important search algorithm is the A* algorithm, which does optimal, heuristically guided search.

UNIFICATION

The major shortcoming of the Prolog search implementation developed here is that the terms are all atoms. They are all Forth variables whose main use is to hold a name. Our Prolog would be much enhanced by providing variables—not Forth variables as such, but logic variables. We could then write rules like these in Prolog:

goat(X) :- mammal(X), has-horns(X).

X is a variable that could stand for a particular goat. With variables, Prolog can be used to return substitutions of atoms for variables (or *instantiated* variables), giving the capability of answering questions or retrieving data using inference.

Variables were used in the definition of **append** earlier in this chapter. To see how they can be used to answer questions, consider the clauses:

goat (billy).
goat (gruffy).

Invoking

?- goat(X).

would return instantiations of X. Both "billy" and "gruffy" could be substituted for X. An example using a rule is:

grandfather(X,Z) :- father(X,Y), father(Y,Z).
father(carl, sam).
father(sam, lewis).

For these clauses, invoking:

?- grandfather(x, lewis).

will return "X = carl" by instantiating the variables in the rule. Variable substitutions are called "bindings", and can be represented as a list of pairs. For the above example, the bindings would be:

((X carl) (Y sam) (Z lewis))

where the first item of each pair is the variable and the second item is its substitution. The variable is *bound* to the substitution. A list of bindings is an *environment*.

The flow of the Prolog interpreter can be followed for the above example, noting the environment at each step. The top-level goal is **grandfather(X, lewis)**. Immediately, **Z** is bound to **lewis**. Then the two goals of the rule are placed on the goals list. Searching for a match with **father(X, Y)**, the interpreter finds the second clause, **father(carl, sam)** and makes substitutions, resulting in:

((Y sam) (X carl) (Z lewis))

The second goal, also with a "father" predicate, matches the same clause and attempts to do the substitutions:

((Y carl) (Z sam))

Both of these substitutions contradict previous ones. At this point, Prolog fails to match and proceeds to look for another clause. The next clause has bindings for Y and Z that agree identically with the previous ones, and the top-level goal succeeds. The substitutions are then displayed.

In this example, the arguments of the predicates are atoms. In the more general case, they could also be predicates or variables. As an example of a more complicated match, the two predicates:

f(X, Y), f(sam, g(X))

have bindings:

((X sam) (Y g(X)))

These predicates can be expressed in list form as:

(f X Y) (f sam (g X))

The process we have briefly surveyed is called *pattern matching*. Two logic expressions attempt to be *unified* by making consistent variable substitutions. An algorithm that produces the most general unifier is the *unification algorithm*, shown in Fig. 9-6.

To appreciate how the unification algorithm, UNIFY, works, we will examine some expressions to be matched that cause problems that must be dealt with by UNIFY. First, consider the two predicates:

(a X X), (a Y b)

The first items match. Both of the second items are variables, with binding (X Y). When the third items are matched, X is bound to b, resulting in bindings:

((X Y) (X b))

In this environment, Y should be bound to b since X is bound to Y, but it is not. Also, X is bound more than once. To produce the environment:

((X Y) (Y b))

instead, the binding of a variable should be matched instead of the variable. Then, X would bind to Y, but when the third items are matched, the binding of X is used to match against b, resulting in (Y b).

The retrieval of the binding of a variable is accomplished by the algorithm, VALUE,

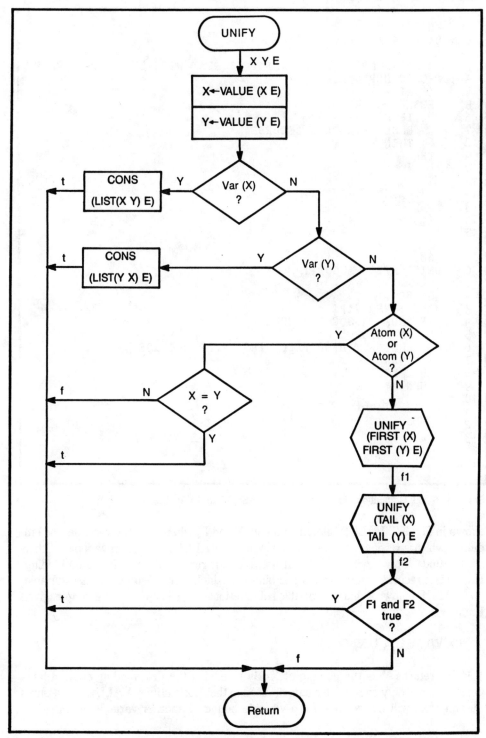

Fig. 9-6. A unification algorithm for Prolog. Variables must occur only once in predicates.

```
      67
0 \ UNIFICATION ALGORITHM
1
2  ( S L1 -> L2) \ 2ASSOC-LIST IS FLAT WITH LVAR-VALUE PAIRS
3 : 2ASSOC DUP NULL
4     IF NIP
5     ELSE 2DUP FIRST =
6         IF NIP
7         ELSE TAIL TAIL RECURSE
8         THEN
9     THEN
10 ;
11
12
13
14
15


      68
0 \ UNIFICATION ALGORITHM
1
2  ( S1 @E -> S2)
3 : VALUE OVER VAR?
4     IF 2DUP 2ASSOC DUP NULL
5         IF 2DROP
6         ELSE ROT DROP TAIL FIRST SWAP RECURSE
7         THEN
8     ELSE DROP
9     THEN
10 ;
11
12
13
14
15
```

Screens 67, 68. Unification algorithm: defining 2ASSOC and VALUE.

shown in Fig. 9-7. VALUE takes arguments X and E, where X is the variable, the binding of which is retrieved from environment list E. VALUE returns non-variables. Otherwise it finds X on E with ASSOC. If not found, it returns X since it has no binding. If found, it recurses on the tail of the binding, which could also be another variable.

VALUE follows a chain of variable substitutions to the last one. For example, given E as:

((X W) (W U) (U V) (V Y))

VALUE returns Y as the binding of X. By returning the first binding created for a given variable, only one variable name is used in the substitutions. VALUE also assures that an atom will be returned for a variable bound to another variable, as in:

((X Y) (Z a) (Y Z))

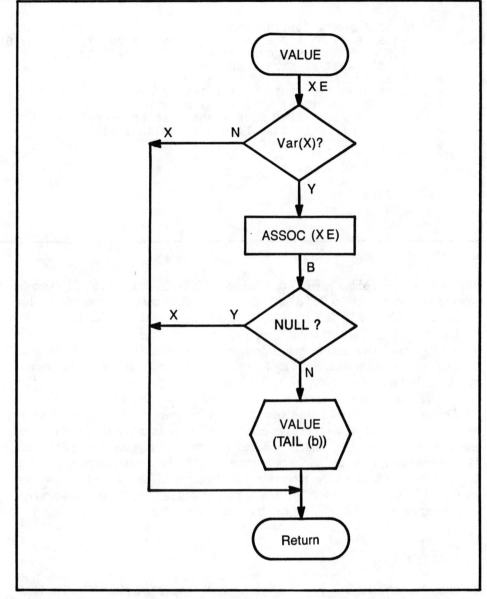

Fig. 9-7. VALUE, used by UNIFY to return the binding of logic variable X in environment E.

The binding for X will be **a**. Although VALUE is initially passed a variable, X, from UNIFY, since VALUE calls itself it must first check to see whether the new X it is passed is a variable. A binding to the initial X might not be.

Returning to UNIFY, the first step taken is to replace X and Y with their bindings. Then, if X is a variable, it is paired with Y and the pair added to the environment, E, and it is returned. If Y is a variable instead, X and Y are swapped so that the variable is the first item of the substitution pair. It is then placed on E. Although the implemen-

```
          69
   0  \ UNIFICATION ALGORITHM
   1  ( S1 S2 E -> F) \ F = TRUE IF S1 AND S2 UNIFY; E HOLDS BINDINGS
   2  : UNIFY DUP >R @ ROT OVER VALUE -ROT VALUE OVER VAR?
   3      IF NIL -ROT R> LIST TRUE
   4    ELSE DUP VAR?
   5        IF SWAP NIL -ROT R> LIST TRUE
   6        ELSE 2DUP ATOM? SWAP ATOM? OR NOT
   7            IF 2DUP FIRST SWAP FIRST SWAP R@ RECURSE
   8                IF TAIL SWAP TAIL SWAP R> RECURSE
   9                ELSE 2DROP R> DROP FALSE
  10                THEN
  11            ELSE R> DROP =
  12            THEN
  13        THEN
  14    THEN
  15  ;
```

Screen 69. Unification algorithm: defining UNIFY.

tation of lists developed in Chapter 7 does not use CONS-cells, in LISP LIST (X Y) would produce a CONS-cell (or "dotted pair") with head of X and tail of Y—and this is A-list structure (see Chapter 7). In the problems, E is implemented as a flat list.

If neither X nor Y are variables, then they are checked for being atoms. If either is, then they must be the same atom in order to match. Otherwise no new binding results, since no variable is involved. Now, for the case where X and Y are neither atoms nor variables, they must be list structure, which is used to represent predicates. In this case, UNIFY is called recursively on the first two items of the lists X and Y.

This call of UNIFY will return an updated environment, E', if any new bindings were added. Then, using this environment, UNIFY is again called on the rest of the lists of X and Y. This is an example of double recursion (used previously in EQUAL). This second call returns the final environment. UNIFY on Screen 69 returns a true flag for a match. After both recursive calls, both flags are ANDed, since matches must occur for both calls for an overall match. If neither flag is false, the match succeeds.

Having examined UNIFY, we can try it on some examples. The first is:

(a X b)
(a (c Y) Y)

X will bind to (c Y) and Y to b. Y in c(Y) is implicitly bound to b since Y is. The bindings are consistent. For a second example, consider:

(a X X X)
(a Y Y Y)

X is bound to Y when matching the second items in each list. For the third items, the binding of X, or Y, is bound to Y. Finally, for the last match, the binding of X is sought by VALUE. It is Y. Then VALUE seeks the binding of Y, which is Y. Then it seeks the binding of Y again. It is in an endless loop or *circularity*. If UNIFY would not bind variables to themselves, this circularity would be eliminated. UNIFY fails to unify properly in this case, where a variable occurs more than once in a predicate.

For the expressions:

(X)
((a X))

UNIFY also fails to produce a consistent binding. X is bound to (a X), but substituting for X produces the result (a (a X)). And again:

(a (a (a X)))

This circularity is due to the occurrence of X in a function to which it is bound. UNIFY lacks an *occurs check*, because no check is made whether X occurs in (a X).

```
         73
 0  \ LVAR-EXTENDED PRINT
 1
 2  ( @ -> FLAG) \ FLAG = TRUE IF @ IS PFA OF VARIABLE
 3  : ATOM? BODY> @ ['] NIL @ = ;
 4
 5  ( @LIST -> )
 6  : PRINTL CR ." ("
 7      BEGIN DUP FIRST DUP ATOM?
 8        IF DUP NULL
 9            IF DROP ELSE BODY> >NAME .ID THEN
10        ELSE DUP VAR?
11            IF 2- BODY> >NAME .ID ELSE RECURSE THEN
12        THEN TAIL DUP NULL
13      UNTIL 8 ( BACKSPACE) EMIT ." ) " DROP
14  ;
15


         74
 0  \ LVAR-EXTENDED PRINT
 1
 2  ( @LIST -> )
 3  : PRINT DUP @ NULL
 4      IF DROP CR ." NIL"
 5      ELSE DUP ATOM?
 6          IF BODY> >NAME .ID
 7          ELSE DUP VAR?
 8              IF 2- BODY> >NAME CR ." LVAR " .ID
 9              ELSE PRINTL
10              THEN
11          THEN
12      THEN
13  ;
14
15
```

Screens 73, 74. LVAR-extended PRINT.

UNIFY is typical of the unification algorithms used in implementations of Prolog. It runs faster at the cost of these restrictions:

1. A variable must occur in a function only once.
2. A variable must not occur in a function it could be bound to.

In practice, these restrictions are not severe for common uses of Prolog. They are allowed in order to gain an increase in execution speed.

To include UNIFY in SEARCH, one other complication must be considered. For the different levels in the deduction tree, the bindings will be different for the same variable names. We saw this in the example with **grandfather(X, Y)**. To keep track of different bindings to the same variable name, two techniques are in use: *structure copying* and *structure sharing*. The structure copying approach makes copies at each level of deduction of the bound expressions, while structure sharing includes with each variable in a binding an index based on the level. In this approach, the bindings are like:

((X i) a)

where i is the index of X indicating which use of X. Many improvements in the efficiency of Prolog implementations have been reported in the literature on logic programming. One of them, parallel computation, will be taken up in Chapter 10.

EXERCISES

1. In the CLAUSES list of Screen 71, reorder the clauses to prevent:
   a. backtracking for the goal GOAT.
   b. any backtracking.
2. Devise an algorithm that keeps track of failed goals on a list called FAILED, and searches this list first before searching for a goal in CLAUSES. If the goal is found in FAILED, the search is abandoned and backtracking is invoked.

```
        66
 0 \ UNIFICATION ALGORITHM
 1
 2
 3
 4 \ LVAR DEFINES LOGICAL VARIABLES
 5 ( -> PFA+2)
 6 : LVAR CREATE HERE 2+ , 0 , DOES>
 7      2+ ;
 8
 9
10 LVAR FOO ' FOO @ FORGET FOO
11
12
13 ( S -> F) \ F IS TRUE IF LVAR
14 : VAR? DUP @ 0= SWAP 4 - @ [ DUP ] LITERAL = AND ;
15 DROP
```

Screen 66. Unification algorithm: defining LVAR and VAR?.

3. Rewrite ADD-GOALS so that new goals are appended to the *end* of GOALS instead of the front. (You may need to define a new list to be used in ordering the goals properly.)
4. Using the modified ADD-GOALS of Exercise 3, write BSEARCH to do breadth-first search. Compare its efficiency with SEARCH for the knowledgebase on Screen 71.
5. Apple II version only: Explain the words used to create logic variables on Screen 66. The number preceding C, in (LVAR) is the processor-specific opcode for a jump. Why can't Forth variables be used as logic variables?
6. Explain the word 2ASSOC on Screen 67 and the data structure it works on. How is it used by VALUE on Screen 68?
7. Modify UNIFY on Screen 69 to allow multiple occurrences of a variable in a predicate.
8. Write the "occurs" check. Write a Forth word that will take two expressions, X and Y, and determine whether X occurs in Y.
9. Incorporate the occurs check of Exercise 8 into UNIFY of Exercise 7.
10. Modify the UNIFY algorithm of Exercise 7 to be incorporated into FIND-CLAUSE.

Chapter 10
Advanced Concepts

L IST PROCESSING, SEARCH, AND PATTERN-MATCHING ARE IMPORTANT KNOWL-
edge system ideas, but they are only the beginning of all the techniques in use.
In this chapter, other ideas that have endured through the growth of AI are briefly
introduced. Each of them is described in more detail in the AI literature references
in the appendix.

PROLOG BUILT-IN PREDICATES

In Chapter 9 a simple Prolog was implemented as a depth-first search algorithm.
It was the only procedure. Programs were a list of assertions in the form of clauses
in the knowledgebase. Writing a Prolog program was descriptive rather than prescriptive. Instead of *prescribing* what should be done to data, the data itself was *described*
instead. Because Prolog implements a form of predicate logic, and because SEARCH
is a logic theorem-prover, this one procedure is powerful enough to be used to solve
a range of AI-oriented problems. It can be used to build expert systems by writing a
list of clauses that capture knowledge in domains of expertise.

Prolog, however, does contain some additional features as built-in predicates. One
of them, called *cut* (symbol !), can be inserted in the body of a rule between goals to
force backtracking. For the rule:

C :– A, !, B.

if B fails, C fails. Cut causes SEARCH to remove alternative paths at the OR level of C and retreat to the previous AND level. The cut predicate is not descriptive since it affects the action of SEARCH. Some other prescriptive predicates in Prolog are:

assert (X)   asserts X as a clause in CLAUSES and succeeds.

retract (X)   removes X from CLAUSES and succeeds. If X does not match any clause in CLAUSES, it fails.

call (X)   calls X as a goal and succeeds if X does.

Prolog has other built-in predicates not described here.

PROCEDURAL ATTACHMENT AND PATTERN-DIRECTED INVOCATION

Some rule interpreters have rules that are condition-action pairs. Instead of asserting a conclusion in the knowledgebase if the conditions are satisfied, the "conclusion" is executed as a procedure instead. This can be more versatile than a purely descriptive scheme, since one of the procedures can be used to assert a conclusion. This technique is known as *procedural attachment*. It can be used to combine prescriptive methods, such as arithmetic, with an otherwise descriptive knowledgebase.

Instead of using the (almost) purely descriptive programming of Prolog, prescriptive rule interpreters can be built as well. By enlarging on the idea of procedural attachment, we could express rules in the form of a pattern paired with a procedure which is executed if the pattern is matched. The procedure would be like a Forth word that is executed by pattern-matching rather than being called by name. The pattern-matcher would correspond to UNIFY in Prolog and the executed procedures would be fragments of SEARCH. Procedures accompanying the patterns could be ADD, REMOVE, or RETRIEVE which add facts to a database of deduced facts, remove facts from it, or retrieve facts, as ?– does in Prolog. This kind of knowledge system has a database for storing deduced facts. In Prolog, **assert (X)** would add X to CLAUSES.

To demonstrate rules as procedures, an example of a backward-chaining rule is:

```
grandfather (X, Z)
      RETRIEVE father (X, Y)
      RETRIEVE father (Y, Z)
      END
```

where **grandfather (X, Z)** is the pattern and END ends the procedure. A forward-chaining rule is:

```
father (X, Y), father (Y, Z)
      ADD grandfather (X, Z)
      END
```

The pattern matcher binds procedure variables to pattern variables. In the backward rule, X of the first RETRIEVE command is bound to X of the pattern. When the second RETRIEVE is called, the binding remains. These bindings are local to the pattern procedure being executed.

NONMONOTONIC REASONING

Nonmonotonic logic goes beyond predicate logic in attempting to overcome some of the latter's limitations. For both forward and backward-chaining inference systems, facts accumulate in a database as they are deduced. If a goal cannot be proved, then it is assumed to be false. This is called the *closed-world assumption*. It is equivalent to assuming that the knowledgebase is complete. Other kinds of reasoning have been developed to allow for the possibility of incomplete knowledge. That is, if a proposition fails as a goal, it is not necessarily false. It may be that the knowledgebase is insufficient to prove the truth of the proposition. Furthermore, conflicting data may be given a knowledge system. It then must weigh evidence for the facts in its database and be able to modify it to achieve consistency.

In knowledge systems of the kind we have studied, a rule interpreter applies facts to rules, producing new facts. These facts are put in a database that continues to fill as new deductions are made. Since all of the new facts are true and certain, they are never retracted from the database. Forward and backward chaining are monotonic forms of reasoning, since the number of facts will increase monotonically with time.

The REMOVE command of the last section could be used in the implementation of a simple kind of nonmonotonic reasoning called *default reasoning*. In addition to normal inference rules, as executed by SEARCH, default inference rules can be added. They are applied like normal rules except that their conclusions are checked against the database for contradictions and added only if none occur.

Default rules themselves may contradict, requiring that they be ordered in priority to maintain consistency in the database. Usually, the more specific a rule is, the higher its priority. For example, a default rule for propulsion of automobiles is:

    propulsion (X, gas) :– auto (X)

But for Stanley steamers this default rule would produce a false conclusion. A more specific rule is needed for Stanleys:

    propulsion (X, steam) :– Stanley (X)

and must be tried before the more general default rule. In rule interpreters that control the choice of which matching rules to fire, this ordering can be built into the control mechanism or into the procedural rules of pattern-directed invocation systems.

A more complex kind of nonmonotonic reasoning involving retraction of database assertions is *truth maintenance*. In a truth maintenance system (TMS), deduced facts with their justifications are called *dependency records* and are kept in the database. In a conventional system, if a fact is in the database it must be true; in a TMS, it is more appropriate to call the database entries *beliefs*, since they rest on justifications which may not be valid. Hypothetical assumptions can be made and later retracted if proved false. If an assumption turns out to be incorrect, all beliefs based on that assumption must also be removed from the database. The grounds for support of beliefs consequently form a network, where the justification of a belief will be other beliefs and rules. Ultimately, this network of dependencies must rest on the well-founded support of beliefs known to be facts.

An advantage of the TMS approach over predicate logic alone is that justifications for beliefs can be used to maintain the database. When it is modified by adding or retracting beliefs, the TMS is invoked to determine whether beliefs are still supported by their justifications. If not, they are removed. Thus, only beliefs which are adequately justified remain. This overcomes the difficulty of maintaining a database which would otherwise grow to an unmanageable size and contain possible inconsistencies. The problem of keeping the database correctly updated is called the *frame problem*.

We have seen already how the SOLVED list of Prolog accumulates the clauses used by SEARCH to prove a given goal. These clauses are the justification for the goal, and they could be attached to the proven goals if they were put in a database. If a clause is later found to be false, the database deductions depending on it would be removed. For example, the goal GOAT, traced in Fig. 9-4, depends on the clauses in SOLVED in the last frame. If any of these clauses, such as the fact HAS-HORNS, were found to be false, the goal GOAT would no longer be justified, and would be removed from the database.

OBJECT-ORIENTED PROGRAMMING

In Prolog, the knowledgebase is not organized into groups of related rules except by the judicious ordering of the programmer. Knowledgebases which have no internal structuring of clauses are called *flat* systems. All the rules are on the same hierarchical level. Although this makes the knowledgebase simple, it also is inefficient: the entire list of clauses is searched every time a goal must be matched. If clauses were grouped instead according to their context, the rule interpreter could index to the appropriate group and try them. Systems which are based on organization of knowledge into distinct groups are called *object-based*.

Smalltalk is an object-based language used to create knowledge systems. It consists of *objects* which are used to represent objects of a domain of knowledge. In Smalltalk programs, objects send *messages* to each other. Although it has descriptive power, Smalltalk is a prescriptive language because it is based on message-sending. These messages cause the receiving object to carry out some procedure and return a message with the result. These procedures are called *methods*.

Smalltalk is different from the languages we have already considered in that each object contains the methods it can carry out. In this approach, instead of having procedures that can be passed data, the data objects themselves own the procedures that can be used on them. This eliminates the problem of calling a procedure which can handle, say, fixed-point numbers, when the data are floating-point numbers instead. The data of an object are compatible with its methods. If an object receives a message to add, it will use its own method to carry out the addition rather than be passed to an unknown procedure.

Since objects often use the same methods, they can be grouped according to *class*.

Objects that belong to the same class, besides having methods unique to them, can inherit methods common to the class they belong to. More generally, objects also can have properties that can be unique to a particular object or be shared by the class of objects to which they belong. These capabilities make object-based languages well-suited for building semantic networks and frame-based systems.

A simple semantic network is shown in Fig. 10-1. In this representation, the nodes (shown by "bubbles") stand for objects or their properties. The links between nodes represent relationships. Two relationships are shown; the IS-A relationship is the most commonly found in semantic networks and indicates to which class an object belongs. GOAT belongs to the class MAMMAL; BILLY belongs to the class GOAT and is an instance of that class. The property links relate properties to objects. GOAT has one property, HAS-HORNS, but by being an instance of MAMMAL, inherits its properties also: GIVES-MILK and HAS-HAIR. Though BILLY has no properties itself, it inherits properties from both GOAT and MAMMAL.

The general form of these networks is that of a *taxonomic hierarchy,* which relates objects through IS-A relationships. The possibilities for expression of relationships among objects in semantic networks is not limited to the taxonomic hierarchy. Links can represent other kinds of relationships among objects. A more complex semantic network could also contain properties with values. Instead of using the general category of property, links could represent particular properties, such as "part-of" for linking HORNS to GOAT.

Semantic networks appear to be a very different form of representation than logic. However, they have an implicit logic to them. The meanings for the relationships must be chosen so that semantic nonsense does not result. Even the seemingly simple IS-A relationship can have more than one meaning. In Fig. 10-1, it has two. The link from

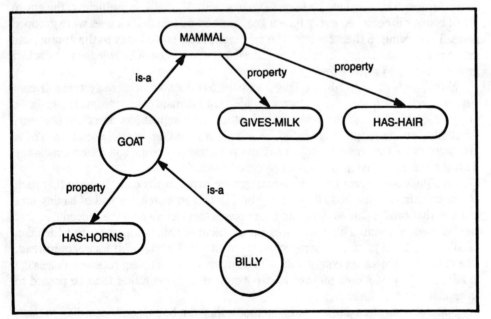

Fig. 10-1. A semantic network. BILLY is a GOAT and inherits the properties of both GOAT and MAMMAL.

BILLY to GOAT is, in logic, a predication statement expressing that BILLY is a member of the class GOAT:

    goat (billy).

This IS-A expresses membership in a class. The other IS-A of Fig. 10-1 is, in Prolog logic:

    mammal (X) : − goat (X).

which means that for all X, if X is a goat, then X is also a mammal. This second meaning for IS-A expresses that goat is a subset of mammal.

Property inheritance is logically not as simple as Prolog statements with variables. In the Prolog case, all variables are *universally quantified*, so that the truth of a proposition holds for all variable substitutions. If all members of a class inherit a property from that class, as GOAT does from MAMMAL, then for all mammals, the MAMMAL properties are true. From Fig. 10-1, the GIVES-MILK property is logically related to MAMMAL as:

    gives-milk (X) : − mammal (X).

Combined with the previous rule, it follows that:

    gives-milk (X) : − goat (X).

Up to this point, the semantic net is equivalent to its logic representation by the two Prolog statements. However, the departure from predicate logic comes when an object can cancel an inherited property by a local relationship. If BILLY was a goat without horns and had that property, it would cancel the HAS-HORNS property inherited from GOAT. In this case, the X in the Prolog statements no longer hold for all X because BILLY is an exception.

This local cancellation feature of the property inheritance mechanism of IS-A is a standard feature found in semantic nets and gives nets a nonstandard logic. The meaning of an inherited property is now what is expected for typical members of the class. Instances of the class that are exceptions obtain their excepted properties through an immediate property relationship. In this use, inherited properties that are not cancelled by local exceptions act as defaults and provide a mechanism for implementing default logic. (See the earlier section on nonmonotonic reasoning.)

The use of semantic networks as a kind of representation is not a refined aspect of knowledge engineering. Only recently have the logical consequences of giving such a fundamental relationship as IS-A different meanings become clearer, suggesting that the possible meanings be "factored out" of IS-A as distinct relationships. In spite of their informal nature, semantic nets have been put to good use, especially in the area of natural language understanding.

METAREASONING: REASONING ABOUT CONTROL

In an earlier section, pattern-directed invocation was introduced as a way to provide more flexible control of the rule interpreter. Also, in the "Breadth-First and Heuristic Search" section of Chapter 9, heuristic search was presented as a way of improving the efficiency of the rule interpreter. If the correct descent path could be chosen based on heuristic knowledge, the search for a solution path to the goal would be shorter. An interesting variation on this idea is to provide the rule interpreter with its own knowledge that can be used to guide search. This control knowledge can furthermore be represented in the same form that the domain knowledge (in CLAUSES) is represented. The interpreter can then run itself on the control knowledge to determine which clause to try next in CLAUSES. The rules providing control knowledge are called *metarules.*.

The search procedure for rule interpreters using metarules is somewhat different than for the SEARCH algorithm of Chapter 9. For a given goal, all the matching clauses are first found. This set of clauses is called the *conflict set*. The "conflict" involved is that of choosing which of these eligible rules to fire. Since they are OR-level alternatives of a deduction tree, each of them will take the search down a different descent path. Metarules are used to choose among these alternatives.

Some metarules are based on simple knowledge of problem-solving itself. For instance, a rule which states that:

The clause in the conflict set with the fewest goals should be chosen.

heuristically anticipates the least search ahead.

An extension of the idea of metarules is to break the search space of the problem into hierarchical levels of abstraction. Then a solution path is found for the highest level. Each step of this solution is solved at the next lower level. This is continued until the bottom level solutions are found. For example, to solve the problem of building a house, an overall sketch is made from which more detailed plans can be developed. After studying this problem, the domain might be decomposed into three levels:

House level:	Location, outer dimensions, and room placement are chosen.
Room level:	Fixtures and utilities are chosen and located.
Fixture level:	Wall composition, plumbing, electrical, and heating are chosen.

Each level of the abstraction hierarchy would be represented by a knowledgebase for that level. By designing the house completely at the house level, the details at lower levels can be ignored. When a satisfactory house-level plan is found, then each room can be designed. With those solutions, the most detailed design of component parts of the rooms can be determined.

The domain of house design was easy to partition into "natural" levels of abstraction because the levels were noninteracting. The details of the bathroom, for instance, would not affect the choices in the design of the kitchen. Possible interaction among the room-level subproblems may come in their shared use of electrical, plumbing, and heating delivery systems. If the routings for these systems are to be minimized, all rooms are involved. This aspect of the problem is global in its extent and is not able to be decomposed into independent subproblems solved locally within individual rooms. For house design, the constraint of minimum wiring length or ductwork can be ignored so that a (nonoptimal) solution can be found by solving independent room-level subproblems.

When subproblems are independent, problem decomposition takes the form of a tree. When subproblems interact, their relationships form a network instead. A technique known as *constraint propagation* has been developed for solving problems expressed as networks. Constraints represent interactions among subproblems by limiting the possible solutions a subproblem can have. In the house design example, the placement of rooms at the house level places constraints on the ductwork routings between rooms.

Constraints can be applied using the *least commitment principle*, in which the weakest constraints necessary to solve the global aspects of the problem are applied to the subproblems, giving them maximum freedom to develop an optimal solution at the local level.

A related technique, *dependency-directed backtracking*, is similar to truth maintenance. Instead of maintaining the database incrementally whenever dependency records are added or removed from it, dependency-directed backtracking uses dependency records to track down failed rules and facts so that backtracking can take into account these failures when choosing an alternative path. Path-independent information gained by going down the wrong path can then be used to keep from repeating the same error.

UNCERTAINTY AND EVIDENCE

Dependency-directed backtracking helps to control reasoning with incomplete data. The reasoning itself, however, is still based on exact inference rules. A departure from exact reasoning has made use of probabilities in describing the certainty of rules. A number between 0 and 1 or 0 and 100 is used to indicate the certainty of the rule, where a larger number means greater certainty. In one common scheme, these numbers are called *certainty factors*. Because probability theory is well-developed, it is plausible to expect that certainty factors are a kind of probability measure, but they are not. A well-known probability formula that would seem the most applicable is *Bayes' Rule*. But it is not used; the difficulty is that to find the probability of a conclusion, the probabilities of the given facts must be independent. But it is almost impossible to establish a knowledgebase in which the certainty of all the rules is independent.

Because standard statistics are too difficult to apply, certainty factors were introduced in a medical diagnostic expert system called MYCIN. Attached to each rule is a certainty factor (CF). To calculate the CF of a deduced fact, the CF of the fact, X, and CF of the rule, Y, are combined in the formula:

$$X + Y - XY$$

where X and Y range from zero to one. M.1 of Teknowledge uses this formula for CFs, with a range from 0 to 100, as:

$$X + Y - XY/100$$

CFs can be propagated through a chain of deductions. The CF will increase as more rules are applied, approaching certainty. This increase in a CF is the result of accumulating evidence for the final conclusion and is independent of the order in which the rules have been applied.

The formula for certainty factors is not based on any theory of evidence. It is used because some of its properties reflect how experts handle evidence. Probability theory implies that a partially certain hypothesis is also partially uncertain. But evidence partially favoring a hypothesis should not be construed also as partial evidence against it.

Rules with certainty factors act as fragments of evidence for hypotheses (their conclusions). Evidence leads to the narrowing of possible hypotheses since each fragment of evidence supports some of the possible hypotheses. For all of these fragments, the individual hypotheses they support form overlapping subsets. The *Dempster-Shafer theory of evidence* is a mathematical theory which includes both Bayesian and CF functions as special cases, but differs from them more generally in that if a hypotheses has X amount of certainty (ranging over 0 to 1), then the certainty $(1-X)$ is the amount remaining for other possible subsets of hypotheses. In D-S theory, X is called the *basic probability assignment* (BPA). It differs from Bayesian probability which would assign $(1-X)$ as the probability of the subset containing all other hypotheses. D-S theory instead assigns $(1-X)$ to all other subsets combined.

The BPA of the intersection of two subsets is the product of their individual BPAs. Several subsets may have this intersection, and the products of their BPAs are added. Since rules having a single conclusion give evidence for sets with one element—the rule conclusion—then the combination of two rules results in four set intersections, given here with their combined BPAs. Let the rule BPAs be X and Y and the conclusion-set be the set containing the conclusion of the two rules. The intersections result from:

1. The sets containing the conclusions of the two rules, with each set having one and the same element: BPA = XY.
2. The conclusion-set of rule one and the other possible subsets containing X: BPA = $X(1-Y)$.
3. The conclusion-set of rule two and the other possible subsets containing Y: BPA = $Y(1-X)$.
4. The other possible subsets with themselves $(1-X)(1-Y)$.

The fourth case is that of intersections of subsets that do not contain the conclusion-set. Only the first three intersections result in the conclusion-set. Thus, the combined BPA is their sum:

$$XY + X(1 - Y) + Y(1 - X)$$

which reduces to:

$$X + Y - XY$$

But this is just the certainty-factor formula, which results from combining the BPAs of rules that both either confirm or disconfirm a hypothesis (the conclusion-set).

A final representation of uncertainty considered here is *fuzzy logic* which also deviates from probability theory. In fuzzy logic, the extent to which something is a member of a set is assigned a number in the range of zero to one. Thus, quantitatively fuzzy ideas such as "large" can be quantified. For example, a long commute could be expressed as:

membership	set (as range of numbers)
0.1	0 to 2km
0.3	2 to 20km
0.5	20 to 50km
0.9	over 50km

Memberships in sets that result from set operations of union and intersection are defined as:

$$m(X \cup Y) = max(m(X), m(Y))$$
$$m(X \cap Y) = min(m(X), m(Y))$$

for memberships in sets X and Y of $m(X)$ and $m(Y)$, respectively.

FORTH VOCABULARIES

An advanced feature of Forth not described in Chapter 6 is *vocabularies*. They can be used to modularize knowledge somewhat like object-oriented programming does. The Forth dictionary consists of a linked list of words. A new defining-word, VOCABULARY, creates a new list:

VOCABULARY *name*

creates a vocabulary with the name following it. For example,

VOCABULARY EDITOR

establishes an editor vocabulary. When EDITOR is invoked, the list of words in this vocabulary are searched by the outer interpreter when encountering words from the input stream. In Forth-83, the root vocabulary is FORTH, which contains the standard Forth words. By invoking WORDS, the list of words of the currently selected vocabulary will be displayed.

Vocabulary words such as FORTH and EDITOR contain a pointer to the nfa of the last word in their vocabulary. It is stored at their pfa. Figure 10-2 shows the whole vocabulary scheme. Notice that the word FORTH is in the dictionary and has a pointer at its pfa to the last FORTH word. The lfa of this word points to the next-to-last (or sixth) FORTH vocabulary word, etc. until the first FORTH word, which contains a zero at its lfa to indicate the end of the list of words. Similarly, the vocabulary word EDITOR contains a pointer to the last defined word of the editor vocabulary. The two

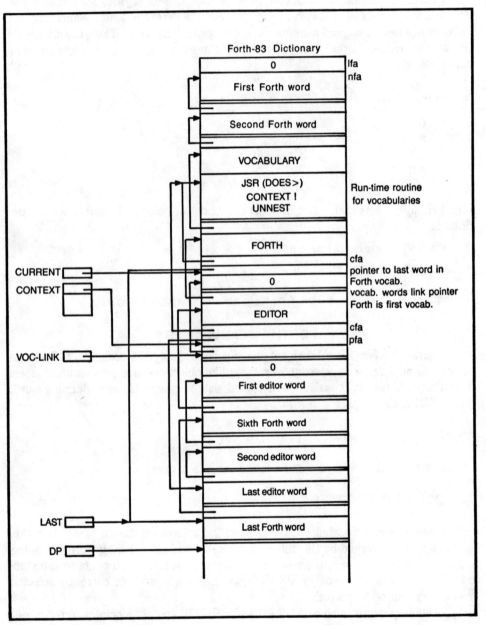

Fig. 10-2. Forth vocabulary structure.

vocabulary words are themselves linked into the FORTH vocabulary. FORTH is in its own vocabulary and both FORTH and EDITOR were defined to be in the FORTH vocabulary.

The system variable CONTEXT holds a pointer to the pfa of the vocabulary word whose vocabulary will be searched by DEFINED (used by the outer interpreter to find words from the input stream). Another system variable, CURRENT, similarly points to the vocabulary into which new word definitions will be linked.

The lists of vocabularies are intertwined in the dictionary, since when a word is defined it will be linked to whatever vocabulary is CURRENT. The compiler uses the system variable LAST to point to the last defined word.

Because vocabulary words are defined by VOCABULARY, the cfa of each contains a pointer to the run-time routine in VOCABULARY. Since (DOES>) leaves the pfa of the vocabulary word on the stack, the run-time routine stores it in CONTEXT, making the invoked vocabulary word the search vocabulary. To set CURRENT to the CONTEXT vocabulary, the word DEFINITIONS is used. It is a standard word and defined as:

```
: DEFINITIONS CONTEXT @ CURRENT ! ;
```

Thus, FORTH DEFINITIONS EDITOR will make FORTH the vocabulary into which new definitions will be linked, and EDITOR the vocabulary for search of words in the word being defined. A side effect of : is that it sets CONTEXT to CURRENT, so that unusual states like this one would have to be done between square brackets within the definition.

Vocabulary words are linked together by pointers at pfa+2 in their bodies. The last vocabulary defined has its "voc-link" pointed at by the contents of the system variable VOC-LINK. The first vocabulary has, as usual, a zero in its voc-link for termination of the list. This vocabulary is FORTH.

An experimental extension to Forth-83 enlarges CONTEXT into a stack of vocabulary pointers, and they are searched in the order that they appear on the CONTEXT stack. The pfa of CONTEXT is the top of this vocabulary stack. The word ALSO will DUP the stack so that if another vocabulary word is invoked, the previous pointer at CONTEXT will be on the stack too. When a word is sought in the dictionary, the top vocabulary on the context stack will be searched. If the word is not found in the top vocabulary, the second vocabulary on the stack is then searched.

At the bottom of every vocabulary stack is the default vocabulary called ONLY. It contains little more than the names of the other vocabularies. ONLY is a special vocabulary. When invoked, it clears the vocabulary stack and puts itself on it. Thus, to establish a search order of EDITOR, FORTH, and then, by default ONLY, invoke:

ONLY FORTH ALSO EDITOR

First, ONLY clears the stack and makes itself the only vocabulary. Since it contains the word FORTH, it will be found in ONLY when invoked. FORTH places itself on top of the stack, replacing ONLY. (Remember, ONLY is always kept also at the bottom of the stack.) Then, ALSO copies FORTH as the second item. Finally, EDITOR replaces FORTH as the top vocabulary. As it stands, EDITOR and then FORTH will be searched, followed by ONLY as a default.

With the ability to control Forth dictionary search, words with the same names can be defined in different vocabularies. Then, which of the words is found depends on which vocabulary containing one of these words is searched first. Vocabularies are able to be used to some extent like objects, each with its own set of procedures (like Smalltalk methods) and local variables. Lacking from this scheme is a property inheritance mechanism. By establishing a search order, however, words can be found in other vocabularies deeper in the CONTEXT stack if they are not found in the top vocabulary. To enable property inheritance, the search order must be established explicitly by the programmer.

To automate class membership and inheritance, other words can be defined which establish search order. If two vocabularies are defined as MAMMAL and GOAT, then IS-A is established between them, as shown in Fig. 10-1, by the word:

```
: GOAT! ONLY MAMMAL ALSO GOAT ;
```

GOAT! establishes a search order that makes MAMMAL the class to which GOAT belongs since it is searched for default properties after GOAT. Properties themselves can be defined as Forth variables or other data-types. To establish BILLY as belonging to GOAT, define:

```
: BILLY! GOAT! BILLY ;
```

Then BILLY inherits the properties of GOAT which in turn inherits properties from MAMMAL.

Forth vocabulary capability has yet to be fully utilized by the Forth community. Other mechanisms useful in the implementation of knowledge systems in Forth have yet to be developed using vocabularies.

PARALLEL COMPUTATION

The rule interpreters we have considered traverse deduction trees one node at a time. With low-cost microprocessors it becomes feasible to consider how problems may be reduced to subproblems that can be solved by multiple rule interpreters, each running on its own microprocessor. We will consider three methods for introducing parallelism into Prolog:

1. Perform unification with parallel processes.
2. Search OR-connected nodes in parallel.
3. Search AND-connected nodes in parallel.

Unification is the most time-consuming part of Prolog and stands to benefit the most from speed-up due to parallelism. Unfortunately, it is an inherently sequential process. It would be nice if the arguments of matching predicates could be matched independently in parallel. As we have seen in Chapter 9, variables must be matched against their previous bindings to maintain consistent substitutions. If processor P1 binds variable X to variable Y before processor P2 can bind X to a, P2 must have the binding of P1 so that it can bind Y to a instead of X. But this makes the overall process sequential, defeating the advantage of parallelism.

Another approach is called *mock unification*. It is unification without binding. Since binding is inherently sequential, the symbol-matching aspect of unification is done instead. Mock unification has the benefit of allowing arguments of predicates to be matched simultaneously. The result is a set of clauses that match except for variable binding. These candidate clauses can then be tried sequentially.

A kind of memory that can perform parallel search for symbol-matching is an *associative memory*. This kind of memory has been produced, but with limited capacity. An associative memory and hardware mock unifier have been developed, but the gains in speed are less than an order of magnitude.

A different approach to parallelism distributes the knowledgebase among parallel processors. A goal is given to all processors simultaneously, and each searches its list of clauses for a match (with unification). The successful matches are returned. This effectively is a breadth-first search at the OR-level in a deduction tree and is OR-parallelism.

Alternatively, each processor can be given an entire list of clauses, and each receive a goal from the goals-lists. Since the goals are conjunctively related, they must all succeed. This AND-parallelism is more complex than OR-parallelism since the goals cannot be solved independently because of shared terms in predicates. However, once partial binding occurs in a goal, other goals can use it to begin their own processing.

Beyond Prolog, *data-flow architecture* is a hopeful alternative to conventional (von Neumann) architecture. The limitation of von Neumann computers is the so-called *von Neumann bottleneck*—the data-rate-limited connection between the CPU and memory. Data-flow machines make functional programming an architectural concept. Multiple CPUs, each capable of doing a set of operations, receive *tokens*. These are units of data that contain an operation name and arguments. They are passed as information packets of a communications network, with "envelopes" that identify them. If a CPU can perform the operation of a token, it does so, passing the result in the same envelope so that the CPU that produced it can identify it and use the result. Data-flow architecture is one of several parallel computing architectures being studied and commercially produced.

EXERCISES

1. Write the following functions for the Prolog implemented in Chapter 9:

   a. ASSERT (X)
   b. CALL (X)

2. Prolog has a backward-chaining inference engine. Explain how forward chaining can be done without modifying the Prolog interpreter.
3. Design algorithms for extending the Prolog interpreter of Chapter 9 by providing the following capabilities:

   a. default reasoning

b. metareasoning
c. certainty factors
d. fuzzy logic
e. multiple knowledgebases on different levels of abstraction

4. Decompose the following domains into structural and functional hierarchical levels of abstraction:

a. automobile
b. digital computer
c. the postal system
d. arm movement
e. the mind/brain

Explain why you chose the levels you did and how they conform or not with existing theories of these domains, if any.

Chapter 11
Learning and Pattern Recognition

A MAJOR ADVANCE TOWARD MORE INTELLIGENT EXPERT SYSTEMS WILL BE EN-abling them to learn. Learning is an important branch of AI that has been studied from the early days of the 1950s. In the 1980s it is again becoming an area of increasing interest.

A form of learning has been used in plan generation such as that used by mobile robots to carry out tasks. Planning is associated with learning. A planner that operates while it carries out its plans (that is, a planner operating in *real time*) will often need to acquire data from its environment. This data can then be used to update its model of the environment.

Not all data is in symbolic form when it is acquired, however. Since expert systems involve *symbolic* rather than *numeric* computing, it has not been necessary to examine numerical methods. However, a robot or instrument-based expert system may have to compute symbolic results from numeric data. This field of study is *pattern recognition (PR)*. Originally, it was part of AI, but later broke off to become a separate discipline. It is not clear that intelligent systems will be able to be built without combining principles from both AI and PR. In this chapter, concepts from these two areas of research will be introduced.

LEARNING

In 1959, A. L. Samuel published the paper, "Some Studies in Machine Learning Using the Game of Checkers." In it he describes a checkers-playing program with the capability of learning how to play better checkers from experience. In game-playing, search trees have large branching factors, resulting in large search spaces. Heuristic rules are needed to determine which moves—that is, which states at the next level in the search space—are the best possibilities. Samuel used a polynomial to evaluate the "goodness" of a move. The terms of the polynomial represented aspects of the situation, such as piece advantage or mobility. The program learned by modifying the coefficients of the polynomial several moves later after evaluating the advantage.

Samuel used two common forms of learning in his checkers program. The first is *rote learning*. The board positions of games were stored along with their scores for future use. Since the outcomes of these positions were known, the state-space of the game would not have to be searched from the current board position if it could be found in a previous game. Having precomputed scores for board positions saves time which can then be used to try other search paths. The limitation of rote learning is that no generalization on experience occurs; memory can quickly fill up with individual board positions. It is advantageous, however, in dealing with specialized situations or for strategies that extend over several moves.

The second kind of learning used in the checkers program generalized on experience by adjusting the polynomial coefficients. The program using this kind of learning never learned to play conventional checkers and had weak openings, but played a good middle game, where search space branches the most. Rote learning was best at opening and closing moves, where the possibilities are limited and are best memorized.

Most forms of learning are based on generalization from experience. The most commonly researched is *concept learning:* from examples of a concept, a general description of it is developed. However, without further constraints, generalization from examples can occur in many ways; many general descriptions are possible. Choosing the least general description consistent with the examples is a straightforward constraint.

Induction is reasoning from the particular to the general. Concept learning—learning by examples—is a form of induction. Some domains for learning by examples are:

- Building finite-state automata from strings of symbols
- Generating mathematical functions from input/output pairs
- Developing general procedures from specific behaviors

From the last example, a mobile robot learns procedures by being led through some specific tasks. It then discovers iterative loops and merges parallel procedural paths that are equivalent in what they accomplish.

Another approach to learning has been researched by Jaime Carbonell of Carnegie-Mellon University, who has investigated learning by analogy. In his approach, the solution paths of problems (corresponding to the SOLVED lists of SEARCH in Chapter 9) are stored. When a new problem is encountered, it will begin to be solved in the usual way. As a solution path takes form from the initial state, and given the goal state, the stored paths of solved problems are compared with the problem.

If similar paths are found, then the problem-solver is *reminded* of these analogous problems. The search space of solved problems (not the search space of the problem being solved) is searched for one which best matches the space of the current problem. The search algorithm for this other space can be the same as that used to solve the given problem. This search of the solution path of solved problems is the means of finding the best match between a known solution path and the partially developed path of the current problem.

Once a known path is found, various techniques are used to apply it to the current problem. Thus, problems with known solutions are compared against the given problem to determine whether they are analogous. If so, the benefit of having the solution of a similar problem is then used to solve the given problem.

Another approach to learning begins by giving the learning program functional descriptions of objects for which the general structural descriptions are to be learned from examples of the objects. This approach is used in image understanding in the ACRONYM vision system developed at Stanford University. To bridge the conceptual gap between function and structure, the system must also be given knowledge about physical constraints and physical behaviors of objects in general.

Strategy learning is another approach to learning in AI. A conceptually simple technique which has been studied recently involves heuristic search of the state-space of a problem. At any state, one of a set of operators can be applied to produce the next state. Heuristics are used to choose which operator most likely will choose a state of the solution path, the last state of which is the goal state.

In Prolog, this amounts to deciding which of several matching rules should be fired. Prolog chooses the first rule it encounters that matches. However, as we have seen in Chapter 9, the first choice is not always the best, since another matching rule may be on the solution path instead. Heuristic rules are used in heuristic search. These rules are intended to choose, using knowledge of the state, which operator to apply. One approach to learning improves the heuristics by crediting correct applications of operators and blaming incorrect applications. This *credit assignment* is done, in this approach, only after a problem has been completely solved.

An example of an implementation in Prolog is Brazdil's ELM. It compares, step-by-step, the operator it would apply to that of the known solution path of a solved problem. When there is a difference, ELM reorders its operators so that the correct one will be encountered first. If learning is performed on several solved problems, ordering conflicts may arise. One problem may require an ordering that conflicts with another problem. In this case, conditions are attached to the operators based on differences between predicates in the two problems. If a predicate is true in one problem but false in another when a certain operator was applied, two constrained operators are created.

Since operators in Prolog are rules, the rule of conflict is used to create two new rules which are placed in front of it so that they are encountered first. Each of the two new rules has the distinguishing predicates added to them as goals, and so constrain the application of the original operator. Credit assignment in ELM is by ordering and constraining the use of a list of operators. By beginning with weak, general heuristics, learning by this approach produces ordered and constrained heuristics that, hopefully, will be more efficient in finding the solution path of new problems of the domain.

PATTERN RECOGNITION

Knowledge engineering lies well within the domain of symbolic computing, but practical expert systems often make use of numeric computing too. For example, inferences with certainty factors require computation of accumulated CF values. The inference mechanisms themselves compute purely symbolically, as do the learning mechanisms of last section. However, Samuel's checkers-playing program used a polynomial as an evaluation function. This heuristic was thus based on numerically oriented decision-making. The field of pattern recognition (not to be confused with pattern-matching of unification or pattern-directed invocation) is based on numerical techniques for classifying *patterns*. Patterns are sets of features that are extracted from input data. A pattern-recognition (PR) system has two stages of processing:

1. *Feature extraction* from input (numerical) data resulting in *patterns* in pattern-space or feature-space
2. *Pattern classification* of patterns, assigning them to one of two or more *classes* in classification-space.

The most difficult part of developing a PR system is in selecting the features to be extracted from data and processing them into a form that makes classification simple (or even possible).

Each pattern can be represented as an ordered set of numbers, where each number is the value of a feature. This value may not be the value of the extracted feature in itself, but could result from scaling, normalization, or other processing. Mathematically, a pattern is a vector and is represented by a point in hyperspace. For *n* features, pattern vectors will be *n*-dimensional and span an *n*-dimensional space, or hyperspace. For our purposes, patterns will be vectors with $n + 1$ values, where the extra value is one.

For pattern **x**, in general:

$$\mathbf{x} = [x_1\, x_2 \ldots x_n\, 1]^T$$

where the superscript T indicates that the vector is transposed—it is really a vertical or column vector. The augmented "1" will have a use that will become apparent later. Pattern-space can be described by a vector of *m* pattern vectors, or matrix, **x**.

Pattern-space can be visualized as a hyperspace with scattered points within it which are the patterns. If feature selection is successful, patterns belonging to the same class will be clustered together away from the clusters of points that belong to other classes. If there is no overlapping of clusters, hyperplanes can be used to separate hyperspace so that the regions defined by these hyperplanes represent the different classes. For example, in 2-space, with two features, a hyperplane is a line. Figure 11-1 illustrates a typical clustering of points in this space. Obviously, the line separates the two clusters of points so that patterns above the line can be assigned to class 1 and those below to class 2.

The mathematical equations for cluster-separating hyperplanes are called *decision functions*. Lines, or hyperplanes in general, are linear decision functions and can correctly classify only linearly separable patterns. If patterns of different classes intermingle in patternspace, either better feature selection and processing is needed, or a more sophisticated decision function will be required. For overlapping clusters, the decision function approach will not work with deterministic functions; statistical functions are required to determine the likelihood that a pattern is in a particular class. Most practical problems require statistical PR.

184

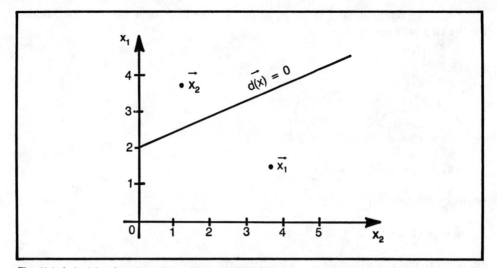

Fig. 11-1. A decision function, $d(\mathbf{x}) = 0$, separates the regions of 2-space occupied by pattern vectors $\mathbf{x}_1$ and $\mathbf{x}_2$.

To demonstrate how to derive a decision function, the 2-dimensional case will be illustrated. It is easily extrapolated to the n-dimensional case. The equation for a line in a plane is:

$$y = mx + b$$

where m is the slope and b is the y-intercept. This equation can be rewritten in the form:

$$x_1 - mx_2 - b = 0$$

where $x_1 = y$ and $x_2 = x$. Going further, this equation could be written as:

$$w_1 x_1 + w_2 x_2 + w_3 = 0$$

where $w_1 = 1$, $w_2 = -m$, and $w_3 = -b$. Extending this form of the equation for a line to n-space, an n-dimensional line would be given as:

$$w_1 x_1 + w_2 x_2 + \cdots + w_n x_n + w_{n+1} = 0$$

This equation can be written more compactly in vector form as:

$$\mathbf{w} \bullet \mathbf{x} = 0$$

where:

$$\mathbf{w} = [w_1\, w_2 \cdots w_{n+1}]^T$$

$$\mathbf{x} = [x_1\, x_2 \cdots x_n\, 1]^T$$

185

A decision function, $d(\mathbf{x})$, is the equation of a line in pattern-space. For example, for the two patterns:

$$\mathbf{x}_1 = [1\ 4]^T$$

$$\mathbf{x}_2 = [3\ 1]^T$$

$$d(\mathbf{x}_1) = [1\ -0.5\ -2][1\ 4\ 1]^T = -3$$

A decision function that separates them is:

$$d(\mathbf{x}) = x_1 - 0.5x_2 - 2 = 0$$

or, in vector notation:

$$d(\mathbf{x}) = [1\ -0.5\ -2][x_1\ x_2\ 1]^T$$

By substituting x_2 into the decision function, the result is:

$$d(\mathbf{x}_2) = [1\ -0.5\ -2][3\ 1\ 1]^T = 0.5$$

For $d(\mathbf{x}) > 0$, the point $\mathbf{x}$ is above the decision function; for $d(\mathbf{x}) < 0$, it is below the line. Thus, for the case of two classes, the sign of $d(\mathbf{x})$ determines the class to which a pattern should be assigned. For $d(\mathbf{x}) = 0$, the point lies on the line and can arbitrarily be assigned to either class, or possibly, to a third class.

For two classes, only one decision function is required. For more than two classes, more than one decision function is needed and three types of classifiers are possible:

1. Consider class 1 as one class and all other classes as class 2, collectively. Then find a decision function that separates these two classes. For n classes, n decision functions result. For a given pattern belonging to class 1, only $d_1(\mathbf{x}) > 0$; all other patterns have a negative decision value. This type of classifier is shown in Fig. 11-2.
2. Separate multiple classes in pairs. Find a decision function that will separate each pair of classes. The decision value will be positive for pattern $\mathbf{x}$ in $d_{ij}(\mathbf{x})$ if $\mathbf{x}$ belongs to class i (where $j \neq i$). This type of classifier is illustrated in Fig. 11-3.
3. Combine types 1 and 2 to eliminate indeterminate regions (where no class assignment is possible). If $\mathbf{x}$ belongs to class i, then $d_i > d_j$ for all $j \neq i$. This classifier is shown in Fig. 11-4.

The type 1 classifier has the most unclassified regions: the center triangle and the wedges radiating out of it. Type 2 leaves the center triangle indeterminate, while type 3 has no unclassifiable regions.

Hyperplane Properties

The three classification schemes use decision functions which must be derived as

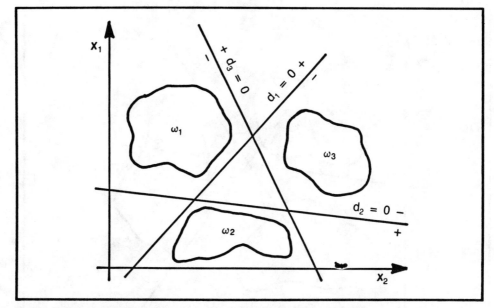

Fig. 11-2. Type 1 classifiers separate a given class from all other classes.

part of the development of classifiers. Decision functions in the general case are *n*-dimensional hyperplanes of the form $\mathbf{w} \bullet \mathbf{x} = 0$, where $\mathbf{w}$ is the *weight vector*. Its components $w_1, w_2, \ldots, w_{n+1}$ are the coefficients of the decision function equation. The hyperplane equation can be expressed as:

$$\mathbf{w}_0 \bullet \mathbf{x} + w_{n+1} = 0$$

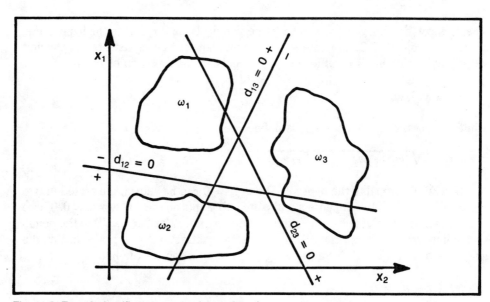

Fig. 11-3. Type 2 classifiers separate classes in pairs.

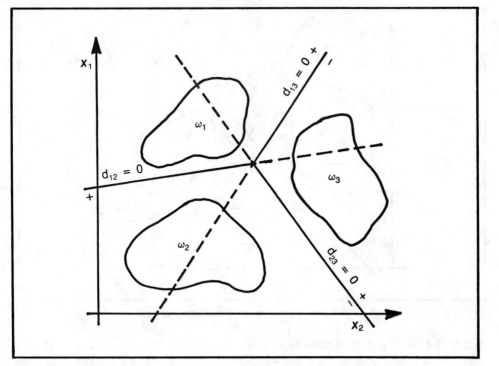

Fig. 11-4. Type 3 classifiers combine types 1 and 2, leaving no indeterminate regions.

where

$$\mathbf{w}_0 = [w_1 \ w_2 \cdots w_n]^T$$

The vector $\mathbf{w}_0$ is orthogonal or *normal* (or perpendicular in 2-space) to the hyperplane, as shown in Fig. 11-5. The orientation of a hyperplane can be represented by the unit vector, $\hat{\mathbf{w}}_0$, which has a *norm* (or length) of unity in the direction of $\mathbf{w}_0$. It is:

$$\hat{\mathbf{w}}_0 = \mathbf{w}_0 / \|\mathbf{w}_0\|$$

while the norm of a vector, $\|\mathbf{w}_0\|$, is defined as:

$$\|\mathbf{w}_0\| = \sqrt{(w_1^2 + w_2^2 + \cdots + w_n^2)}$$

That $\hat{\mathbf{w}}_0$ is normal to the hyperplane $\mathbf{w} \bullet \mathbf{x} = 0$ can be shown, illustrated in two dimensions by Fig. 11-5. Suppose $\mathbf{x}$ and $\mathbf{p}$ are two points on the line $\mathbf{w} \bullet \mathbf{x} = 0$. These vectors can be represented also as directed line segments (or "arrows") to the points on the line which also represent them. By vector subtraction, $\mathbf{x} - \mathbf{p}$ also lies on the line, as shown in Fig. 11-6. Substituting into the equation for the line:

$$\mathbf{w} \bullet (\mathbf{x} - \mathbf{p}) = 0$$

188

or

$$\mathbf{w} \bullet \mathbf{x} = \mathbf{w} \bullet \mathbf{p}$$

Expanding $\mathbf{w}$ and canceling w_{n+1} from both sides gives:

$$\mathbf{w}_0 \bullet \mathbf{x} = \mathbf{w}_0 \bullet \mathbf{p}$$

or

$$\mathbf{w}_0 \bullet (\mathbf{x} - \mathbf{p}) = 0$$

The zero dot product implies that $\mathbf{w}_0$ is normal to $(\mathbf{x} - \mathbf{p})$, which lies along the line. Thus, $\mathbf{w}_0$ is normal to the line.

Notice from Fig. 11-4 that the distance from the origin to the line is the length of $\mathbf{w}_0 \bullet \mathbf{p}$. This is true for any point $\mathbf{x}$ on the line, since

$$\mathbf{w}_0 \bullet \mathbf{x} = \mathbf{w}_0 \bullet \mathbf{p}$$

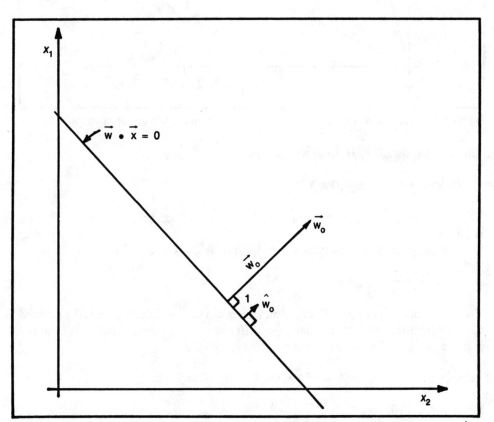

Fig. 11-5. A line, $\mathbf{w} \bullet \mathbf{x} = 0$, has orientation vector $\mathbf{w}_0$ of length $||\mathbf{w}_0||$ and unit orientation vector $\hat{\mathbf{w}}_0$.

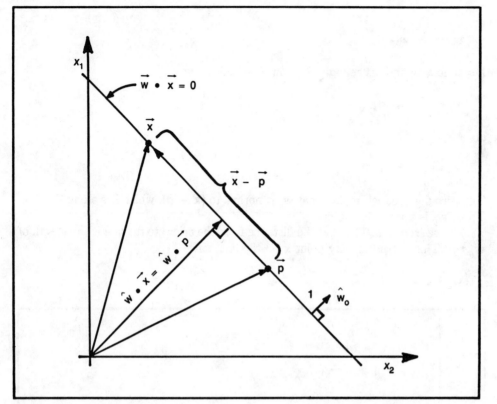

Fig. 11-6. The distance from the origin to the line is $\mathbf{w}_0 \bullet \mathbf{x}$, where $\mathbf{x}$ is any point on the line.

The directed distance, D, to $\mathbf{w} \bullet \mathbf{x} = 0$ is:

$$D = \hat{\mathbf{w}}_0 \bullet \mathbf{x} = -w_{n+1}/\|\mathbf{w}_0\|$$

The directed distance is signed, indicating in which direction from the line the distance is measured.

For any point $\mathbf{y}$ in hyperspace, the distance from $\mathbf{w} \bullet \mathbf{x} = 0$ to $\mathbf{y}$ is:

$$D_y = \hat{\mathbf{w}}_0 \bullet \mathbf{y} - \hat{\mathbf{w}}_0 \bullet \mathbf{x}$$

The first term is the directed distance from the origin to $\mathbf{y}$, and the second is the directed distance from the origin to the line. The difference is the directed distance from the point to the line. The second term can be expanded as:

$$\hat{\mathbf{w}}_0 \bullet \mathbf{x} = \mathbf{w}_0 \bullet \mathbf{x}/\|\mathbf{w}_0\| = \mathbf{w} \bullet \mathbf{x}/\|\mathbf{w}_0\| - w_{n+1}/\|\mathbf{w}_0\|$$

Since $\mathbf{w} \bullet \mathbf{x} = 0$, then:

$$\hat{\mathbf{w}}_0 \bullet \mathbf{x} = - w_{n+1}/\|\mathbf{w}_0\|$$

190

Finally, the directed distance from a point y to the hyperplane with orientation vector $\mathbf{w}_0$ *is:*

$$D_y = (\mathbf{w}_0 \bullet \mathbf{y} + w_{n+1})/\|\mathbf{w}_0\|$$

To summarize these derivations, the major properties of hyperplanes are:

☐ The unit vector $\mathbf{w}_0$ is normal to the hyperplane $\mathbf{w} \bullet \mathbf{x} = 0$ and represents its orientation.
☐ The constant term in the hyperplane equation, w_{n+1}, is proportional to the distance of the hyperplane from the origin. When $w_{n+1} = 0$, the hyperplane passes through the origin.

Therefore, by examining the components of $\mathbf{w}$, much can be learned about the hyperplane it represents.

Minimum-Distance Classifiers

Having established some hyperplane properties, we can now turn our attention to the development of decision functions. To construct a decision function as a hyperplane separating two clusters of points (belonging to two different classes), two points in hyperspace must be found which represent each entire cluster. A *prototype* point or cluster-center is usually taken as the point that is an average distance from all the points in the cluster, and can be found by averaging the N points in the cluster:

$$\mathbf{z} = (\mathbf{x}_1 + \mathbf{x}_2 + \ldots + \mathbf{x}_N)/N$$

Having a means of establishing prototypes, some measure of similarity of a given pattern to a prototype is needed. One common measure is Euclidean distance, the absolute value of directed distance. For a given point to be classified, whichever prototype is closest is considered the most similar and is assigned to the same class as the prototype. This approach is called *minimum-distance classification.*

The distance from a point $\mathbf{x}$ to prototype $\mathbf{z}$ is

$$D = \|\mathbf{x} - \mathbf{z}\|$$

For 2-space this is (expressing distance by the square):

$$D^2 = (x_1 - z_1)^2 + (x_2 - z_2)^2$$
$$= x_1^2 - 2x_1z_1 + z_1^2 + x_2^2 - 2x_2z_2 + z_2^2$$

In general, for multiple classes, the distance to the prototype of class i is:

$$D_i^2 = \|(\mathbf{x} - \mathbf{z}_i)\|^2 = (\mathbf{x} - \mathbf{z}_i) \bullet (\mathbf{x} - \mathbf{z}_i)$$
$$= \mathbf{x} \bullet \mathbf{x} - 2\mathbf{x} \bullet \mathbf{z}_i + \mathbf{z}_i \bullet \mathbf{z}_i$$

We will now use this result for D^2 to create a decision function for minimum-distance classification. Since $\mathbf{x} \bullet \mathbf{x}$ is independent of class, it can be eliminated. Then, multiplying by $-1/2$, the decision function is:

$$d_i\,(\mathbf{x}) = \mathbf{x} \bullet \mathbf{z}_i - (1/2)\mathbf{z}_i \bullet \mathbf{z}_i$$

In multiplying D^2 by negative $1/2$ to obtain d_i, the largest value for d_i represents the closest similarity or minimum distance.

Finally, we can now determine the components of $\mathbf{w}$. Since

$$d(\mathbf{x}) = \mathbf{w} \bullet \mathbf{x} = 0$$

then

$$w_i = z_i, \text{ for } i = 1, \ldots, n$$
$$w_{n+1} = -(1/2)\mathbf{z}_i \bullet \mathbf{z}_i$$

A geometric interpretation of d_i is shown in Fig. 11-7. The first term of d_i is the projection of $\mathbf{x}$ onto $\mathbf{z}$ and the second term is half the length of $\mathbf{z}$. If the projection of $\mathbf{x}$ onto $\mathbf{z}$ is more than halfway to $\mathbf{z}$, then the decision function d_i is positive.

For minimum-distance classification using a type-3 classifier, the decision functions (in two dimensions) are lines which are the perpendicular bisectors of the lines joining the prototype points. Thus, the distance from a decision function to the prototypes on

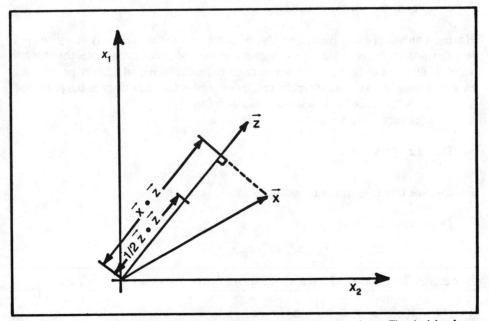

Fig. 11-7. Minimum-distance classification of $\mathbf{x}$ with respect to prototype point, $\mathbf{z}$. The decision function, $d(\mathbf{x}) = \mathbf{x} \bullet \mathbf{z} - (1/2)\mathbf{z} \bullet \mathbf{z}$ is illustrated graphically. If the projection of $\mathbf{x}$ onto $\mathbf{z}$ is greater than half the length of $\mathbf{z}$, then $d > 0$.

192

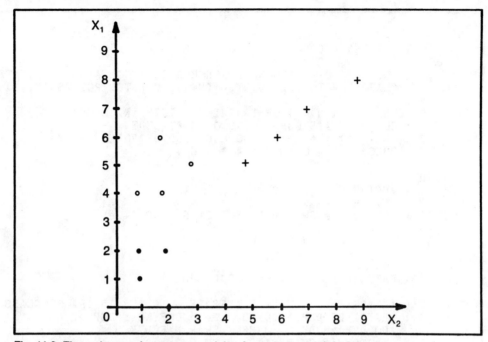

Fig. 11-8. Three classes of patterns containing four patterns each in 2-space.

each side of it is the same. By running midway between the clusters, the decision functions intuitively suggest minimum-distance classification.

As an example of constructing a minimum-distance classifier, consider the patterns shown in Fig. 11-8 with three clusters and thus three classes. A Forth program has been written to perform the needed computations, and is given on Screens 90 through 95. Data structures are created by CLASS, on Screen 90 and CLASSES, on Screen 92. CLASS creates individual classes of cluster points used in determining the decision functions. The allotted memory for a CLASS word is:

at pfa:	number of cluster points in class
pfa + 2:	x-value of prototype point
pfa + 4:	y-value of prototype point
pfa + 6:	w_{n+1}
pfa + 8:	first cluster point x-value

.
.
.

A CLASS-defined word, when executed, takes an index number off the stack and returns a pointer to the indexed cluster point. DOT takes the dot product of two points whose pointers are on the stack. A number, the dot product, is returned.

On Screen 91, PROTOTYPE takes the cfa of a class word and calculates the prototype point and w_{n+1} for it, storing these values in the appropriate data fields of the class-word itself. D(X) is the decision function. It takes a pointer to a point to be classified

193

```
        90
0 \ PATTERN-RECOGNITION ALGORITHMS
1
2 \ CLASS IS DEFINING-WORD FOR CLASSES; CONTAINS: # POINTS IN
3 \ CLASS, PROTOTYPE POINT, W(N+1), CLUSTER POINTS (X, Y)
4
5  ( N -> ) \ N = # OF TRAINING POINTS IN CLASS
6 : CLASS CREATE DUP , 6 ALLOT 4 * ALLOT
7  ( N -> @) \ @ POINTS TO LOCATION OF POINT (X, Y)
8    DOES> DUP -ROT @ MIN 4 * + 8 +
9 ;
10
11 \ VECTOR DOT PRODUCT
12  ( @v1 @V2 -> N)
13 : DOT 2DUP @ SWAP @ * -ROT 2+ @ SWAP 2+ @ * + ;
14
15


        91
0 \ PATTERN-RECOGNITION ALGORTIHMS
1
2 ( 'CLASS -> ) \ VECTOR AVERATE - 'CLASS IS CFA OF CLASS
3 : PROTOTYPE DUP >BODY DUP 2+ 6 0 FILL @ DUP >R 0
4    DO DUP >BODY 2+ OVER I SWAP EXECUTE
5        2DUP @ SWAP +! 2+ @ SWAP 2+ +!
6    LOOP >BODY 2+ DUP DUP @ R@ / OVER ! 2+ DUP @ R> / SWAP !
7    DUP 4 + SWAP DUP DOT 2/ SWAP ! \ CALC W(N+1)
8 ;
9
10 \ MINIMUM-DISTANCE DECISION FUNCTION
11  ( 'CLASS @X -> N)
12 : D(X) SWAP >BODY 2+ DUP 4 + @ -ROT DOT SWAP - ;
13
14
15


        92
0 \ PATTERN-RECOGNITION ALGORTIHMS
1
2  ( N -> )
3 : CLASSES CREATE DUP , 2* ALLOT
4  ( N -> 'CLASSN)
5    DOES> DUP @ ROT MIN 2* + 2+ @
6 ;
7
8  ( @X 'CLASSES -> N) \ CLASSIFIES POINT (X, Y) AT @X
9 : CLASSIFY DUP 0 0 ROT >BODY @ 0
10    DO I 3 PICK EXECUTE 4 PICK D(X) DUP 3 PICK >
11        IF -ROT 2DROP I ELSE DROP THEN
12    LOOP NIP NIP NIP
13 ;
14
15
```

Screens 90, 91, 92. Pattern recognition algorithms, including definitions of CLASS, DOT, PROTOTYPE, D(X), CLASSES, and CLASSIFY.

```
      93
 0 \ PATTERN-RECOGNITION ALGORITHMS
 1
 2  ( X1 Y1 Y2 ... XN YN N 'CLASS -> )
 3  : >CLASS >BODY DUP >R 8 + DUP ROT DUP R> ! 4 * + 2-
 4    DO I ! -2 +LOOP
 5  ;
 6
 7  ( 'CLASS1 'CLASS2 ... 'CLASSN -> )
 8  : >CLASSES ' >BODY DUP >R 2+ DUP ROT DUP R> ! 2* + 2-
 9    DO I ! -2 +LOOP
10  ;
11
12
13
14
15


      94
 0 \ PATTERN-RECOGNITION ALGORITHMS
 1
 2 \ EXAMPLE
 3
 4 4 CLASS CLASS1  0 2  1 1  2 1  2 2  4 ' CLASS1 >CLASS
 5
 6 4 CLASS CLASS2  5 3  4 1  4 2  6 2  4 ' CLASS2 >CLASS
 7
 8 4 CLASS CLASS3  6 6  5 5  8 9  7 7  4 ' CLASS3 >CLASS
 9
10 3 CLASSES CLASSES1
11 ' CLASS1 ' CLASS2 ' CLASS3 3 >CLASSES CLASSES1
12
13 VARIABLE X 2 ALLOT
14
15


      95
 0 \ PATTERN-RECOGNITION ALGORTIHMS
 1
 2 ' CLASS1 PROTOTYPE
 3 ' CLASS2 PROTOTYPE
 4 ' CLASS3 PROTOTYPE
 5
 6 4 X ! 4 X 2+ ! \ X = (4, 4)
 7
 8 X ' CLASSES1 CLASSIFY
 9
10
11
12
13
14
15
```

Screens 93, 94, 95. Pattern recognition algorithms, including definitions of > CLASS and > CLASSES.

and the cfa of a class and returns a number relating to the similarity of the point with the class. The larger the number, the greater the similarity. On Screen 92, CLASSES defines the classes in a pattern-space. At its pfa is the number of classes, followed by the cfas of each class, in order (so that class 0 is first). Finally, CLASSIFY takes a pointer to a data point, ^X, and the cfa of a pattern-space, and returns the number of the assigned class.

On Screen 93 are two words used to easily fill the allotted memory in a CLASS or CLASSES word with data. Their use is illustrated on Screen 94 where class 1 (CLASS1) is defined by four points in pattern-space: (0,2), (1,1), (2,1), and (2,2). On Screen 95, each class prototype point and w_{n+1} are calculated. Then the point to be classified is put in X. On Screen 95, it is set to (4,4). Finally, CLASSIFY is called on X and CLASSES1, containing the three classes. The results of this are:

class	prototype point	w_{n+1}
0	(1,1)	1
1	(4,2)	10
2	(6,7)	36

CLASSIFY assigns (4,4) to class 1.

PATTERN RECOGNITION AND LEARNING

For the minimum-distance classifier, the prototype points, z_i, are calculated from a set of points with given classifications. New points can then be classified based on the decision functions derived from the prototypes. More generally, a weight vector **w**, used to define a decision hyperplane, is derived from a prototype point.

We will now examine a few algorithms that automatically classify patterns. These clustering techniques are *unsupervised* when they determine their own classes. Algorithms that learn how to correctly classify patterns based on feedback they receive after making a classification are *supervised*. Both forms of learning are applicable in expert systems.

A simple clustering algorithm is the *threshold algorithm,* shown in Fig. 11-9. It uses a distance threshold T as a basis for determining the class membership of a pattern. If a pattern is within distance T of a prototype, it is assigned to its cluster. If the pattern is farther than T from any prototype, it becomes a new prototype. Initially, a prototype point is arbitrarily chosen. This can be the first pattern, x_1. Then the distance of the next pattern to z_1 (and any other prototypes, as they appear) is calculated. The pattern is assigned based on comparison of its distance with T.

The threshold algorithm is simple, but is weak in several ways. First, the order of the patterns greatly affects which points become prototypes. Performance is improved if approximate values of prototypes are given. Second, T affects the resolution of the clustering. Figure 11-10A shows the number of clusters formed versus T. The "natural" value of T would lie in a range over which this function is flat (between T_1 and T_2). In this range, the algorithm is relatively insensitive to T and results in optimal clustering. In Fig. 11-10B the corresponding situation is shown in pattern-space. The two clusters, A and B, will be correctly separated by any T between T_1 and T_2. In the case where A and B overlap, no value of T will separate them. In fact, they are

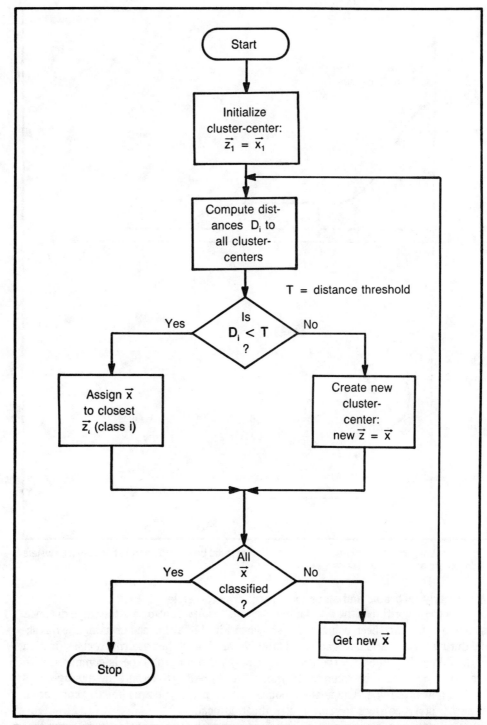

Fig. 11-9. The threshold classification algorithm. Distance threshold, T, is used to determine whether a pattern is close enough to an existing cluster or whether it should be made a new prototype.

197

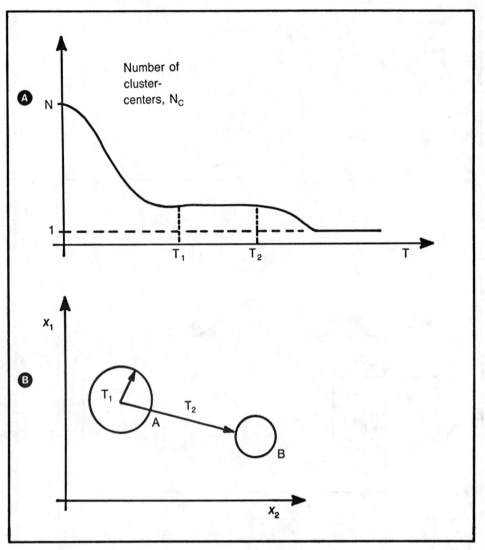

Fig. 11-10. Variation of number of clusters with T at (A) is flat between T_1 and T_2 because (B) clusters A and B are separated in this range.

not linearly separable and statistical classifiers are needed.

A better algorithm is the *maximim-distance algorithm*. It also uses the same distance measure as we have been using, and is shown in Fig. 11-11. Instead of fixing the threshold during classification, it is adjusted after classifying all the patterns; reclassification is then done. To adjust T, the pattern farthest from its prototype is compared with the average distance between prototypes. If it is greater than half the average, it is made a new prototype. The farthest points in each prototype are similarly compared. If new prototypes were formed, reclassification occurs.

The maximim algorithm is an improvement over the threshold algorithm in that it adjusts T. However, it is still sensitive to the order in which patterns are considered

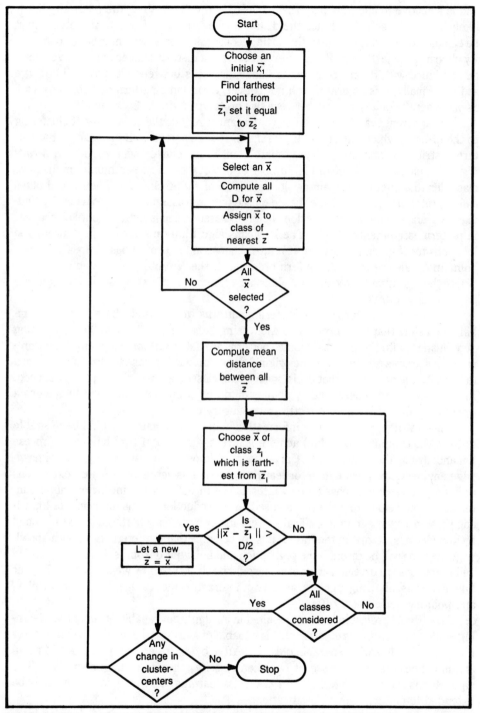

Fig. 11-11. The maximim algorithm. The extent of cluster points from their prototypes versus the distances between prototypes provides an improved basis for determining clusters over the threshold algorithm.

and is sensitive to spurious patterns (or noise in the data), since the farthest point is likely to be a noise point. Since the distance of every point from its prototype must be calculated to find the largest, this is time-consuming for a large number of patterns. By choosing the farthest point as a new prototype, a distinct cluster may inadvertently be combined with the nearest cluster, since distances between clusters will be large at first. Finally, this algorithm will not converge for some pattern distributions such as one where a point is midway between two prototypes with an equal number of points.

It is apparent that the next improvement must reduce the sensitivity of clustering to the order in which patterns are presented. It seems good to first examine the pattern distribution and make approximate choices for cluster centers. The *K-Means algorithm* chooses (or is given) K number of prototypes. It uses a minimum-distance classifier to assign the remaining points to one of the K clusters. Then it computes a new prototype for each cluster based on the patterns assigned to the cluster (by finding the average point, as we have done before). Classification is repeated until no changes in pattern assignments results. The K-Means algorithm, in effect, adjusts prototype locations for K given prototypes. If it must choose initial prototypes, it does so at random, and is also sensitive to pattern ordering. If the K prototypes are approximated before the algorithm is executed, then it is not as "automatic" as the maximim algorithm in choosing prototypes.

A more general approach to clustering patterns would also include means of combining clusters that have grown together (using "death rules"), as well as generating new clusters (with "birth rules"). Since patterns are data from some domain of measurement (or features derived from the original data), knowledge-based rules could be used to describe the domain so that decisions made in classification could be partly deduced. In this way, both numeric and symbolic computing would be combined to achieve a system capable of learning directly from sensory data.

Since learning requires new information about the domain, it would be desirable to have the computer (or robot) acquire it directly instead of first having to process it manually into the form of rules. Currently, most knowledge systems depend on knowledge engineers to provide data for learning. They thus act as the sensory extensions of knowledge systems, passing new information through rather inefficient human interfaces. The field of robotics has focused on the reduction of this interface for knowledge systems by integrating artificial sensory-motor systems with the cognition provided by knowledge systems. In the future, it is conceivable that our interactions with knowledge systems will be through the perception and behavior of robots, both self-initiated and in response to us. Such an interface would be similar to how we interact with other human beings, allowing a greater variety of interaction modes than keyboard, display, and pointing device now offer.

An early AI project in learning resulted in an algorithm capable of supervised learning, called the *perceptron algorithm*. It is capable of learning the correct weight vector for classifying linearly separable clusters. After being trained on patterns of known classification (the *training set*), it can then classify patterns of unknown class. The algorithm is shown in Fig. 11-12 for two-class learning. The technique can easily be extended to multicategory classification.

The training set consists of N patterns in each of the two classes. A decision func-

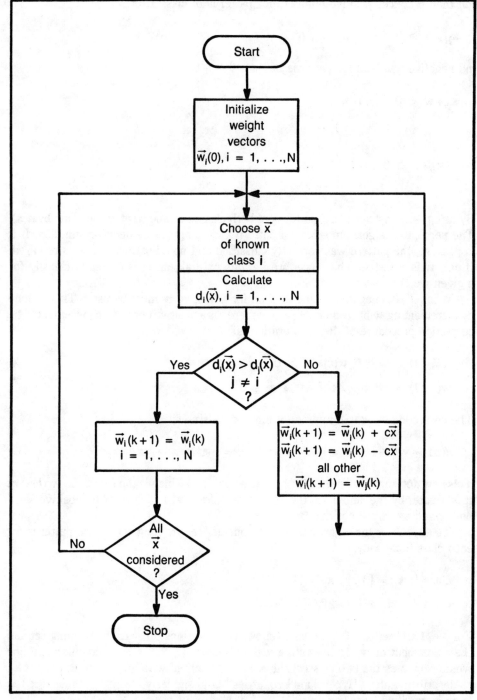

Fig. 11-12. The perceptron algorithm. Supervised learning is accomplished by training *w* to align with the sequence of patterns presented to it.

tion then produces positive numbers for patterns of class 1, or:

$$\mathbf{x}_{1i} \bullet \mathbf{w} > 0, i = 1, 2, \ldots, N$$

and negative numbers for patterns of class 2:

$$\mathbf{x}_{2i} \bullet \mathbf{w} < 0, i = 1, 2, \ldots, N$$

or

$$-\mathbf{x}_{2i} \bullet \mathbf{w} > 0, i = 1, 2, \ldots, N$$

By using $-\mathbf{x}_{2i}$ instead of $\mathbf{x}_{2i}$, patterns of both classes can be treated the same by $d(\mathbf{x})$. The perceptron algorithm selects a pattern and computes its decision function. If it is positive, the pattern was correctly classified and no adjustment of $\mathbf{w}$ is required. If not, $\mathbf{w}$ is adjusted. The procedure iterates until all patterns correctly classify for a given weight vector.

When $d(\mathbf{x})$ is negative, some method for adjusting $\mathbf{w}$ must be used. This is done by incrementing $\mathbf{w}$ by an amount $c \bullet \mathbf{x}$, where c is a positive correction increment. The correction procedure of the kth iteration is:

$$\mathbf{w}(k+1) = \mathbf{w}(k) \text{ if } \mathbf{w}(k) \bullet \mathbf{x} > 0$$

$$\mathbf{w}(k+1) = \mathbf{w}(k) + c\mathbf{x} \text{ if } \mathbf{w}(k) \bullet \mathbf{x} \leq 0$$

The correction of $\mathbf{w}$ will improve it since $d(\mathbf{x})$ is now:

$$d(\mathbf{x}) = \mathbf{w}(k+1) \bullet \mathbf{x} = (\mathbf{w}(k) + c\mathbf{x}) \bullet \mathbf{x} = \mathbf{w}(k) \bullet \mathbf{x} + c\mathbf{x} \bullet \mathbf{x}$$

This new $d(\mathbf{x})$ must be greater than the previous $d(\mathbf{x})$ which is the first term, $\mathbf{w}(k) \bullet \mathbf{x}$. It is greater by the amount of the second term, $c\mathbf{x} \bullet \mathbf{x}$, which must be positive since both c and $\mathbf{x} \bullet \mathbf{x}$ are positive ($\mathbf{x} \neq \mathbf{0}$).

To show how the algorithm works, consider the training set of two patterns for each class in 2-space:

class 1: $\mathbf{x}_1 = [3 \; 1]^T, \mathbf{x}_2 = [1 \; 2]^T$

class 2: $-\mathbf{x}_3 = [1 \; -2]^T, -\mathbf{x}_4 = [2 \; -1]^T$

For $c = 1$ and $\mathbf{w}(0) = \mathbf{0}$, Fig. 11-13 shows the iterations through the training set and the adjustment of $\mathbf{w}$. The resulting weight vector $[4 \; -1]^T$ is perpendicular to a line which separates the two classes; the $\mathbf{x}$ are augmented with an x_{n+1} component of 1 as described under "Hyperplane Properties" (and similarly for $\mathbf{w}$). Because $d(\mathbf{x}_1) = 0$, $\mathbf{w}$ is modified, resulting in $\mathbf{w}(1) = [3 \; 1 \; 1]^T$:

$$\mathbf{w}(1) = \mathbf{w}(0) + 1 \bullet \mathbf{x}_1 = [0 \; 0 \; 0]^T + [3 \; 1 \; 1]^T = [3 \; 1 \; 1]^T$$

Iteration	Class	w	x	d(x)	Modify w
0	1	(0,0,0)	(3,1,1)	0	yes
1	1	(3,1,1)	(1,2,1)	6	no
2	2	(3,1,1)	(1,-2,-1)	0	yes
3	2	(4,-1.0)	(2,-1,-1)	9	no
4	1	(4,-1,0)	(3,1,1)	11	no
5	1	(4,-1,0)	(1,2,1)	2	no
6	2	(4,-1,0)	(1,-2,-1)	6	no

Fig. 11-13. An example of the perceptron algorithm for initial **w** = **0** and four patterns in 2-space with *c* = 1.

Next,

$$d(\mathbf{x}_2) = \mathbf{w} \bullet \mathbf{x}_2 = [3\ 1\ 1][1\ 2\ 1]^T = 6$$

which is positive; **w** remains the same, or **w**(2) = **w**(1). The procedure continues, as shown in Fig. 11-11.

Why does the perceptron algorithm work? We know from previous work that *w* is perpendicular to the decision surface of the decision function $d(\mathbf{x}) = 0$. For a given pattern, **x**, **w** lies in the same general direction when $\mathbf{w} \bullet \mathbf{x} > 0$. The angle between them is less than 90° because the dot product of two vectors is:

$$\mathbf{w} \bullet \mathbf{x} = \|\mathbf{w}\| \bullet \|\mathbf{x}\| \bullet \cos\theta$$

where θ is the angle between **w** and **x**.

Since the norm of vectors is always nonnegative, the dot product has a sign determined by the orientation of the vectors. The decision function is therefore a measure of the extent to which **w** and **x** point in the same direction. For the perceptron algorithm, a **w** must be found which points in the same direction as the pattern vectors (with class 2 patterns negated). Adding $c \bullet \mathbf{x}$ to **w** causes it to point more in the direction of **x**. The result is that $\mathbf{w} \bullet \mathbf{x}$ always improves after adjustment. By adding patterns $\mathbf{x}_i$ to **w**, the effect on **w** is to cause it to tend toward the mean of $\mathbf{x}_i$. The mean is:

$$\mathbf{m} = \Sigma \mathbf{x}_i / N, i = 1, \ldots, N$$

As the algorithm proceeds, **w** approaches **m**. In effect, this is just minimum-distance classification. The difference is that **w** is learned rather than calculated from a set of patterns of known classification.

The adjustment of **w** can be optimized by choosing *c* differently than was done above. Instead of arbitrarily fixing the value of *c* at one, the algorithm would converge much faster if *c* were made just large enough to have the correct classification occur after weight adjustment. In one iteration, for a given pattern, $d(\mathbf{x})$ would be positive. For this value of *c*, $\mathbf{w}(k+1) \bullet \mathbf{x} > 0$, or:

$$\mathbf{w}(k+1)\bullet \mathbf{x} = (\mathbf{w}(k) + c\mathbf{w})\bullet \mathbf{x} > 0$$

Solving for c,

$$c > -\mathbf{w}(k)\bullet \mathbf{x}/\mathbf{x}\bullet \mathbf{x} = -\mathbf{w}(k)\bullet \mathbf{x}/\|\mathbf{x}\|^2$$

Since $\mathbf{x}\bullet \mathbf{x} > 0$ and $\mathbf{w}(k)\bullet \mathbf{x} < 0$ (having been wrongly classified), then $-\mathbf{w}(k)\bullet \mathbf{x} \leq 0$. By setting c equal to the above expression, called the *absolute-correction increment,* the *absolute-correction perceptron algorithm* is obtained.

Although any of the three multicategory classifiers can be used for more than two-class perceptron algorithms, the type 3 classifier allows a more general form of this algorithm. For a pattern of class i, if d_i is not greater than d_j $(j \neq i)$, then the weight vector of d_i is increased and that of d_j decreased. The other weight vectors are unaffected.

The field of pattern recognition has been briefly introduced here since some of its basic ideas are similar in a numerical way to AI techniques, which are based on symbols instead. A major area of PR, that of *statistical pattern recognition* has not been covered here, though for real applications it is almost always a necessity. Deterministic classification provides a foundation on which to build an understanding of statistical methods.

EXERCISES

1. Extend the Forth words for classification given on Screens 90 through 95 to handle vectors of arbitrary length, up to a maximum length, N. These more general words could then classify patterns in up to N-space.
2. Write a program for the threshold algorithm, create some test patterns, and test its performance.
3. Determine the function $N_c(T)$, which is the number of cluster centers as a function of threshold T of the threshold algorithm from Exercise 2. Plot N_c.
4. Write a program for the maximim algorithm and test it on some chosen patterns.
5. Write a program for the K-Means algorithm and test it on selected patterns. Let it select the prototypes randomly and then initialize the prototypes to approximations of the cluster centers. Report on the difference in performance between the two cases.
6. Write a perceptron learning program for two classes with patterns in 2-space. Print a table of $\mathbf{w}$, $\mathbf{x}$, and $d(\mathbf{x})$ for each iteration for:
   a. $c = 1$
   b. $c =$ the absolute-correction increment

Appendix A

Source Listing

PRESENTED IN THIS APPENDIX IS THE COMPLETE SOURCE CODE LISTING FOR THE PROLOG implementation developed in Chapters 7, 8, and 9. Enter these screens according to the instructions provided with the version of Forth-83 you are using.

If you are using an IBM PC and the Perry and Laxen F83 (available from the publisher as part of the program disk), the following are some general comments on getting the IBM PC version of the Prolog interpreter operational.

1. Copy the contents of this disk to another disk or to a hard disk.
2. Start the program by entering FORTH. This will bring up the FORTH program.
3. Open the Prolog blocks using:

   OPEN PROLOG.BLK

   Remember that all entries must be in capital letters.
4. Experiment with your FORTH:
   a) You can print a block range using SHOW as:

   37 74 SHOW

   b) You can display any block using the LIST command:

   37 LIST

   c) You can use WORDS to see a list of available words.
   d) You can use SEE to decompile any word, as in:

   SEE LIST

5. The load screen for the Prolog is Screen 38. Load the new words using:

   37 LOAD

The Prolog should load, and you will see several "... isn't unique" messages. This is normal—you are redefining some of FORTH basic words. For example, LIST is now a Prolog word. To list a block, you should now use XLIST:

   37 XLIST

6. After loading, the last screen loaded (which is Screen 72—see Screen 38) should have created some lists (try 72 XLIST). To see these lists:

205

```
L1 @ PRINT
L2 @ PRINT
L3 @ PRINT
```

7. Test the READL function by loading block 50 and examining these lists:

```
50 LOAD
I1 @ PRINT
I2 @ PRINT
I3 @ PRINT
```

8. Load a knowledgebase and try it:

```
70 LOAD
GOALS @ PRINT
CLAUSES @ PRINT
TRACE
```

9. Repeat this with Screen 71.

```
71 LOAD
GOALS @ PRINT
CLAUSES @ PRINT
TRACE
```

Read Chapters 6-10 to get more insights on how the words work.

Note: You can save the memory image at any time using the F83 SAVE-SYSTEM command with a file name as:

```
SAVE-SYSTEM ANIMAL.COM
```

The .COM file thus created now will act as a command in DOS, thus bypassing the loading procedures.

```
Scr # 36          C:PROLOG.BLK
 0
 1
 2
 3
 4
 5
 6
 7
 8
 9
10
11
12
13
14
15

Scr # 37          C:PROLOG.BLK
 0 \ LOAD SCREEN FOR PROLOG
 1 ONLY FORTH ALSO DEFINITIONS
 2 DECIMAL
 3 : XLIST LIST ;
 4 39 49 THRU
 5 51 52 THRU
 6 60 63 THRU
 7 66 68 THRU
 8 73 74 THRU
 9 69 LOAD
10 64 65 THRU
11 53 54 THRU
12 72 LOAD
13
14
15

Scr # 38          C:PROLOG.BLK
 0
 1
 2
 3
 4
 5
 6
 7
 8
 9
10
11
12
13
14
15
```

```
Scr # 39          C: PROLOG.BLK
 0 \ MODIFIED CASE STATEMENT TO WORK WITH PERRY AND LAXEN
 1
 2 : CASE 0 ; IMMEDIATE
 3
 4 : OF COMPILE OVER
 5     COMPILE =
 6     [COMPILE] IF
 7     COMPILE DROP ; IMMEDIATE
 8
 9 : ENDOF [COMPILE] ELSE ; IMMEDIATE
10
11 : ENDCASE COMPILE DROP BEGIN ?DUP WHILE
12     [COMPILE] THEN REPEAT ; IMMEDIATE
13
14
15


Scr # 40          C: PROLOG.BLK
 0 \ LISP LIST-BUILDING WORDS IN FORTH-83
 1
 2 VARIABLE NIL NIL NIL ! \ THE EMPTY LIST
 3
 4 ( #ITEMS -> ) \ #ITEMS = MAXIMUM NUMBER OF ITEMS THIS LIST
 5
 6 : NEWLIST CREATE HERE 2+ , NIL , 2* ALLOT ;
 7
 8 ( @LIST -> @FIRST) \ @FIRST IS A POINTER TO FIRST ITEM OF LIST
 9 : FIRST @ ;
10
11 ( @LIST | NIL -> FLAG) \ FLAG = TRUE IF LIST IS EMPTY
12 : NULL @ NIL = ;
13
14 ( @LIST -> @TAIL) \ @TAIL IS A POINTER TO THE TAIL OF THE LIST
15 : TAIL DUP NULL IF @ ELSE 2- THEN ;


Scr # 41          C: PROLOG.BLK
 0 \ LISP LIST-BUILDING WORDS IN FORTH-83
 1
 2 ( I -> ) \ SET LIST TO NIL (EMPTY LIST)
 3 : EMPTY DUP 2+ DUP ROT ! NIL SWAP ! ;
 4
 5 ( I @LIST -> ) \ SETS LIST-ID I TO POINT TO @LIST
 6 : SET DUP NIL = IF DROP EMPTY ELSE SWAP ! THEN ;
 7
 8 ( @ITEM I -> ) \ ADDS @ITEM TO THE HEAD OF LIST-ID I
 9 : CONS 2 OVER +! @ ! ;
10
11 \ RECURSION WORD
12 : RECURSE LAST @ NAME> , ; IMMEDIATE
13
14
15
```

```
Scr # 42          C:PROLOG.BLK
 0 \ LISP LIST-BUILDING WORDS IN FORTH-83
 1
 2  ( NIL S1 S2 . . . SN I -> ) \ BUILDS LIST AT I
 3 : LIST >R
 4    BEGIN DUP NULL NOT
 5    WHILE R@ CONS
 6    REPEAT R> 2DROP
 7 ;
 8
 9  ( @LIST I -> ) \ RECURSIVE WORD FOR 2APPEND
10 : 2APPEND OVER NULL
11    IF 2DROP
12    ELSE OVER TAIL OVER RECURSE
13       SWAP FIRST SWAP CONS
14    THEN
15 ;

Scr # 43          C:PROLOG.BLK
 0 \ LISP LIST-BUILDING WORDS IN FORTH-83
 1
 2  ( @ -> FLAG) \ FLAG = TRUE IF @ IS PFA OF VARIABLE
 3 : ATOM? BODY> @ [´] NIL @ = ;
 4
 5  ( @LIST -> )
 6 : PRINTL CR ." ("
 7    BEGIN DUP FIRST DUP ATOM?
 8       IF DUP NULL NOT
 9          IF BODY> >NAME .ID ELSE DROP THEN
10       ELSE RECURSE
11       THEN TAIL DUP NULL
12    UNTIL 8 ( BACKSPACE) EMIT ." ) " DROP
13 ;
14
15

Scr # 44          C:PROLOG.BLK
 0 \ LISP LIST-BUILDING WORDS IN FORTH-83
 1
 2  ( @LIST -> )
 3 : PRINT DUP @ NULL
 4    IF DROP CR ." NIL"
 5    ELSE DUP ATOM?
 6       IF BODY> >NAME .ID
 7       ELSE PRINTL
 8       THEN
 9    THEN
10 ;
11
12
13
14
15
```

```
Scr # 45        C:PROLOG.BLK
  0 \ LISP LIST-BUILDING WORDS IN FORTH-83
  1
  2  ( -> C) \ RETURN NEXT CHARACTER FROM INPUT STREAM
  3 : READCH
  4    BEGIN SOURCE >IN @ /STRING
  5       IF C@ 1 >IN +! TRUE
  6       ELSE DROP [´] SOURCE >BODY @ [´] (SOURCE) =
  7          IF QUERY ELSE 1 BLK +! 0 >IN ! THEN FALSE
  8       THEN
  9    UNTIL
 10 ;
 11
 12  ( -> CFA) \ IF WORD IS NOT IN DICTIONARY, CREATE IT AS VARIABLE
 13 : ?CREATE >IN @ DEFINED
 14    IF NIP ELSE DROP >IN ! HERE VARIABLE 4 + NAME> THEN
 15 ;

Scr # 46        C:PROLOG.BLK
  0 \ LISP LIST-BUILDING WORDS IN FORTH-83
  1
  2  ( I -> )
  3 : READL >R
  4    BEGIN READCH
  5       CASE BL
  6          OF FALSE ENDOF ASCII (
  7          OF NIL FALSE ENDOF ASCII )
  8          OF R@ LIST TRUE ENDOF ASCII @
  9          OF @ FALSE ENDOF
 10          -1 >IN +! ?CREATE EXECUTE FALSE ROT
 11       ENDCASE
 12    UNTIL R> DROP
 13 ;
 14
 15

Scr # 47        C:PROLOG.BLK
  0 \ LISP LIST-BUILDING WORDS IN FORTH-83
  1
  2 UNNEST
  3
  4  ( @LIST -> @LAST) \ RETURNS POINTER TO LAST ITEM OF @LIST
  5 : LAST DUP TAIL NULL NOT
  6    IF TAIL RECURSE
  7    THEN
  8 ;
  9
 10 \ ITERATIVE LAST
 11 : LAST
 12    BEGIN DUP TAIL NULL NOT
 13    WHILE TAIL
 14    REPEAT
 15 ;
```

```
Scr # 48          C:PROLOG.BLK
 0 \ LISP LIST-BUILDING WORDS IN FORTH-83
 1
 2  ( @LIST -> N) \ RETURNS NUMBER OF ITEMS OF LIST
 3 : LENGTH DUP NULL
 4    IF DROP 0
 5    ELSE TAIL RECURSE 1+
 6    THEN
 7 ;
 8
 9 UNNEST
10 \ ITERATIVE LENGTH
11 : LENGTH 0
12    BEGIN OVER NULL NOT
13    WHILE 1+ SWAP TAIL SWAP
14    REPEAT NIP
15

Scr # 49          C:PROLOG.BLK
 0 \ LISP LIST-BUILDING WORDS IN FORTH-83
 1
 2  ( ITEM @LIST -> @TAIL) \ IF ITEM IS IN LIST, @TAIL IS REST OF
 3                         \ LIST BEGINNING WITH ITEM; ELSE NIL
 4 : MEMB SWAP OVER NULL
 5    IF 2DROP NIL
 6    ELSE OVER FIRST OVER =
 7       IF DROP
 8       ELSE SWAP TAIL RECURSE
 9       THEN
10    THEN
11 ;
12
13
14
15

Scr # 50          C:PROLOG.BLK
 0 \ SOME LISTS
 1
 2 20 NEWLIST I1
 3 20 NEWLIST I2
 4 20 NEWLIST I3
 5
 6 VARIABLE S1
 7 VARIABLE S2
 8 VARIABLE S3
 9
10 I1 READL (S1 S2 S3 )
11 I2 READL (S1 I1 @ S2 S3 )
12 I3 READL (S3 )
13
14
15
```

```
Scr # 51        C:PROLOG.BLK
 0 \ LISP LIST-BUILDING WORDS IN FORTH-83
 1
 2  ( S L1 -> L2)
 3 : ASSOC DUP NULL
 4   IF NIP
 5   ELSE 2DUP FIRST FIRST =
 6      IF FIRST NIP
 7      ELSE TAIL RECURSE
 8      THEN
 9   THEN
10 ;
11
12
13
14
15


Scr # 52        C:PROLOG.BLK
 0 \ LISP LIST-BUILDING WORDS IN FORTH-83
 1
 2  ( L1 N -> L2)
 3 : NTH DUP 1 <
 4   IF 2DROP NIL
 5   ELSE
 6      BEGIN 1- DUP
 7      WHILE SWAP TAIL SWAP
 8      REPEAT DROP
 9   THEN
10 ;
11
12
13
14
15


Scr # 53        C:PROLOG.BLK
 0 \ PROLOG UNIFICATION IN FORTH-83
 1
 2  ( S1 S2 -> F)
 3 : EQUAL 2DUP =
 4   IF 2DROP TRUE
 5   ELSE 2DUP ATOM? SWAP ATOM? OR
 6      IF 2DROP FALSE
 7      ELSE 2DUP FIRST SWAP FIRST SWAP RECURSE
 8          -ROT TAIL SWAP TAIL SWAP RECURSE AND
 9      THEN
10   THEN
11 ;
12
13
14
15
```

```
Scr # 54          C: PROLOG.BLK
 0 \ RECURSION EXAMPLE: FACTORIAL
 1
 2  ( N M -> )
 3 : *FACTORIAL OVER 0=
 4    IF NIP
 5    ELSE OVER * SWAP 1- SWAP RECURSE
 6    THEN
 7 ;
 8
 9  ( M -> M!)
10 : FACTORIAL 1 *FACTORIAL ;
11
12
13
14
15

Scr # 55          C: PROLOG.BLK
 0
 1
 2
 3
 4
 5
 6
 7
 8
 9
10
11
12
13
14
15

Scr # 56          C: PROLOG.BLK
 0
 1
 2
 3
 4
 5
 6
 7
 8
 9
10
11
12
13
14
15
```

```
Scr # 57          C: PROLOG.BLK
 0 \ PROLOG RULE INTERPRETER
 1
 2 ( -> FLAG TRUE | FALSE) \ FLAG = TRUE => SUCCEED
 3 : XSEARCH
 4    GOALS @ NULL NOT
 5
 6    IF GET-GOAL CLAUSES @ FIND-CLAUSE?
 7       IF ADD-GOALS FALSE
 8       ELSE BACKTRACK
 9          IF FALSE ELSE FALSE TRUE THEN
10       THEN
11    ELSE TRUE DUP
12    THEN
13 ;
14
15

Scr # 58          C: PROLOG.BLK
 0
 1
 2
 3
 4
 5
 6
 7
 8
 9
10
11
12
13
14
15

Scr # 59          C: PROLOG.BLK
 0
 1
 2
 3
 4
 5
 6
 7
 8
 9
10
11
12
13
14
15
```

```
Scr # 60          C:PROLOG.BLK
  0 \ PROLOG RULE INTERPRETER
  1
  2 20   NEWLIST GOALS
  3 20   NEWLIST SOLVED
  4 200 NEWLIST CLAUSES
  5
  6  ( -> GOAL)
  7 : GET-GOAL GOALS @ DUP FIRST SWAP TAIL GOALS SWAP SET ;
  8
  9  ( GOAL @CLAUSES1 -> GOAL @CLAUSES2)
 10 : FIND-CLAUSE
 11   BEGIN 2DUP FIRST FIRST DUP >R = R> NULL OR NOT
 12   WHILE TAIL
 13   REPEAT
 14 ;
 15

Scr # 61          C:PROLOG.BLK
  0 \ PROLOG RULE INTERPRETER
  1
  2  ( GOAL @ CLAUSE -> FLAG) \ FIND MATCHING CLAUSE AND PUT ON SOLV
  3                           \ FLAG IS TRUE IF CLAUSE IS FOUND
  4 : FIND-CLAUSE? FIND-CLAUSE DUP NULL DUP >R
  5   IF 2DROP
  6   ELSE SOLVED CONS SOLVED CONS
  7   THEN R> NOT
  8 ;
  9 : ADD-GOALS SOLVED @ TAIL FIRST FIRST TAIL GOALS 2APPEND ;
 10
 11  ( -> FLAG) \ FLAG = FALSE IF SOLVED LIST EMPTY
 12 : BACKTRACK SOLVED @ DUP FIRST SWAP TAIL FIRST TAIL
 13   SOLVED DUP @ TAIL TAIL SET FIND-CLAUSE? DUP
 14   IF ADD-GOALS THEN
 15 ;

Scr # 62          C:PROLOG.BLK
  0 \ PROLOG RULE INTERPRETER
  1
  2  ( -> FLAG TRUE | FALSE) \ FLAG = TRUE => SUCCEED
  3 : (SEARCH)
  4   GOALS @ NULL NOT
  5   IF GET-GOAL CLAUSES @ FIND-CLAUSE?
  6      IF ADD-GOALS FALSE
  7      ELSE BACKTRACK
  8         IF FALSE ELSE FALSE TRUE THEN
  9      THEN
 10   ELSE TRUE DUP
 11   THEN
 12 ;
 13
 14
 15
```

```
Scr # 63          C:PROLOG.BLK
  0 \ PROLOG RULE INTERPRETER
  1
  2 ( -> FLAG) \ FLAG = TRUE => SUCCEED
  3 : SEARCH
  4   BEGIN (SEARCH)
  5   UNTIL
  6 ;
  7
  8 DEFER INFER ~ SEARCH IS INFER
  9
 10 : ?- SOLVED NIL SET GOALS DUP NIL SET READL INFER CR
 11   ['] INFER >BODY @ ['] SEARCH = \ IS INFER SEARCH ?
 12   IF
 13       IF ." SUCCEED" ELSE ." FAIL" THEN
 14   THEN
 15 ;

Scr # 64          C:PROLOG.BLK
  0 \ PROLOG RULE INTERPRETER
  1
  2 \ MAXIMUM GOALS/RULE = 4
  3 : RULE: CREATE HERE DUP 2+ , NIL , 10 ALLOT READL ;
  4
  5 : .KB CLAUSES @ PRINT ;
  6 : .GOALS GOALS @ PRINT ;
  7
  8 : HOW? SOLVED @ DUP NULL
  9   IF PRINT
 10   ELSE
 11      BEGIN DUP NULL NOT
 12      WHILE DUP TAIL FIRST FIRST PRINT TAIL TAIL
 13      REPEAT DROP
 14   THEN
 15 ;

Scr # 65          C:PROLOG.BLK
  0 \ PROLOG RULE INTERPRETER
  1 : NUF? KEY?
  2      IF KEY DROP KEY 13 =
  3          ELSE FALSE
  4      THEN
  5 ;
  6
  7 \ TRACE SEARCH
  8 : TRACE
  9   BEGIN CR ." GOALS:" GOALS @ PRINT
 10       CR ." SOLVED:" HOW? CR (SEARCH) DUP >R
 11       IF
 12         IF ." SUCCEED" ELSE ." FAIL" CR THEN
 13       THEN R> NUF? OR
 14   UNTIL
 15 ;
```

216

```
Scr # 66          C: PROLOG.BLK
 0 \ UNIFICATION ALGORITHM
 1
 2
 3
 4 \ LVAR DEFINES LOGICAL VARIABLES
 5 ( -> PFA+2)
 6 : LVAR CREATE HERE 2+ , 0 , DOES>
 7      2+ ;
 8
 9
10 LVAR FOO ´ FOO @ FORGET FOO
11
12
13 ( S -> F) \ F IS TRUE IF LVAR
14 : VAR? DUP @ 0= SWAP 4 - @ [ DUP ] LITERAL = AND ;
15 DROP

Scr # 67          C: PROLOG.BLK
 0 \ UNIFICATION ALGORITHM
 1
 2 ( S L1 -> L2) \ 2ASSOC-LIST IS FLAT WITH LVAR-VALUE PAIRS
 3 : 2ASSOC DUP NULL
 4    IF NIP
 5    ELSE 2DUP FIRST =
 6       IF NIP
 7       ELSE TAIL TAIL RECURSE
 8       THEN
 9    THEN
10 ;
11
12
13
14
15

Scr # 68          C: PROLOG.BLK
 0 \ UNIFICATION ALGORITHM
 1
 2 ( S1 @E -> S2)
 3 : VALUE OVER VAR?
 4    IF 2DUP 2ASSOC DUP NULL
 5       IF 2DROP
 6       ELSE ROT DROP TAIL FIRST SWAP RECURSE
 7       THEN
 8    ELSE DROP
 9    THEN
10 ;
11
12
13
14
15
```

```
Scr # 69          C.PROLOG.BLK
 0 \ UNIFICATION ALGORITHM
 1 ( S1 S2 E -> F) \ F = TRUE IF S1 AND S2 UNIFY; E HOLDS BINDINGS
 2 : UNIFY DUP >R @ ROT OVER VALUE -ROT VALUE OVER VAR?
 3    IF NIL -ROT R> LIST TRUE
 4    ELSE DUP VAR?
 5       IF SWAP NIL -ROT R> LIST TRUE
 6       ELSE 2DUP ATOM? SWAP ATOM? OR NOT
 7          IF 2DUP FIRST SWAP FIRST SWAP R@ RECURSE
 8             IF TAIL SWAP TAIL SWAP R> RECURSE
 9             ELSE 2DROP R> DROP FALSE
10             THEN
11          ELSE R> DROP =
12          THEN
13       THEN
14    THEN
15 ;

Scr # 70          C:PROLOG.BLK
 0 \ KNOWLEDGEBASE
 1
 2 : MARKER ;
 3 RULE: GIVES-MILK   (GIVES-MILK )
 4 RULE: HAS-HAIR     (HAS-HAIR )
 5 RULE: HAS-HORNS    (HAS-HORNS )
 6 RULE: MAMMAL       (MAMMAL GIVES-MILK HAS-HAIR )
 7 RULE: GOAT1        (GOAT IS-BILLY )
 8 RULE: GOAT2        (GOAT MAMMAL HAS-HORNS )
 9
10 CLAUSES NIL SET CLAUSES READL
11 (GIVES-MILK @ HAS-HAIR @ HAS-HORNS @ MAMMAL @ GOAT1 @ GOAT2 @ )
12
13 SOLVED NIL SET
14 GOALS NIL SET
15 NIL GOAT GOALS LIST

Scr # 71          C:PROLOG.BLK
 0 \ KNOWLEDGEBASE
 1 : MARKER ;
 2 RULE: GIVES-MILK   (GIVES-MILK )
 3 RULE: HAS-HAIR1    (HAS-HAIR IS-GRUFFY )
 4 RULE: HAS-HAIR2    (HAS-HAIR )
 5 RULE: HAS-HORNS    (HAS-HORNS )
 6 RULE: MAMMAL       (MAMMAL GIVES-MILK HAS-HAIR )
 7 RULE: GOAT1        (GOAT IS-BILLY )
 8 RULE: GOAT2        (GOAT IS-GRUFFY )
 9 RULE: GOAT3        (GOAT MAMMAL HAS-HORNS )
10 CLAUSES NIL SET CLAUSES READL
11 (GIVES-MILK @ HAS-HAIR1 @ HAS-HAIR2 @ HAS-HORNS @
12  MAMMAL @ GOAT1 @ GOAT2 @ GOAT3 @ )
13 SOLVED NIL SET
14 GOALS NIL SET
15 NIL GOAT GOALS LIST
```

```
Scr # 72          C: PROLOG.BLK
  0 \ LVARS AND ENV LIST
  1
  2 LVAR X1
  3 LVAR X2
  4 LVAR X3
  5
  6 VARIABLE A1
  7 VARIABLE A2
  8 VARIABLE A3
  9 20 NEWLIST ENV
 10 20 NEWLIST L1 NIL A2 X3 L1 LIST
 11 20 NEWLIST L2 NIL A1 X2 L1 @ L2 LIST
 12 20 NEWLIST L3 NIL A1 X1 X2 L3 LIST
 13
 14
 15

Scr # 73          C: PROLOG.BLK
  0 \ LVAR-EXTENDED PRINT
  1
  2 ( @ -> FLAG) \ FLAG = TRUE IF @ IS PFA OF VARIABLE
  3 : ATOM? BODY> @ [´] NIL @ = ;
  4
  5  ( @LIST -> )
  6 : PRINTL CR ." ("
  7     BEGIN DUP FIRST DUP ATOM?
  8        IF DUP NULL
  9           IF DROP ELSE BODY> >NAME .ID THEN
 10        ELSE DUP VAR?
 11           IF 2- BODY> >NAME .ID ELSE RECURSE THEN
 12        THEN TAIL DUP NULL
 13     UNTIL 8 ( BACKSPACE) EMIT ." ) " DROP
 14 ;
 15

Scr # 74          C: PROLOG.BLK
  0 \ LVAR-EXTENDED PRINT
  1
  2  ( @LIST -> )
  3 : PRINT DUP @ NULL
  4     IF DROP CR ." NIL"
  5     ELSE DUP ATOM?
  6        IF BODY> >NAME .ID
  7        ELSE DUP VAR?
  8           IF 2- BODY> >NAME CR ." LVAR " .ID
  9           ELSE PRINTL
 10           THEN
 11        THEN
 12     THEN
 13 ;
 14
 15
```

```
Scr # 90          C.PROLOG.BLK
  0 \ PATTERN-RECOGNITION ALGORITHMS
  1
  2 \ CLASS IS DEFINING-WORD FOR CLASSES; CONTAINS: # POINTS IN
  3 \ CLASS, PROTOTYPE POINT, W(N+1), CLUSTER POINTS (X, Y)
  4
  5   ( N -> ) \ N = # OF TRAINING POINTS IN CLASS
  6 : CLASS CREATE DUP , 6 ALLOT 4 * ALLOT
  7   ( N -> @) \ @ POINTS TO LOCATION OF POINT (X, Y)
  8   DOES> DUP -ROT @ MIN 4 * + 8 +
  9 ;
 10
 11 \ VECTOR DOT PRODUCT
 12   ( @v1 @V2 -> N)
 13 : DOT 2DUP @ SWAP @ * -ROT 2+ @ SWAP 2+ @ * + ;
 14
 15

Scr # 91          C:PROLOG.BLK
  0 \ PATTERN-RECOGNITION ALGORTIHMS
  1
  2 ( ´CLASS -> ) \ VECTOR AVERATE - ´CLASS IS CFA OF CLASS
  3 : PROTOTYPE DUP >BODY DUP 2+ 6 0 FILL @ DUP >R 0
  4    DO DUP >BODY 2+ OVER I SWAP EXECUTE
  5       2DUP @ SWAP +! 2+ @ SWAP 2+ +!
  6    LOOP >BODY 2+ DUP DUP @ R@ / OVER ! 2+ DUP @ R> / SWAP !
  7    DUP 4 + SWAP DUP DOT 2/ SWAP ! \ CALC W(N+1)
  8 ;
  9
 10 \ MINIMUM-DISTANCE DECISION FUNCTION
 11   ( ´CLASS @X -> N)
 12 : D(X) SWAP >BODY 2+ DUP 4 + @ -ROT DOT SWAP - ;
 13
 14
 15

Scr # 92          C PROLOG.BLK
  0 \ PATTERN-RECOGNITION ALGORTIHMS
  1
  2   ( N -> )
  3 : CLASSES CREATE DUP , 2* ALLOT
  4   ( N -> ´CLASSN)
  5   DOES> DUP @ ROT MIN 2* + 2+ @
  6 ;
  7
  8   ( @X ´CLASSES -> N) \ CLASSIFIES POINT (X, Y) AT @X
  9 : CLASSIFY DUP 0 0 ROT >BODY @ 0
 10    DO I 3 PICK EXECUTE 4 PICK D(X) DUP 3 PICK >
 11       IF -ROT 2DROP I ELSE DROP THEN
 12    LOOP NIP NIP NIP
 13 ;
 14
 15
```

```
Scr # 93          C.PROLOG.BLK
 0 \ PATTERN-RECOGNITION ALGORITHMS
 1
 2  ( X1 Y1 Y2 ... XN YN N ´CLASS -> )
 3 : >CLASS >BODY DUP >R 8 + DUP ROT DUP R> ! 4 * + 2-
 4    DO I ! -2 +LOOP
 5 ;
 6
 7  ( ´CLASS1 ´CLASS2 ... ´CLASSN -> )
 8 : >CLASSES ´ >BODY DUP >R 2+ DUP ROT DUP R> ! 2* + 2-
 9    DO I ! -2 +LOOP
10 ;
11
12
13
14
15


Scr # 94          C:PROLOG.BLK
 0 \ PATTERN-RECOGNITION ALGORITHMS
 1
 2 \ EXAMPLE
 3
 4 4 CLASS CLASS1  0 2  1 1  2 1  2 2  4 ´ CLASS1 >CLASS
 5
 6 4 CLASS CLASS2  5 3  4 1  4 2  6 2  4 ´ CLASS2 >CLASS
 7
 8 4 CLASS CLASS3  6 6  5 5  8 9  7 7  4 ´ CLASS3 >CLASS
 9
10 3 CLASSES CLASSES1
11 ´ CLASS1 ´ CLASS2 ´ CLASS3 3 >CLASSES CLASSES1
12
13 VARIABLE X 2 ALLOT
14
15


Scr # 95          C:PROLOG.BLK
 0 \ PATTERN-RECOGNITION ALGORTIHMS
 1
 2 ´ CLASS1 PROTOTYPE
 3 ´ CLASS2 PROTOTYPE
 4 ´ CLASS3 PROTOTYPE
 5
 6 4 X ! 4 X 2+ ! \ X = (4, 4)
 7
 8 X ´ CLASSES1 CLASSIFY
 9
10
11
12
13
14
15
```

Appendix B

The Diagnostis Routines

═══

T HE SCREENS IN THIS SECTION CAN BE USED TO MODIFY THE PROLOG SYSTEM OF APPENDIX A to use as a rule interpreter. With this extension, the system supports user dialog and the use of a working memory.

To implement these new routines, three new lists have been added:

1. HYPOTHESES: This list stores each tentative hypothesis for which the system will test. One of these may be the eventual conclusion (see Screen 80).
2. SOLUTIONS: This is a very short list that stores the final conclusion.
3. FACTS: This list is used as a working memory or database for true propositions.

The top-level word of this extension is DIAGNOSE. This word tries each hypothesis on the hypothesis list, putting each in turn on the GOALS list and attempting to verify it using backward chaining through the clauses using (SEARCH). Once an hypothesis is proven true, DIAGNOSE stops and prints the final conclusion.

The (SEARCH) word has been modified to permit user dialog and the use of working memory (the FACTS list). For each goal, (SEARCH) tries first to find it in the FACTS list (already proven true). This is done using FIND-FACT?, a minor modification of the earlier FIND-CLAUSE? routine. If the goal is not found in the FACTS list, (SEARCH) then tries to find a rule using FIND-CLAUSE? If it fails in this, it asks the user for the verification. If the user answers "Y," the goal is added to the FACTS list as true. If the answer is "N," then (SEARCH) backs up one level in the SOLUTIONS trace list as before and continues.

In summary:

(SEARCH)	modified
TRACE	modified
SEARCH	modified
GET-HYPO	gets hypothesis (similar to GET-GOAL)
FIND-FACT?	tries to find fact in FACT list, similar to FIND-CLAUSE?
DIAGNOSE	new high-level word
DIALOG	get user's answer

Note: It would seem simpler to add a fact to the clauses when it is proven true (rather than adding it to a FACT list), but this cannot be done with this system. CLAUSES is a list of lists,

222

and you cannot add the goal to CLAUSES without creating a list from the goal and then CONS-ing this list to the clauses.

With this system, you cannot create dynamic lists. You can always tell whether something is an atom or a list with this system using the PRINT command. If the item is returned with parentheses, it is a list; otherwise it is an atom. GET-GOAL PRINT returns an atom, the top item of the GOALS list. CLAUSES @ PRINT returns a list.

Although this is only a basic diagnostic system, you may want to modify it to include the following:

1. Add a word that is a routine so that when facts are added to the FACTS list, a backward trace is made to check to see if any rule conclusions are proved by the added fact. If so, the conclusion is added to the FACTS list. For example, if HAS-FEATHERS is proven true, IS-BIRD could be added to the facts list. This word would replace each FACTS CONS in the (SEARCH) routine.
2. Add a new list, FACTS, that stores facts that are not true. As the system is now, if a fact is true it is stored in FACTS, eliminating the need to ask that question again with the next hypothesis. If a fact is false, however, the fact is not saved and the question will reappear for the next hypothesis. The (SEARCH) routine must be modified to check this list as well.

From this example, you can modify the knowledgebase of Screens 80-83. For example, you might try to implement the knowledgebase for the automobile repair example. What would be the final hypotheses in that example? What are the symptoms to query about? What will be the intermediate goals?

Forth Notes

Load these screens as you did the Prolog knowledge system (Appendix A) according to the instructions supplied with your particular Forth-83 implementation.

If you are using the Laxen and Perry F83 (available from the publisher as part of the program disk) on an IBM PC, here's what to do:

1. First load the basic system according to the instructions in Appendix A.
2. To load these screens, type

   75 83 THRU

3. Turn on the trace by typing

   ' TRACE IS INFER

4. Then you can execute the system using the word **DIAGNOSE**. Note: To run **DIAGNOSE** again, you must first load the knowledgebase by using the expression 80 83 THRU. Be sure to turn the trace on again.

You can save the system after loading using **SAVE-SYSTEM ANIMAL.COM**. Be sure you have enough room (32K) before saving, or F83 Forth will crash. Once it is saved this way, you can restart the system directly from DOS (simply by typing **ANIMAL**) and omit the use of the load screens. Be sure to set the infer word (such as **' TRACE IS INFER**) before saving.

```
      Scr # 75          C:PROLOG.BLK
   0 \ PROLOG DIAGNOSIS ROUTINES
   1 : DIALOG CR ." Is this true (Y/N)?"
   2   KEY DUP EMIT CR ASCII Y =
   3   ;
   4
   5 : BACKUP
   6    BACKTRACK
   7      IF FALSE ELSE FALSE TRUE THEN
   8 ;
   9 20 NEWLIST HYPOTHESIS
  10 20 NEWLIST FACTS
  11 20 NEWLIST SOLUTIONS
  12 VARIABLE ENDFLG
  13
  14 : GET-HYPO HYPOTHESIS @ DUP FIRST
  15     SWAP TAIL HYPOTHESIS SWAP SET ;

      Scr # 76          C:PROLOG.BLK
   0 \ PROLOG DIAGNOSIS ROUTINES
   1 ( GOALS @FACTS1 -> GOALS @FACTS2 )
   2 : FIND-FACT
   3  BEGIN 2DUP FIRST DUP >R = R> NULL OR NOT
   4    WHILE TAIL
   5    REPEAT
   6 ;
   7
   8 ( -> FLAG) \ FLAG TRUE IF FACT IS FOUND
   9 : FIND-FACT? FIND-FACT DUP NULL DUP >R
  10      IF 2DROP
  11      ELSE SOLVED CONS SOLVED CONS
  12      THEN R> NOT
  13 ;
  14
  15

      Scr # 77          C:PROLOG.BLK
   0 \ PROLOG DIAGNOSIS ROUTINES
   1 \ PROLOG RULE INTERPRETER
   2 ( -> FLAG TRUE | FALSE) \ FLAG = TRUE => SUCCEED
   3 : (SEARCH) GOALS @ NULL NOT
   4    IF GET-GOAL DUP FACTS @ FIND-FACT?
   5      IF DROP FALSE
   6      ELSE  DUP CLAUSES @ FIND-CLAUSE?
   7        IF ADD-GOALS DROP FALSE
   8        ELSE DUP CR PRINT DIALOG
   9          IF FACTS CONS FALSE
  10          ELSE DROP BACKUP
  11          THEN
  12        THEN
  13      THEN
  14    ELSE TRUE DUP
  15    THEN ;
```

```
Scr # 78          C:PROLOG.BLK
  0 \ PROLOG DIAGNOSIS ROUTINES
  1 : SEARCH
  2    BEGIN
  3       (SEARCH) DUP >R
  4       IF IF TRUE ENDFLG ! ELSE FALSE ENDFLG ! THEN
  5       THEN R>
  6    UNTIL ;
  7 \ TRACE SEARCH
  8 : TRACE
  9    BEGIN CR ." GOALS:" GOALS @ PRINT
 10       CR ." SOLVED:" HOW? CR (SEARCH) DUP >R
 11       IF
 12          IF TRUE ENDFLG ! ELSE FALSE ENDFLG ! THEN
 13       THEN R> NUF? OR
 14    UNTIL
 15 ;

Scr # 79          C:PROLOG.BLK
  0 \ PROLOG DIAGNOSIS ROUTINES
  1
  2
  3 : DIAGNOSE SOLVED NIL SET FACTS NIL SET
  4 BEGIN SOLUTIONS NIL SET GET-HYPO DUP NULL NOT
  5    IF DUP GOALS NIL SET NIL SWAP GOALS LIST
  6    NIL SWAP SOLUTIONS LIST INFER
  7    ENDFLG @
  8    THEN
  9 UNTIL
 10 CR ." CONCLUSION:" SOLUTIONS @ PRINT CR
 11
 12 ;
 13
 14
 15

Scr # 80          C:PROLOG.BLK
  0 \ ANIMAL CLASSIFICATION EXAMPLE
  1 : MARKER ;
  2 HYPOTHESIS NIL SET HYPOTHESIS READL
  3 (IS-ALBATROSS IS-PENGUIN IS-OSTRICH IS-ZEBRA
  4  IS-GIRAFFE IS-TIGER IS-CHEETAH )
  5
  6
  7
  8
  9
 10
 11
 12
 13
 14
 15
```

```
Scr # 81          C:PROLOG.BLK
  0 \ ANIMAL CLASSIFICATION EXAMPLE
  1 RULE: IS-MAMMAL1? (IS-MAMMAL HAS-HAIR )
  2 RULE: IS-MAMMAL2? (IS-MAMMAL GIVES-MILK )
  3 RULE: IS-BIRD1? (IS-BIRD HAS-FEATHERS )
  4 RULE: IS-BIRD2? (IS-BIRD FLIES LAYS-EGGS )
  5 RULE: IS-CARNIVORE1? (IS-CARNIVORE EATS-MEAT )
  6 RULE: IS-CARNIVORE2? (IS-CARNIVORE HAS-POINTED-TEETH
  7       HAS-CLAWS HAS-FORWARD-EYES )
  8 RULE: IS-UNGULATE1? (IS-UNGULATE IS-MAMMAL HAS-HOOFS )
  9 RULE: IS-UNGULATE2? (IS-UNGULATE IS-MAMMAL CHEWS-CUD )
 10 RULE: IS-CHEETAH? (IS-CHEETAH IS-MAMMAL
 11       IS-CARNIVORE HAS-TAWNY-COLOR HAS-DARK-SPOTS )
 12 RULE: IS-TIGER? (IS-TIGER IS-MAMMAL IS-CARNIVORE
 13       HAS-TAWNY-COLOR HAS-BLACK-STRIPES )
 14 RULE: IS-GIRAFFE? (IS-GIRAFFE HAS-LONG-NECK
 15       HAS-LONG-LEGS HAS-DARK-SPOTS )

Scr # 82          C:PROLOG.BLK
  0 \ ANIMAL CLASSIFICATION EXAMPLE
  1 RULE: IS-ZEBRA? (IS-ZEBRA IS-UNGULATE HAS-BLACK-STRIPES )
  2 RULE: IS-OSTRICH? (IS-OSTRICH IS-BIRD DOES-NOT-FLY
  3       HAS-LONG-NECK HAS-LONG-LEGS )
  4 RULE: IS-PENGUIN? (IS-PENGUIN IS-BIRD DOES-NOT-FLY
  5       SWIMS IS-BLACK-AND-WHITE )
  6 RULE: IS-ALBATROSS? (IS-ALBATROSS IS-BIRD FLIES-WELL )
  7
  8
  9
 10
 11
 12
 13
 14
 15 CLAUSES NIL SET

Scr # 83          C:PROLOG.BLK
  0 \ ANIMAL CLASSIFICATION EXAMPLE
  1 CLAUSES READL
  2 (IS-MAMMAL1? @ IS-MAMMAL2? @ IS-BIRD1? @
  3  IS-BIRD2? @ IS-CARNIVORE1? @ IS-CARNIVORE2? @
  4  IS-UNGULATE1? @ IS-UNGULATE2? @ IS-CHEETAH? @
  5  IS-TIGER? @ IS-GIRAFFE? @ IS-ZEBRA? @
  6  IS-OSTRICH? @ IS-PENGUIN? @ IS-ALBATROSS? @ )
  7
  8
  9
 10
 11
 12
 13 SOLVED NIL SET
 14 GOALS NIL SET
 15 NIL IS-ALBATROSS GOALS LIST
```

Forth Vocabulary

!	(n a – >)	"store"	Store **n** at address **a**.
,	(– > cfa)	"tick"	Return the **cfa** of the next word in the input stream.
(	– >)	"paren"	Skip characters from the input stream until after the next right parenthesis. This word is used for comments.
*	(n1 n2 – > n3)	"times"	Multiply **n1** and **n2**, returning product **n3**.
*/	(n2 n2 n3 – > n4)	"times-divide"	Multiply **n1** by **n2**, retaining a double-number result, which is then divided by **n3**. This word is useful for scaling in fixed-point arithmetic.
*/MOD	(n1 n2 n3 – > r q)	"times-divide-mod"	Do */ but leave quotient **q** and remainder **r**.
+	(n1 n2 – > n3)	"plus"	Add **n1** and **n2**, returning the sum **n3**.
+!	(n a – >)	"plus-store"	Add **n** to the contents at address **a**.
+LOOP	(n – >)	"plus-loop"	Add **n** to the loop index. If the resulting index crossed the boundary between *limit-1* and *limit,* then leave loop; else, branch back to the code after DO.
,	(n – >)	"comma"	Compile n into the dictionary by alloting space and storing it.
–	(n1 n2 – > n3)	"minus"	Subtract **n2** from **n1**, leaving difference **n3**.
.	(n – >)	"dot"	Display the number **n**.
."	(– >)	"dot-quote"	Used during compila-

			tion, ." compiles a string literal beginning with the character after a blank following ." and terminated by ". The string will be displayed when the word containing ." is executed.
/	(n1 n2 – > n3)	"divide"	Divides n1 by n2, leaving quotient n3.
/MOD	(n1 n2 – > r q)	"divide-mod"	Same as / but leaves quotient q and re-mainder r.
0<	(n – > f)	"zero-less"	If n < 0, the flag f is true.
0=	(n – > f)	"zero-equals"	Returns a true flag if n = 0.
0>	(n – > f)	"zero-greater"	Returns a true flag if n > 0.
1+	(n1 – > n2)	"one-plus"	n2 = n1 + 1
1–	(n1 – > n2)	"one-minus"	n2 = n1 – 1
2+	(n1 – n2)	"two-plus"	n2 = n1 + 2
2–	(n1 – > n2)	"two-minus"	n2 = n1 – 2
2/	(n1 – > n2)	"two-divide"	n2 = n1/2 by arithmetically shifting n1 right one bit.
2*	(n1 – > n2)	"two-times"	n1 = 2*n2 by shifting n1 left one bit.
:	(– >)	"colon"	Defines a word in Forth by creating a header and compiling text from the input stream until a ; is en-countered.
;	(– >)	"semicolon"	Terminates a colon-definition, returning Forth to the inter-preted state.
<	(n1 n2 – > f)	"less-than"	Flag is true if n1 < n2.
=	(n1 n2 – > f)	"equals"	Flag is true if n1 = n2.
>	(n1 n2 – > f)	"greater-than"	Flag is true if n1 > n2.
>BODY	(cfa – > pfa)		Converts cfa to pfa, the location of a word body.
>R	(n – >)	"to-r"	Push n on the return stack.

Word	Stack	Pronunciation	Description
?DUP	(n1 – > [n1] n1)	"question-dupe"	DUP n1 if n1 is not zero.
@	(a– > n)	"fetch"	Return the contents of address a.
ABS	(n1 – > n2)	"absolute"	Return the absolute value of n1.
ALLOT	(n – >)		Allocate n bytes of memory in the dictionary.
AND	(n1 n2 – > n3)		n3 is the bitwise logical conjunction of n1 and n2.
BASE	(– > pfa)		A system variable containing the number base for numerical I/O.
BEGIN	(– >)		Used to mark the beginning of interactive control constructs ending in UNTIL or containing WHILE.
.C!	(n a – >)	"c-store"	Store the LSB of n at address a. This is a byte-wide store.
C@	(a – > n)	"c-fetch"	Fetch the LSB of the contents of address a. Set the MSB of n to zero. This is a byte-wide fetch.
CONSTANT	compile-time: (n – >) run-time: (– > n)		A defining-word that at compile-time creates a word which at run-time returns a number, n, when invoked.
COUNT	(a – > a+1 u)		Converts a string pointer into string notation on the stack by fetching the string character count, u, at address a, and leaving the address of the first string character at address a+1.
CR	(– >)		Outputs a carriage-return (ASCII 13) character.
CREATE	(– >)		A defining-word used to create headers of Forth words. It takes the following word as the name and builds link, name, and code-

DECIMAL	(->)	fields. The run-time routine of VARIABLE is placed in the cfa. Sets the numeric conversion base to 10 by storing 10 in the system variable BASE.
DEFINITIONS	(- >)	Sets the compilation vocabulary to be the same as the first vocabulary in the search order (at CONTEXT).
DO	(*limit index* ->)	A compiling-word used to begin a DO-loop. The starting index of the loop is *index*. The loop terminates when *limit* is crossed (in either direction). The loop will always execute at least once.
DOES>	compile-time: (->) run-time: (-> pfa)	Defines the run-time action of words defined by the defining-word DOES> is used in. At run-time, it leaves pfa of the word being executed on the stack.
DROP	(n ->)	Removes the top item from the stack.
DUP	(n -> n n)	Pushes a copy of the top item of the stack.
ELSE		A compiling-word used in IF-ELSE-THEN constructs. The words between ELSE and THEN are executed if the flag for IF is false.
EMIT	(n ->)	Outputs n as a character to the output stream.
EXECUTE	(cfa ->)	Executes the word whose cfa is on the stack.
FLUSH	(->)	Saves updated disk buffers and unassigns them.

FORGET	(->)	Takes the following word from the input stream and forgets all words defined before this word. If the word is protected, an error message will be given.
FORTH	(->)	The vocabulary containing the standard Forth words.
HERE	(-> a)	Returns the address of the next available address (past the end of the dictionary).
I	(-> n)	Used in DO-LOOP or DO - +LOOP constructs to return the current index of the loop.
IF	(f ->)	A compiling-word which, at run-time, will execute the words following IF if the flag, f, is true. Otherwise, the words after ELSE or THEN (if there is no ELSE) are executed.
IMMEDIATE	(->)	Makes the last defined word a compiling-word which will execute rather than be compiled when in the compiling state.
J	(-> n)	Used in double-nested DO-loops, returns the outer loop index. (See I.)
KEY	(-> n)	Returns a character from the input stream.
LITERAL	(n ->)	A compiling-word which, at run-time, causes n to be returned on the stack.
LOAD	(n ->)	A disk word used to take the input stream from block n of the disk.
LOOP		A compiling-word

231

			which, at run-time, increments the DO-loop index by one. If the new index crossed the boundary between *limit*-1 and *limit*, the loop terminates and words following LOOP are executed. Otherwise, words after DO are executed.
MAX	(n1 n2 – > n3)		Returns the larger of n1 and n2.
MIN	(n1 n2 – > n3)		Returns the smaller of n1 and n2.
NEGATE	(n – > –n)		Returns the two's complement or negation of n.
NOT	(n1 – > n2)		Returns the bitwise logical negation of n1.
OR	(n1 n2 – > n3)		Returns the bitwise disjunction of n1 and n2.
OVER	(n1 n2 – > n1 n2 n1)		Pushes a copy of the second item of the stack on the stack.
R>	(– > n)	"r-from"	Pops the top item of the return stack onto the parameter stack.
R@	(– > n)	"r-fetch"	Copies the top item of the return stack onto the parameter stack.
REPEAT	(– >)		A compiling-word used in BEGIN-WHILE-REPEAT loops to jump back to the word following BEGIN.
ROT	(n1 n2 n3 – > n2 n3 n1)		Moves the third item on the stack to the top.
SAVE-BUFFERS	(– >)		Saves all updated disk buffers on the disk.
SPACE	(– >)		Outputs a space (ASCII 32) character.
STATE	(– > pfa)		A system variable that indicates Forth as interpreting if zero and compiling if non-zero.
SWAP	(n1 n2 – > n2 n1)		Swaps the top two stack items.

232

THEN	(– >)		A compiling-word used in IF-THEN or IF-ELSE-THEN constructs. (See IF and ELSE.)
TYPE	(a u – >)		Outputs the string given on the stack.
UNTIL	(f – >)		A compiling-word used in BEGIN-UNTIL constructs. At run-time, if the flag, f, is true, the loop terminates and the words following UNTIL are executed; otherwise, the words following BEGIN are executed.
VARIABLE	(– >)		A defining-word that creates variables. At run-time, the **pfa**, where the value of the variable is stored, is returned.
VOCABULARY	(– >)		A defining-word that defines vocabularies.
WHILE	(f – >)		A compiling-word used in BEGIN-WHILE-REPEAT constructs. At run-time, if the flag, f, is true, the words following WHILE are executed. Otherwise, the words following REPEAT are executed.
XOR	(n1 n2 – > n3)	"x-or"	Returns the bitwise exclusive-or of n1 and n2.
[	(– >)	"left-bracket"	A compiling-word that sets the state to interpret.
[']	compile-time: (– >) run-time: (– > cfa)	"bracket-tick"	A compiling-word used within colon definitions to compile the **cfa** of the following word in the input stream. At run-time, the **cfa** is returned. This word acts as ' does when interpreting.

]   (->)   "right-bracket"   Sets state to compile.

For a complete glossary of Forth-83 standard words, see the *FORTH-83 STANDARD,* published by the Forth Standards Team.

Appendix D

Expert System Tools

A N EXPERT SYSTEM TOOL IS A SOFTWARE PACKAGE THAT SIMPLIFIES THE EFFORT IN-
volved in building an expert system. Tools contain the inference engine, a user interface, and knowledge acquisition routines that enable a user to build a complete system by adding a knowledgebase.

Each tool will also have restrictions that make it easy to apply in certain domains but have limited applicability in other domains. In designing an expert system with a tool, one must use caution to select a tool that is appropriate for the desired expert system.

This appendix includes a listing of the major tools available for expert system developers.

Name	Manufacturer	Price	User Interface	Knowledge Representation	Language	Computers	Applications	Notes
Advisor	Ultimate Media, Inc.	$99.50		Rule	Assembly	Apple II Commodore 64 Atari 800	Education	Backward and forward chaining to 255 rules
Advice Language/X	J. Reiter, S. Barth, & A. Patterson University of Edinburgh Scotland		Diagnosis/Prescription	Rule	Pascal	Apple II	DEC classroom assignments	A-V pairs, forward chaining
Duck	Smart Systems Technology Suite 421 North 7700 Leesburg Pike Falls Church, VA 22209 (703) 448-8562	$6,000	Diagnosis/Prescription	Rule		Apollo Symbolics DEC VAX	Government & universities	Rule-based with nonmonotonic reasoning
ESP/Advisor	Expert Systems Inter. 1150 First Ave. King of Prussia, PA 19406 (215) 337-2300	$895	Diagnosis/Prescription	Rule	Prolog	IBM PC	Small knowledge systems	A-V pairs, no limits on rules, backward chaining, depth first
EXPERT	Weiss & Kulikowski Rutgers University New Brunswick, NJ 08903		Diagnosis/Prescription	Rule	FORTRAN		serum protein, diagnosis, rheumatic disease	A-V pairs, confidence factors, trace
EXPERT-2	Mountain View Press P.O. Box 4656 Mountain View, CA 94040 (415) 961-4103	$100	Diagnosis/Prescription	Rule	Forth	IBM PC Apple II CP/M-80	Small expert systems	
Expert-Ease	Jeffrey Perrone & Assoc. 3685 17th Street San Francisco, CA 94114 (415) 431-9562	$695	Example Driven	Example		IBM PC DEC Rainbow Victor 9000	Small knowledge systems	Requires USCS-P operating system, all conclusions must have same attribute, no rule hierarchy, to 255 rules
ExperOPS V	ExperTelligence 559 San Ysidro Rd. Santa Barbara, CA 93108 (805) 969-7874	$325	Planning	Rule	ExpertLISP	Macintosh	Small knowledge systems	O-A-V triplets, to 500 rules, forward chaining

Product	Company	Price	Application	Representation	Language	Hardware	Domain	Features
EXSYS	Exsys, Inc. P.O. Box 75158, Sta. 14 Albuquerque, NM 87194 (505) 836-6676	$295	Multiple Choice	Rule		IBM PC	Small expert systems	Permits 700 rules per 64K of memory over 192K, certainty factors
INSIGHT-1	Level 5 Research 4980 S-A1A Melbourne Beach, FL 32951 (305) 729-9046	$95	Diagnosis/ Prescription	Rule	Pascal	IBM PC DEC Rainbow Victor 9000	Education	O-A-V triplets to 625 rules, backward & limited forward chaining, certainty factors, accepts unknowns, rule entry with word processor
INSIGHT-2	Level 5 Research 4980 S: A-1-A Highway Melbourne Beach, FL 32951 (305) 729-9046	$485	Diagnosis/ Prescription	Rule	Pascal	IBM PC DEC Rainbow Victor 9000	Education	O-A-V triplets to 2000 rules, backward & limited forward chaining, certainty factors, accepts unknowns, rule entry with word processor
KDS Development System	KDS	$795	Example	Rule	Assembly	IBM PC	Small knowledge systems	Backward & forward chaining
Knowledge Craft	Carnegie Group, Inc. 4616 Henry St. Pittsburgh, PA 15213 (412) 578-3450	$50,000	Planning	Frame	Common LISP	DEC VAX	Manufacturing & industrial	Frames & rules, object-oriented
Knowledge Engineering Environment (KEE)	IntelliCorp 707 Laurel Street Menlo Park, CA 94025 (415) 323-8300	$60,000	(hybrid)	Frame	LISP	Symbolics 3600 TI Explorer LMI LAMBDA Xerox 1100	Genetic engineering, others	Multiple objects, inheritance, can include rules, graphic support, backward & forward chaining
Knowledge Engineering System (KES)	Software A & E 1500 Wilson Blvd, #800 Arlington, VA 22209 (703) 276-7910	$4000 for IBM PC version	Diagnosis/ Prescription	Rules	IQLISP and other LISPS	IBM PC DEC VAX CDC CYBER (others)		A-V pairs, multiple objects, inheritance, probabilities, explanation, trace
LOOPS	Xerox Palo Alto Research 3333 Coyote Hill Rd. Palo Alto, CA 94304 (415) 494-4000	$300	(hybrid)	Frame	INTERLISP	Xerox 1100	Demonstration system	Graphic support

Name	Manufacturer	Price	User Interface	Knowledge Representation	Language	Computers	Applications	Notes
M.1	Teknowledge, Inc. 525 University Ave. Palo Alto, CA 94301 (415) 327-6600	$5,000	Diagnosis/Prescription	Rules	PROLOG	IBM PC	Large expert systems	A-V pairs to 1000 rules. Certainty factors, backward & limited forward chaining, depth first, trace & explanation, accepts unknowns, word processor rule entry, variable rules
Micro Expert	McGraw Hill Book Co. 1221 Ave. of the Americas New York, NY 10020 (212) 512-2000	$49.95	Diagnosis/Prescription	Rule	Pascal	IBM PC Apple II	Small expert systems, educational	Backward chaining, includes source code
Nexpert	Neuron Data, Inc. Palo Alto, CA 94304	$5,000		Rule		Macintosh		Backward and forward searching
OPS5	Dept. of Computer Sci. Carnegie-Mellon Univ. Pittsburgh, PA 15213		Planning	Rules	LISP	VAX 11/780	Computer configuration	O-A-V triplets, forward chaining, trace
OPS5e	Verac, Inc. 10975 Torreyana, #300 P.O. Box 26669, Dept 418 San Diego, CA 92126-0669	$3000	Planning	Rules	ZetaLISP	Symbolics 3600		O-A-V triplets, forward chaining, trace, graphics
OPS5+	Artelligence, Inc. 14902 Preston Rd. Suite 212-252 Dallas, TX 75240 (214) 437-0361	$3,000	Planning	Rule		IBM PC + color (others)	Large expert systems	O-A-V triplets, to 1500 rules, interfaces to Lattice C, forward chaining
Personal Consultant	Texas Instruments P.O. Box 809063 Dallas, TX 95380 (800) 527-3500	$950	Diagnosis/Prescription	Rules	IQLISP	TI Professional & MS-DOS	Small knowledge systems	O-A-V triplets to 400 rules, backward chaining, depth first, certainty factors, multiple objects, accepts unknowns

Product	Company	Price	Type	Frames	Language	Hardware	Application	Features
Personal Consultant Plus	Texas Instruments P.O. Box 809063 Dallas, TX 95380 (800) 527-3500	$3000	Diagnosis/ Prescription	Frames	IQLISP	TI Professional	Small knowledge systems	Frames plus features (including rules) of Personal Consultant. Also meta-rules and graphics.
Rule-Master	Radian Corporation 8501 Mo-Pac Blvd. P.O. Box 9948 Austin, TX 78766 (512) 454-4797	$5K for IBM XT to $25K for VAX	Example	Rule	C	IBM XT, IBM AT, 68000 UNIX machines & VAX	Diagnostic & control, defense, insurance	Backward & forward chaining, no DBMS interface, run-time available as option
SeRIES-PC	SRI International 333 Ravenswood Ave. Menlo Park, CA 94025 (415) 859-2464	$5000	Diagnosis/ Prescription	Rules	IQLISP	IBM PC		A-V pairs, backward chaining, depth first, explanation, trace
S.1	Teknowledge, Inc. 525 University Ave. Palo Alto, CA 94301 (415) 327-6600	$50,000-$80,000	Diagnosis/ Prescription	Rules	LISP	DEC VAX Xerox 1100 (others)		O-A-V triplets, multiple objects, backward chaining, depth first, inheritance, certainty factors, accepts unknowns
TIMM	General Research Corp. P.O. Box 6770 Santa Barbara, CA 93160 (805) 964-7724	$39,500	Example driven	Rule	Fortran	IBM, DEC VAX, Prime, IBM PC	Simulation of helicopter pilot's battle decisions	Certainty and reliability factors, A-V pairs, up to 500 rules compiled from examples
TIMM-PC	General Research Corp. P.O. Box 6770 Santa Barbara, CA 93160 (805) 964-7724	$9,500	Example driven	Rule	Fortran	IBM PC (others)	Educational	Certainty and reliability factors, A-V pairs, up to 100 rules compiled from examples

Appendix E

Expert Systems

S EVERAL EXPERT SYSTEMS HAVE ALREADY BEEN SUCCESSFUL IN SOLVING PROBLEMS THAT were formerly solved only by experts. This appendix is an overview of the most significant of these. Each of these systems includes both a shell and knowledgebase. It should also be recognized that this is only a portion of the working systems in operation and development today.

Selected Expert Systems

Name	Developer	Date	Development Tools*	Domain & Purpose	Knowledge Representation	Language	Computer	Notes
DELTA-CATS	General Electric	1981-		Locomotive repair	Rules	Forth		
DENDRAL	Stanford University	1965-1970		Organic chemistry-mass spectrometry		LISP		15 person-year development
DRILLING ADVISOR	Teknowledge		KS300	Diagnosis drilling problems				Currently has about 250 rules
GENESIS	Intellicorp	1981-	MOLGEN	Genetic engineering applications	Frame		IBM 370 DEC VAX	Also can be used remotely by accessing a DEC-20
HEARSAY II	Carnegie-Mellon University	1970-1975	AGE & HEARSAY III	Speech understanding	Blackboard	SAIL		

cont.

Selected Expert Systems

Name	Developer	Date	Development Tools*	Domain & Purpose	Knowledge Representation	Language	Computer	Notes
INTERNIST/ CADUCEUS	University of Pittsburgh	1970-		Medical diagnosis	Rule	LISP		Now has 500 diseases in database
MACSYMA	MIT	1969-1980		Symbolic mathematics		LISP	KL-10	Now contains about 100 person-years of design; ARPA access available
PRO-SPECTOR	SRI International	1970-1978	KAS	Exploratory geology	Rule-like semantic net	LISP		
PUFF	Stanford University	1979-1981	EMYCIN	Pulmonary analysis	Rule	BASIC LISP	PDP-11	
MYCIN	Stanford University	1970-1975	EMYCIN	Bacteremia & meningitis; infections diagnosis	Rule	LISP	PDP-11	
XCON, XSEL	Carnegie-Mellon University & DEC	1978-	OPS5	VAX computer configuring	Rule		DEC VAX	
------	Rutgers University & Helena Laboratories	1980-	EXPERT	Electrophoresis analysis	Rule	Fortran	(6800)	This is an 82-rule system that is cost-effective

Glossary

algorithm—An effective procedure that will terminate.

alpha-beta algorithm—A game-playing strategy that attempts to reduce a search by cutting off branches in the search space that are not to be evaluated.

artificial intelligence (AI)—A subfield of computer science concerned with the concepts and methods of knowledge representation and problem solving.

association-list—A LISP data structure in which attribute-value pairs are stored in CONS-cells. Also called an *A-list*. (See *property-lists*.)

atom—A fundamental symbol in LISP. Atoms are used to represent objects. Atoms and lists are symbolic expressions.

attribute—A property of an object. For example, if the color of the elephant is gray, we could say that *the elephant* is the object, *color* the attribute, and *gray* is the value.

attribute-value pair (A-O-V)—A method of representing factual knowledge in which attributes can be assigned values. Example: For the fact, "The animal has hair," the attribute would be ANIMAL, the value would be HAS HAIR. (See *object-attribute-value triplet*.)

backtracking—The process of moving backward through a series of inferences to discover or trace a reasoning pattern or to explore an alternative path.

backward chaining—An inference engine control strategy in which inferences are made by starting with a conclusion and working backward in an attempt to find the facts to support the conclusion.

blackboard systems—A type of knowledge system in which several representations are used in a single knowledge system.

body—In Prolog, the goals of a clause.

boolean operators—The operators used in propositional calculus, which include AND, OR, and NOT.

breadth-first search—A search strategy in which all nodes at one level are pursued before moving to the next level of detail.

CAR—In LISP, an address pointer to a list item; also called HEAD or FIRST.

CDR—In LISP, an address pointer to the next CONS-cell in a list; also called TAIL or REST.

certainty factor (CF)—A measure of the confidence of a fact or relationship. This contrasts with probability.

cfa—In Forth, the code field address. The location of a pointer to the run-time location of the Forth word.

chunk—A collection of knowledge stored and retrieved as a single unit.

clause—A conjunctively related term.

cognitive modeling—The development of theories, concepts and models of the human mind and how it functions.

243

common LISP—A version of LISP that is increasingly accepted as standard and will function on many different computers.

compiled knowledge—Knowledge that has been abstracted from an expert and organized in a form that can be accessed and used by an expert or knowledge system. This generally implies some knowledge structuring, such as chunks and hierarchies.

compiler—A procedure which parses an input stream and stores the data for future execution in a more efficient form.

conflict resolution—In a production system, the process of determining which rule to fire when two or more rules match the specified facts in the working memory.

connectives—The boolean operators used in first-order logic to relate terms, including operators such as IMPLIES and EQUIVALENT (see Table 4-1).

CONS-cells—A LISP data type which consists of two components, a HEAD and a TAIL. (See *CAR, CDR.*)

consultation mode—A particular user interface used in knowledge systems, in which the user is moved through the problem space to a solution with a series of interactive questions. (See planning mode.)

control component—The inference engine or rule interpreter, which determines the sequence of use of rules.

dangling references—In LISP, a memory allocation fault in which a cell is assumed to be free when actually it is in use. This leaves pointers from active cells "dangling". (See *garbage collection.*)

database—In a knowledge system, this generally refers to the working memory. (See *working memory.*)

data structure—In LISP, a way of organizing data and defining access to it.

deduction tree—In Prolog, a graphical representation of search activity.

deep knowledge—Knowledge of basic theories about a domain (See Chapter 5 and *shallow knowledge.*)

defining words—Forth words that are used to define other words.

demons—Hidden or virtual procedures in a knowledge system that are activated by data.

depth-first search—A search strategy in which the details are pursued as far as possible until a conclusion is unable to be proved true.

diagnostic systems—A type of knowledge system that is used to relate behavioral faults to faulty structures.

dictionary—The list of Forth words.

domain—A definable extent of knowledge about a subject-matter. Computer science is a broad domain, while cognitive modeling would be a much narrower domain.

dynamic allocation—The run-time allocation of memory.

expert systems—See *knowledge systems.*

expertise—Heuristics and knowledge possessed by some humans in a particular domain. Expertise is gained by amassing large amounts of knowledge in a domain and organizing it into appropriate hierarchical chunks so that it can be applied to the solution of problems in the domain.

extended variable—A Forth variable with additional memory allotment.

facets—Constraint values stored in slots of a frame-based knowledge representation.

fact—A statement or premise that is true. A fact can consist of an attribute and an associated value.

firing—The action in a production system inference cycle in which a conclusion is added to the working memory or a specific output action is initiated. (See *triggering*.)

FIRST—See *CAR*.

first-order logic—An extension of propositional calculus with quantified variables.

flat—Any knowledge representation without hierarchical relationships of knowledge.

forward chaining—An inference engine control strategy in which inferences are made by applying facts to rules, resulting in conclusions that are supported by the facts.

frame representation—A type of knowledge representation in which objects are stored with one or more attributes. The value for each attribute is stored in a slot. A frame, then, is a set of slots related to a specified object.

functional programming—A style of programming based on passing arguments between functions.

garbage—In LISP, a type of memory allocation fault in which a cell appears active even though it is actually free. (See *dangling references*.)

garbage collection—In LISP the recovery of unused list cells.

heuristic—Informal knowledge used to improve the efficiency of search in a given problem space.

hierarchy—A relationship of concepts or objects in which some are subordinate to others.

IF-THEN rule—A statement of a relationship between premises and a conclusion, also called a *production*.

inference—A reasoning process in which new facts are derived from known facts.

inference engine—That part of a production system that derives new facts from known facts in the knowledgebase.

inheritance—A process in which attribute values of one object are derived from an object class in a hierarchy.

inner interpreter—That part of the Forth virtual machine that interprets threaded code.

interpreter—A procedure that parses an input data stream, converts it to an executable form, and executes it immediately.

interpretive systems—A type of knowledge system used to establish conclusions from observed data.

knowledge—A collection of facts, relationships, and heuristics which can be used to solve problems.

knowledgebase—That portion of a knowledge system that consists of facts and rules. In a production system it consists of the rulebase and working memory.

knowledge engineer—An individual skilled in assessing problems and building knowledge systems. The term implies training in cognitive science, computer science, knowledge systems, and other aspects of artificial intelligence.

knowledge representation—The method that is used to encode facts and relationships in a knowledgebase.

knowledge systems—A class of computer programs that use knowledge and inference procedures to solve problems.

LISP—A programming environment that is used to solve problems involving symbolic relationships.

list—An ordered set of connected LISP CONS-cells. (See *atom.*)

list identifier—Forth variables whose values are pointers to the list they name; also called *list-id.*

list-id—See *list identifiers.*

list pointer—The address of the head of a list.

list-space—The part of the computer memory used for storing lists.

long-term memory—That part of the human mind that is used for storing knowledge that is not currently being used for long periods of time. Similar to disk storage in a computer or a rulebase in a knowledge system.

mark and sweep—A LISP list management scheme in which all active cells are marked and then any unmarked cells are put on the free list.

modus ponens—A rule of inference that states:

IF (A AND IF A THEN B) THEN B

monotonic reasoning—A kind of reasoning in which facts in the working memory are not deleted.

MYCIN—A knowledge system developed at Stanford University in the mid-1970s for the diagnosis and treatment of meningitis and bacteremia infections.

natural language understanding—A branch of artificial intelligence concerned with language translation, intelligent information retrieval, and the development of computer systems that can communicate in human languages.

network database management system—A type of database management system in which data can be stored in hierarchical relationships in which a "child" record can have more than one owner or "parent" record.

nfa—In Forth, the name field address; the location of the Forth word name.

NIL—A LISP atom that is also the empty list.

nonmonotonic reasoning—A kind of reasoning in which facts in the working memory can be deleted.

nucleus—The machine-dependent level of Forth from which all other Forth words are defined.

object—An entity in a knowledge system that can have one or more attributes. (See *attributes.*)

object-attribute-value triplet (A-O-V)—A method of representing factual knowledge in which objects can have properties, which in turn have values. Example: For the fact "The brother of the patient is John," the object is PATIENT, the attribute is BROTHER, and the value is JOHN. (See *attribute-value pair.*)

outer interpreter—The Forth interpreter that interacts with the user.

parallel architecture—Any computer architecture in which multiple processes occur simultaneously.

parameter stack—In Forth, a stack used to pass data between words.

parenthesis notation—A list notation in LISP wherein list items are enclosed in parentheses, such as (A B C).

parsing—The act of decomposing a statement into its component symbols and determining its syntax.

pattern-directed module (PDM)—See *production.*

pfa—In Forth, the parameter field address; the location of the Forth word body.

planner system—A knowledge system that determines a sequence of actions to achieve a goal.

246

planning mode—A particular user interface used in knowledge systems in which the user creates a matrix or other representation of a desired goal and the knowledge system defines the state space needed to reach the goal.

postfix notation—A syntax in which a function follows its arguments.

predicate—A function with a value of true or false.

predicate calculus—An extension of propositional logic that permits the use of quantified variables. Propositions can have the value TRUE or FALSE. The language provides a means of expressing symbolic relationships. (See *propositional logic, first-order logic.*)

prefix notation—A syntax in which a function precedes its arguments.

predicate logic—See *predicate calculus.*

prediction systems—A type of knowledge system used to predict future results from a given state.

problem reduction—A control heuristic in which goals are defined in terms of subgoals in a hierarchical goal structure.

problem solving—The process of achieving a desired goal starting from an initial state. The solution involves moving through a problem space in a sequence of operations.

problem space—A representation of all the possible states in the solution of a problem and the operations between the states.

production—An IF-THEN rule that consists of a premise or antecedent and conclusion or consequence. Also called a *pattern-directed module (PDM).*

production rule—See *production.*

production system—A type of knowledge system in which the knowledge is stored as productions or a collection of IF-THEN rules. A production system consists of a knowledgebase, an inference engine, and working memory.

Prolog—A logic programming language based on predicate calculus used in AI.

property—An attribute.

property-list—A database list structure wherein properties are associated with an atom. For example, to create a phone directory the names could be assigned as atoms, each with a property list that included the address and phone number properties. Property-lists can be used to create frame representations. (See *association-lists.*)

proposition—An expression in which a predicate affirms or denies something about a subject.

propositional logic—A formal logic language in which variables can only have the value of true or false and boolean operations can be performed between the variables.

prototype—A preliminary version of a knowledge system.

pruning—The reduction of search space through the use of heuristics or algorithms to reduce search time.

quantifiers—Operators used in first-order logic to express quantification; includes THERE-EXISTS and FOR-ALL operators (see Table 4-1).

reasoning—The application of inference rules to facts.

reference counting—A Forth list memory managment scheme in which each cell has a count of the number of pointers to the cell.

relational database management system—A type of database management system in which data is stored in any number of two-dimensional files or relations viewed as a single unit.

representation—See *knowledge representation.*

resolution—A general inference rule used in logic programming.

robotics—A branch of artificial intelligence involving the development of sensors, manipulators, and heuristics for object- and space-oriented environmental problem solving.

rule—See *production.*

rulebase—That part of a knowledgebase that is used to store the productions or rules; the static part of the knowledgebase in a production system.

run-time procedure—A procedure in Forth which interprets a Forth word when the word is executed.

script—A frame-like knowledge structure used to represent a sequence of events. The slots contain data concerning the event, and the slots are linked in a chain.

semantics—The meaning of an expression or statement. (See *syntax.*)

semantic network—A type of knowledge representation in which the objects and values are represented as nodes with links indicating relationships between the nodes.

shallow knowledge—Heuristic knowledge gained from experience in a particular domain that is used when facts are not available to support a particular conclusion. Also called *surface knowledge.* (See *deep knowledge.*)

shell—A tool that can be used to develop a complete knowledge system; consists of the inference engine, a working memory, and optional auxiliary components such as a knowledge acquisition subsystem or explanatory interface.

short-term memory—That portion of human memory that is used for temporarily storing particulars about a problem as it is being solved.

slot—A component of a frame (object) in a frame-based knowledge representation. Slots can contain intrinsic features (object name, hierarchical pointers), attribute values, procedures or productions used to evaluate attributes, or constraint values for attributes (facets).

stack—A data structure for which the last item pushed on the structure will be the first to be popped from it.

state—A node in a problem space.

state space—See *problem space.*

static allocation—Compile-time allocation of memory.

static frame—A frame in which the values of the attributes do not change during the course of the consultation.

surface knowledge—See *shallow knowledge.*

symbol—Any component of a knowledge structure.

symbolic expression—In LISP, an atom or a list; also called an *s-expression.* (See *atom.*)

symbolic computing—The use of symbols and symbolic relationships to solve a problem.

syntax—Refers to the order of symbols of an expression. Computers are good at resolving syntax, but have a very difficult time resolving semantics. (See *semantics.*)

TAIL—See *CDR.*

taxonomy—The hierarchical classification of objects by IS-A relationships.

tool—Any device (hardware or software) that can be used to improve the efficiency of the knowledge system design.

triggering—A process in the inference cycle of a production system in which a rule is selected for firing. (See *firing.*)

uncertainty—See *certainty.*

unification—A kind of variable-matching and instantiation in predicate logic.

value—A quantity or quality of an attribute. (See *attribute.*)

von Neumann architecture—A type of computer architecture in which a single memory is used to store the data and program, separate from the CPU.

well-formed formulas (WFFs)—Syntactically correct symbolic expressions in first-order logic.

windows—The sectioning of the display screen of a computer to permit viewing different types of data at the same time. These are particularly useful in frame-based systems in which hierarchical relationships can be displayed graphically.

word—A Forth procedure.

working memory—The storage used for the facts (attribute-value pairs) in a production type of knowledge system that have been ascertained as true or not true during a particular consultation; also called a *database.*

Resources

T HIS IS A SELECTIVE BIOGRAPHY BY SUBJECT AREA FOR THOSE WHO WISH TO pursue additional research on topics covered in this book.

ARTIFICIAL INTELLIGENCE

Barr, Avron; Feigenbaum, Edward; and Cohen, Paul R. *The Handbook of Artificial Intelligence*. Los Altos, Calif.: William Kaufmann, Inc., 1982.

> The Handbook is a four-volume encyclopedia on the history and status of artificial intelligence research. The first volume is of particular importance for expert systems researchers. This is not meant to be a textbook, but rather a reference book to be used selectively for particular subject areas. It is written at a very technical level and includes a good section on representation schemes.

Feigenbaum, Edward A. and McCorduck, Pamela, *The Fifth Generation: Artificial Intelligence and Japan's Computer Challenge to the World*. Reading, Mass.: Addison-Wesley Publishing Company, 1983.

> This book is a nontechnical and historical perspective on the international development of expert systems.

Winston, Patrick Henry. *Artificial Intelligence, 2nd Edition*. Reading, Mass.: Addison-Wesley Publishing Co., 1984.

> This book is a classic introductory text on artificial intelligence with emphasis on the use of LISP in AI. (See also "Languages" in this appendix.)

_____, and Prendergast, Karen A. *The AI Business: Commercial Uses of Artificial Intelligence*. Cambridge, Mass.: The MIT Press, 1984.

> This book is a nontechnical overview of the current status of several expert systems operational on large computers. It contains a collection of papers presented at an AI colloquium that attracted representatives from the academic perspective, the business and financial community, and the industrial research and development community.

BYTE, Volume 6, No. 9 (September 1981).

> This issue contains five articles on artificial intelligence, including an article on natural language processing.

BYTE, Volume 10, No. 4 (April 1985).

> This issue contains a collection of thirteen articles on artificial intelligence with specific articles on the human brain, LISP, learning in parallel networks, and expert systems. Authors include Marvin Minsky and Patrick Winston.

EXPERT SYSTEMS

Forsyth, Richard. *Expert Systems: Principles and Case Studies*. London: Chapman and Hall, 1984.

Overview of expert systems, particularly using rule-based representations on large computers.

Freiling, M.; Alexander, J.; Messick, S.; Rehfuss, S.; and Shulman, S. "Staring a Knowledge Engineering Project—A Step by Step Approach." *AI Magazine*, Vol. 6 No. 3 (Fall 1985).

Genesereth, Michael R., and Brown, Dennis. *Fundamentals of Artificial Intelligence*. Palo Alto, Calif.: Teknowledge, 1982.
> This is an excellent introduction to predicate logic and symbolic processing. Available from Teknowledge, Inc., 525 University Ave., Palo Alto, CA 94301

Gevarter, William B. *An Overview of Expert Systems*.
> Washington, D.C.: National Bureau of Standards (NBSIR 82-2505) October, 1982. (Prepared for NASA Headquarters, Washington, D.C. 20546)

Hayes-Roth, Frederick; Waterman, Donald; and Lenat, Douglas B. *Building Expert Systems*. Reading, Mass.: Addison-Wesley Publishing Company, 1983.
> This is a classic overview of expert system research, with collaborative writings of 38 top researchers. It contains a historical overview, tutorial material, and an introduction to the basic concepts. It is intended as a textbook, and is primarily oriented toward expert systems on large computers.

Harmon, Paul, and King, David. *Expert Systems: Artificial Intelligence in Business*. New York: John Wiley & Sons, Inc., 1985.
> This book is directed to a business person or researcher interested in learning the fundamentals of expert systems and applying them commercially to solve problems. The emphasis is on the application of expert systems to commercial problem solving as opposed to the more research and laboratory emphasis of most books. Includes good material on personal computer systems.

Stefik, Mark, et. al. *The Organization of Expert Systems: A Prescriptive Tutorial*. Palo Alto, Calif.: Xerox Palo Alto Research Center, (3333 Coyote Hill Road, Palo Alto, CA 94304, VLSI-82- January 1982.

Communications of the ACM, Volume 28 No. 5 (September 1985).
> This series of articles describes various knowledge system architectures.

BYTE, Volume 4, No. 8 (August 1979).
> This issue features LISP, cognitive modeling, and pattern-directed invocation.

FORTH-BASED KNOWLEDGE SYSTEMS

Johnson, H., and Bonissone, P. "Expert System for Diesel Electric Locomotive Repair." *Journal of Forth Application and Research* (September 1983).

Redington, D. "Outline of a Forth Oriented Real-time Expert System for Sleep Staging: a FORTES Polysomnographer." Forth Modification Laboratory: Sixth FORML conference, November 1984.

Park, Jack. *MVP-FORTH Expert System Toolkit*. Mountain View, Calif.: Mountain View Press, 1984.
> This is a simple and complete Forth Expert System that is useful for demonstration and tutorial purposes. A separate tutorial manual is available by Mitch and Linda Derick from the same publisher.

LANGUAGES

Brodie, Leo. *Starting Forth*. Englewood Cliffs, N.J.: Prentice-Hall, 1981.
> This book still remains one of the best introductory books on Forth, but is not typeset and as a result is difficult to read.

Meehan, James R. *The New UCI LISP Manual*. Hillsdale, N.J.: Lawrence Erlbaum Associates, 1979.

Winston, Patrick Henry, and Horn, Berthold Klaus Paul. *LISP: Second Edition*. Reading, Mass.: Addison Wesley Publishing Company, 1984.
> This is a classic book on the LISP programming language and includes several chapters on rule and frame-based expert systems.

BYTE, Volume 10, No. 8 (August 1985).
> This issue features declarative languages and logic programming, including Prolog (6 articles).

BYTE, Volume 6, No. 8 (August 1981).
> This issue features Smalltalk and object-oriented software (13 articles).

TOOLS

Goldenberg, Janet. "Experts on Call." *PC World* (September 1985): 192-201.
> Overview of expert system shells available for personal computers.

PC Magazine Volume 4, No. 8 (April 16, 1985)
> This issue contains nine articles by several writers reviewing the expert system tools available for personal computers.

KNOWLEDGE REPRESENTATION

Communications of the ACM, Volume 28, Number 9 (September 1985).
> This is an excellent tutorial overview of frame, production, and predicate logic representations.

OTHER RESOURCES

1. *FORTH 83 Standard*
   This publication is available from:
   Forth Standards Team
   P.O. Box 4545
   Mountain View, CA 94040

2. Public domain versions of LISP and Forth are available from:
   PC-SIG
   1030 E. Duane, Suite J,
   Sunnyvale, CA 94086.
   Order XLISP as Disk 148 and the Perry & Laxon F83 Forth as Disks 263 and 264. Disks are $6.00 each plus $4.00 shipping fee per order.

3. A large number of Forth resources (books and software) are available from the following address:

Mountain View Press, Inc.
Box 4656
Mountain View, CA 94040
(415) 961-4103

Inside F83, a manual describing the Perry & Laxon F83 Forth, is available from this address for $25.00. For the Apple II, get *Mastering FORTH* by Anderson and Tracy, for $20.00.

4. Publications:
   The AI Magazine
   AAAI Conference Proceedings
The American Association of Artificial Intelligence (AAAI)
   445 Burgess Drive
   Menlo Park, CA 94025-3496

5. International Joint Conference on Artificial Intelligence (IJCAI)
   Order proceedings from:
   Morgan Kaufmann Publishers, Inc.
   95 First Street
   Los Altos, CA 94022

6. International Symposium of Logic Programming
   IEEE Computer Society
   Box 80452, Worldway Postal Center
   Los Angeles, CA 90080

7. AI Memos, technical reports, and books are available from the following major AI research centers:

   a) Massachusetts Institute of Technology (MIT) AI Lab
      Elizabeth Heepe
      Publications Rooms NE43-818
      MIT Artificial Intelligence Laboratory
      545 Technology Square
      Cambridge, MA 02139
   b) Stanford University
      Department of Computer Science
      Stanford, CA 94305
   c) SRI International
      Artificial Intelligence Center
      Mail Stop EJ257
      333 Ravenwood Ave.
      Menlo Park, CA 94025
   d) Carnegie-Mellon University
      Department of Computer Science
      Pittsburgh, PA 15213

8. A Forth compiler is available from Laboratory Microsystems. Order CFORTH for $300.00 from:
   Laboratory Microsystems, Inc.
   Box 10430
   Marina del Rey, CA 90295
Note: Additional addresses of product suppliers can be found in Appendix D and E.

Index

A

* algorithm, 156
absolute-correction increment, 204
absolute-correction perceptron algorithm, 204
abstraction hierarchy, 172
ACRONYM, 183
address interpreter (Forth), 100
algorithm, 26
algorithmic computing, 26
alpha-beta algorithm (search strategy), 42
AND-parallelism, 179
animal game, 48-52, 63-64
  network diagram, 52
  operation, 63-64
  production rules, 50
antecedent (production rule), 33
antecedent-driven search, 40
architecture, von Neumann, 30
artificial intelligence
  cost-effectiveness, 15
  game development, 9-11
  history, 3
  knowledge representation, 9
  problem solving, 9
  scope, 9
  scope (diagram), 10
Asimov, Isaac, 15
association-list, 122
associative memory, 179
atom (LISP), 120
atom (predicate logic), 60
atomic formula, logical, 59
atomic proposition (predicate logic), 60
attached procedure (frame-based representation), 55
attribute-object-value (A-O-V) triplet, 51
attribute-value pair (production rule), 33
attribute-value pairs, 49

B

backtracking, 146
  dependency-directed, 173
backward chaining, 40, 49, 145, 168
backward planning, 69
backward reasoning, 34
BASIC, 27, 60, 79, 110
basic probability assignment (BPA), 174

C

Bayes' Rule, 173
behavioral hierarchy, 72
belief (truth maintenance system), 168
binding
  logical, 59
  Prolog, 157
birth rules, 200
blackboard knowledge representation, 62
Boeing Computer Services Company, 21
boolean operator, 60, 89
by-example knowledge representation, 62

C (language), 27, 60, 79
Carbonell, Jaime, 182
causal hierarchy, 72
"caused-by" semantic network link, 56
certainty factor, 173
  formula, 174
character strings (Forth), 96-97
  pointers, 96
  stack representation, 96
  structure, 96
chunking, 6-8, 27, 46
circularity (Prolog), 162
clause (Prolog), 142
CLAUSES list (Prolog interpreter), 145
closed-world assumption, 168
CLOUT, 15
clustering, unsupervised, 196
code field, 98
code-field address, 98
cognitive modeling, 14
colon (Forth word), 80
comments (Prolog), 143
compiler layer (Forth), 83
compiling-word (Forth), 102-103
computer interfacing, natural language, 11
computer language
  declarative, 141
  functional, 141
computer systems, classification of, 26-28
computing
  algorithmic, 26

heuristic, 26
numeric, 181
symbolic, 181
concept learning, 182
conclusion, 51
  production rule, 33
conflict resolution (production system cycle), 40
conflict set, 172
CONS-cell (LISP), 112
consequence (production rule), 33
consequence-driven search, 40
constant
  logical, 59
  Prolog, 142
constraint propagation, 173
consultation mode, 18-19
control constructs (Forth), 90-95, 103
  diagram, 92
control procedure, nondeterministic, 36
convergent reasoning, 28
Cray-1, 4
credit/blame assignment, 183
cyclic search strategy, 42

D

dangling references, 137
data stack (Forth), 81
data structures, 110
data types
  list processing, 120
  Prolog, 142
data-driven search, 40
data-flow architecture, 179
database, viii
  production system, 33
database manager, and knowledge systems, 25
dBASE II, 26
death rules, 200
decision function, 184
decompiler (SEE), 100
deduction, 9
deduction tree, 155
deep knowledge, 72-74
default reasoning, 168
defining-word (Forth), 80, 103

definitional semantic network link, 57
demon, 36
Dempster-Shafer theory of evidence, 174
DENDRAL, 42
dependency records (truth maintenance
  system), 168
dependency-directed backtracking, 173
destructive list functions, 124-127, 138
  and reference counting, 139
DETEKTR, 37-39
device layer (Forth), 82
dictionary (Forth), 80
dictionary management (Forth), 98-100
Diebold, John, viii
Digital Equipment Corporation, 15, 21, 69
divergent reasoning, 28
document generation, natural language,
  11
domain, 8
  defined, 27
  defining, 66
  formal language representation, 71
  formal representation of, 68
  object identification, 70
  problem area identification, 71
  taxonomic, 71
dotted pair (LISP), 112
double recursion, 131, 133

E

ELM, 183
empty list (Prolog), 143
EMYCIN, 43
entropy, 36
environment (Prolog), 157
EURISKO, 22
EVAL-APPLY loop (LISP), 111
execution vector (Forth), 97, 153
expert and knowledge systems
  advantages, 24-25
  and personal computers, 15, 25-26
  and traditional computer systems, 29
  applications, 20, 22-23
  characteristics, 20
  components, 30-46
  computer languages, 45, 79
  consultation mode, 18-19
  cost-effectiveness vs. knowledgebase
    size, 25
  cyclic function, 18
  defined, 11, 17, 141
  design problems, 65
  development, 25
  diagram, 18
  frame-based, 36, 46
  interdisciplinary, 22
  interpretive, 21
  limitations, 22-24
  mainframe, 15
  mechanical and electrical diagnostic,
    21
  medical diagnostic, 20
  monitoring and control, 21
  natural language research, 11
  planning, 21
  predictive, 20
  scope, 11-16
  system architecture, 75
  tutorial, 22

types of knowledge, 18
expert systems, development of, viii
Expert-Ease, 26, 62, 75
explanatory interface (production
  system), 38
extended variable (Forth), 114

F

facet (frame-based representation), 55
feature extraction (pattern recognition),
  184
Feigenbaum, Edward, 17
"fetch" operation, 81
Fifth Generation Project (Japan), viii, 141
Fig-Forth, 79
first (of list), 112
first-order logic knowledge representation, 57
flags (Forth), 89
flatness (of knowledge system), 53, 169
FOO (Forth), 102
FOR-NEXT loop (BASIC), 93
Forth, 45, 79-108
  advantages as knowledge system
language, 80
  arithmetic, 83-86
  assembly language capabilities, 81
  boolean operators, 89-90
  compiler layer, 83
  debugging, 82
  decomposition of levels, 82
  delimiters, 80
  device layer, 82
  extensibility, 105, 111
  interpreter layer, 83
  levels of abstraction, 82
  memory allocation, 81
  modularity, 82
  nucleus layer, 82
  numeric data types, 83
  outer interpreter, 83
  procedural nature of, 81
  prompt, 81
  range of abstraction, 81
  required word set, 83-84
  similarity to LISP, 111-112
  standard integer, 83
Forth control words
  action during compilation, 93
  BEGIN-UNTIL, 90
  BEGIN-WHILE-REPEAT, 90
  CASE-OF-ENDOF-ENDCASE, 94
  DO-LOOP and DO-+LOOP, 93
  IF-ELSE-THEN, 90
  LEAVE, 90
Forth Interest Group (FIG), 79
Forth "LISP"/Prolog implementation
  2APPEND, 117, 133-136, 144
  ADD-GOALS, 150-151, 153
  2ASSOC, 160
  ASSOC, 123
  ATOM?, 117, 120
  BACKTRACK, 150-151
  ?CREATE, 118
  CONS, 115
  EQ, 124
  EQUAL, 124, 131
  FIND-CLAUSE, 150-151
  FIND-CLAUSE?, 150-151
  FIRST, 113

GET-GOAL, 150-151, 153
.GOALS, 154-155
HOW?, 154-155
.KB, 154-155
LAST, 126, 129
LENGTH, 126, 132
LIST, 117-118
LVAR, 164
MEMB, 124, 127
MEMBER, 124
NEWLIST, 113
NIL, 120
NTH, 126
NUF?, 154-155
NULL, 113
PRINT, 116-117, 163
PRINTL, 117, 163
query (?-), 153-154
READCH, 118
READL, 94, 118-119
RECURSE, 115, 130
REMPROP, 124
RULE:, 154-155
SEARCH, 149-164, 167
(SEARCH), 150
search algorithm, 145
SET, 115
TAIL, 113
TRACE, 153-154
UNIFY, 151, 162, 167
VALUE, 160
VAR?, 164
Forth pattern-recognition implementation
  CLASS, 191, 194
  >CLASS, 195
  CLASSES, 191, 194
  >CLASSES, 195
  CLASSIFY, 194
  D(X), 194
  DOT, 194
  PROTOTYPE, 191, 194
Forth system variables
  BASE, 86
  CONTEXT, 177
  CURRENT, 177
  DP, 104
  FENCE, 100
  STATE, 102
  VOC-LINK, 177
Forth word structure, 97
  code field, 98
  code-field address, 98
  default field, 98
  link field, 97
  link-field address (lfa), 97
  name field, 98
  name-field address, 98
  parameter field, 98
  parameter-field address, 98
Forth words
  ABS, 86
  ALLOT and 2ALLOT, 104
  ALSO, 177
  ARRAY, 105
  >BODY, 106
  BEGIN-UNTIL, 129
  BEGIN-WHILE-REPEAT, 129
  BL, 97
  BRANCH and ?BRANCH, 103
  C-fetch (C@), 88

C-store (C!), 88
CASE-OF-ENDOF-ENDCASE, 129
(;CODE), 105
CODE, 80
colon, 80
comment, 97
comment line (½), 97
compile (]), 102
(CON), 103
CONSTANT, 80-81
COUNT, 96
CR, 97
CREATE, 103
DECIMAL, 86
DEFER, 97, 106
DEFINED, 177
DEFINITIONS, 177
device, 97
disk handling, 108
divide (/), 85
divide by two (2/), 85
DO-COLON, 102
DOES> and (DOES>), 105
DROP and 2DROP, 86
DUP and 2DUP, 86
?DUP, 87
EDITOR, 175
EMIT and (EMIT), 97
EMPTY-BUFFERS, 108
END-CODE, 80
EXECUTE, 106
fetch (@), 88
FLUSH, 108
FOO, 102
FORGET, 100
HERE, 104
HEX, 86
IF-ELSE-THEN, 129
IMMEDIATE, 102
incrementation/decrementation, 85
INFER, 153
INTERPRET, 102
.ID, 98
IS, 106-108
JSR, 106
KEY, 97
LAST, 98
LITERAL and (LIT), 103
LOAD, 108
machine-dependent, 82
MAX, 85
memory access, 87-89
memory allocation, 104
MIN, 85
multiply (*), 85
multiply by two (2*), 85
NEGATE, 85
NEST, 102
NEXT, 100
NIP, 87
NOOP, 106
OFF, 89
ON, 88
OVER, 87
PICK, 87
plus-store (+!), 88
(PREMIT), 97
R-fetch (R@), 95
R-from (R⁴), 95
removing, 98

return stack access, 95
ROLL, 87
ROT and -ROT, 87
SAVE, 100
SAVE-BUFFERS, 108
SEE, 100
SET, 116, 137
single-byte access, 88
SPACE, 97
stack duplication, 86
stack manipulation, 86-87
state change ([), 102
store (!), 88
string literal delimiter (."), 96
subtract (-), 85
SWAP, 87
THRU, 108
tick ('), 98
to-R (>R), 95
TYPE, 96
UNNEST, 102
(VAR), 103
VARIABLE, 80, 81
VLIST, 98
VOCABULARY, 175
WORDS, 98
Forth-83 Standard, 83
Fortran, 27, 79, 110
forward chaining, 40, 49, 145, 168
forward reasoning, 34
frame, 53
    hierarchical organization of, 55
frame problem, 169
frame-based knowledge representation,
    53-56
    advantages, 56
    disadvantages, 56
frame-based system, 170
function (predicate logic), 60
functional hierarchy, 73
functional programming, 82
functor, Prolog, 142-143
fuzzy logic, 175

G

Galen, Robert S., 25
game development
    control strategy, 11
    goal, 11
    paradigm, 11
    representation, 11
    rules, 11
garbage, 137
garbage collection, 136
    schemes, 137-138
General Electric locomotive division, 21
goal-driven search, 40
GOALS list (Prolog interpreter), 145

H

"has-a" semantic network link, 56
HASP/SIAP, 21
head (of list), 112
HEARSAY, 62
heuristic computing, 26
heuristic search, 172
heuristics, 11, 17, 26-27, 32, 36, 53, 73,
    156, 183
    robotic, 15

hierarchy
    behavioral, 72
    causal, 72
    functional, 73
    structural, 72
hierarchy of abstraction, 172
human mind
    indexing system, 6-7
    information access, 6
    knowledge processing (diagram), 5
    memory, 4
    thinking process, 4-8
hyperplane, 184
    properties, 186
hypothesis, 51

I

implication, 51
induction, 9, 182
INFER (Forth execution vector), 153
inference engine
    control component, 35-36
    inference component, 34
    production system, 34
infix notation, 143
Infocom, Inc., 11, 13, 38
information indexing, human, 6
information retrieval, natural language, 11
inner interpreter (Forth), 100
    diagram, 101
    registers, 100-102
input stream (Forth), 97
instantiated variable (Prolog), 157
INTERNIST, 42
interpretation, logical, 59
interpreter layer (Forth), 83
"is-a" semantic network link, 56
iteration primitive (Forth), 129

K

K-Means algorithm, 200
KEE system, 56
knowledge
    acquisition of, 75
    deep, 72, 73, 74
    implementation of, 74
    operational, 37
    parenthetical, 37
    shallow, 72, 74
    structural, 18, 36
    structural dynamic, 18, 36
    supporting, 37
    working, 18, 36
knowledge acquisition module, produc-
    tion system, 36
knowledge engineer, 20
knowledge engineering, 65-76
knowledge processing, human (diagram),
    5
knowledge representation, 9, 48-64
    blackboard representation, 62
    by example, 62
    first-order logic, 57
    frame-based, 53
    rules, 49
    semantic network, 56
knowledgebase, viii, 17
    compiled, 62
knowledgebase construction, 65-76
    cyclic nature of, 65

domain definition, 66
  problem identification, 68
Kulikowski, Casimir A., 25

L

language, object-based, 170
learning, 11, 181-183
  and applications programs, 14
  as subfield of AI, 181
  by-analogy, 182
  concept, 182
  rote, 182
  strategy, 183
least committment principle, 173
Lenat, Douglas, 22
link
  semantic network, 56
  types, 56
link field, 97
link-field address, 97
LISP, 45, 79
  similarity to Forth, 111-112
LISP functions
  *APPEND, 124
  APPEND, 125
  ASSOC, 122
  ASSOC#, 122
  ATTACH, 124, 138
  CAAR, 114
  CADR, 114
  CAR, 112, 114
  CDAR, 114
  CDDR, 114
  CDR, 112, 114
  COND, 129
  CONS, 114, 124
  DREMOVE, 124, 138-140
  DREMOVE1, 138
  DREVERSE, 124, 138-140
  EQ, 123-124, 127
  EQUAL, 123-124, 127
  FIRST, 114
  GET, 121
  GETL, 121
  LIST, 127
  MEMB, 127
  MEMBER, 127
  MEMQ, 127
  NCONC, 124, 138
  *NCONC, 138
  NIL, 113
  PUT, 121-122
  PUTPROP, 121
  RC+, 137
  RC-, 137
  REMOVE, 125, 127
  REMPROP, 121-122
  REVERSE, 124-125, 127
  RPLACA, 124, 138
  RPLACA*, 138
  RPLACD, 124, 138
  RPLACD*, 138
  SETQ, 137
  SUBST, 127
list
  components, 112-114
  defined, 112
  empty (Prolog), 143
  parenthesis notation, 113
  Prolog, 143
  proper, 121
list operations, primitive, 114-116
list pointer, 116
list processing, 110-128
list-id, 114, 116
list-space, management of, 136
lists, merging, 124
local variable, 82, 178
logic
  nonmonotonic, 168
  propositional, 59
Logic Theorist, 9
logical implications (Prolog), 143
logical operators (Forth), 89
logical proposition (predicate logic), 61
"logically follows," 59
long-term memory, human, 4, 6
loop
  endless, 162
  iterative, 93
  negative step, 93
loop index, 93

M

M.1, 174
machine translation, natural language, 11
MACSYMA, 110
manipulator, robotic, 15
mark and sweep (garbage collection), 137
Martin, James, viii
matching (production system cycle), 40
maximin algorithm, 198-200
Maxwell's demon, 36
McCarthy, John, 110
memory, human, 4
memory management
  dynamic, 112
  static, 112
message (Smalltalk), 169
metareasoning, 171
metarule, 172
method (Smalltalk), 169
Microsoft Word, 14
minimum-distance classification, 191-196
Minsky, Marvin, 9
missing information, 35
mock unification, 179
Modula-2, 79
modus ponens (34-35), 34
MYCIN, 15, 20, 23, 42, 43, 51, 173

N

name field, 98
name-field address, 98
natural language interface, 11
  production system, 38
natural language research
  computer interfacing, 11
  document generation, 11
  information retrieval, 11
  machine translation, 11
von Neumann architecture, 30
von Neumann bottleneck, 179
Newell, Allen, 9
node, semantic network, 56
nonmonotonic reasoning, 168
notation
  infix, 143
  prefix, 143
nucleus layer (Forth), 82

numeric computing, 27, 181
  in expert systems, 183

O

object, grouping by class, 169
object-oriented programming, 55, 169
OBLIST (LISP), 111
occurs check, 163
ONLY (Forth vocabulary), 177
operational knowledge, 37
OR-parallelism, 179
orientation vector (of line), 189
outer interpreter (Forth), 83
output stream (Forth), 97

P

Pandemonium model, 36
Paradox (database manager), 16
parallel computation, 164, 178
  and Prolog, 178
parameter field, 98
parameter stack (Forth), 81
parameter-field address, 98
parenthesis notation, 113
parenthetical knowledge, 37
parsing, 38
Pascal, 27, 60, 79
pattern
  antecedent, 33
  defined, 184
  vector representation of, 184
pattern matching, 158
pattern matching inference system, 30
pattern recognition, 181, 183-204
  feature extraction, 184
  pattern classification, 184
  processing stages, 184
pattern-directed invocation, 167, 171
pattern-space, 184
PEEK statement (BASIC), 88
perceptron algorithm, 200-204
  absolute-correction, 204
Personal Consultant, 21
point. prototype, 191
pointer, 81
  list, 116
  list item, 114
POKE statement (BASIC), 88
postfix notation, 111
predicate
  built-in (Prolog), 166-167
  logical, 58
  predefined (Prolog), 143
predicate logic, 59-62, 141
  atom, 60
  function, 60
  predicate symbol, 60
  proposition types, 60
  syntax, 60
  term, 60
  well-formed formulas, 61
predicate symbol (predicate logic), 60
prefix notation, 111, 143
prefix predicate calculus, 59-62
probability theory, 174
problem reduction (search strategy), 42
problem solving, 9
procedural analysis, 9
procedural attachment, 167
processing

descriptive, 27
numeric, 27
prescriptive, 27
symbolic, 27
production rule, 33
production system, 30-42
  advantages, 53
  compared to human brain, 45-46
  components, 30-40
  control strategies, 40-42
  database, 33
  diagram, 31
  disadvantages, 53
  explanatory interface, 38
  inference engine, 34
  knowledge acquisition module, 36
  monotonic, 34
  natural language interface, 38
  nonmonotonic, 34
  operating cycle, 40
  rule interpreter, 34
  rulebase, 30
  working memory, 33
production system tools (43-45), 43
production systems
  and personal computers, 42
  commercial, 42
program, object-oriented, 55
program code, unstructured, 91
programming
  "AI-style", 111
  assembly language, 100
  bottom-up, 111
  functional, 82
  list-oriented, 110
  object-oriented, 169
  recursive, 82
  top-down, 111
Prolog, 45, 74, 79
  data types, 142
  development of, 141
  "if" operator (:-), 142
  logical implications, 143
  program structure, 142, 166
Prolog built-in predicates
  assert, 167
  call, 167
  cut (!), 166
  retract, 167
Prolog interpreter, 145-164
proper list, 121
property inheritance, 171
property-list, 121-122
proposition
  atomic, 60
  logical, 58
propositional logic, 59
PROSPECTOR, 15, 21, 42
prototype point, 191
PUFF, 42

Q

quantified proposition (predicate logic),
  61

R

reasoning
  by analogy, 9
  convergent, 28
  divergent, 28

recursion, 111, 129-136
  ascent, 132
  descent, 131
  double, 131, 133
  stack activity, 131
  tail, 130
  terminating condition, 129
recursion diagram, 133
recursive programming, 82
reference counting (garbage collection),
  137
reminding (learning theory), 182
resolution (rule of inference), 61, 143
rest (of list), 112
return stack, 93, 95
  restriction in do-loops, 95
robotics, 14
  and knowledge systems, 200
robotics research, 14
rote learning, 182
rule interpreter, 80
  production system, 34
rule of conflict, 183
rule-based knowledge representation, 30,
  49
rulebase, 30
rules of inference
  completeness, 59
  resolution, 61
  soundness, 59
run-time address (Forth), 106
run-time procedure (Forth), 80

S

S-expression, 120
SACON, 42
Samuel, A.L., 181
Savvy, 15
screens (Forth), 108
search
  antecedent-driven, 40
  breadth-first, 42, 156
  consequence-driven, 40
  data-driven, 40
  depth-first, 42, 145
  goal-driven, 40
  heuristic, 156, 172
  improving efficiency, 42
search algorithm, uniform-cost, 156
selection (production system cycle), 40
Selfridge, Oliver, 36
semantic network, 170
semantic network knowledge representation, 56
semantics, 11
semicolon (Forth word), 80
sensor, robotic, 15
shallow knowledge, 72, 74
Shannon, Claude, 9
shell, production system, 43
short-term memory, human, 4
slot (frame-based representation), 53
Smalltalk, 79, 169, 178
SOLVED list (Prolog interpreter), 145
source code, 96
stack, 80
  data, 81
  parameter, 81
  pop operation, 81
  push operation, 81

return, 93, 95
stack notation, 81-82
statistical pattern recognition, 204
"store" operation, 81
strategy learning, 183
string length, 96
string literal, 96
structural dynamic knowledge, 18, 36
structural hierarchy, 72
structural knowledge, 18, 36
structure copying (Prolog), 164
structure sharing (Prolog), 164
style sheet, 14
sublist, 125
supporting knowledge, 37
symbol, definition, 27
symbolic computing, 27, 181
syntax, 11, 58

T

tail (of list), 112
tail recursion, 130
taxonomic hierarchy, 170
text processing (Forth), 96
threaded code, 98
  direct, 100
  indirect, 100
  instruction pointer, 100
"Three Laws of Robotics", 15
threshold algorithm, 196-198
token, 179
Traveller T.C.S., 22
truth maintenance, 168-169
Turing, A.M., 3
two's complement arithmetic, 89

U

unification (predicate calculus), 61
unification (Prolog), 157
unification algorithm, 158-164
unifier, 61
uniform-cost algorithm, 156
universally quantified variable (Prolog),
  171

V

validity, logical, 59
variable
  bound, 157
  instantiated, 157
  local, 178
  Prolog, 142
  universally quantified, 171
Vaucanson's duck, 14
vision, machine, 14

W

weight vector, 187
Weiss, Sholom M., 25
well-formed formula (WFF), 61
"Winning on Wall Street", 20
Wishbringer (game), 13
word (Forth), 80
working knowledge, 18, 36
working memory, 49
  production system, 33

X

XCON, 21, 42, 69
XSEL, 21

Designing and Programming
Personal Expert Systems

If you are intrigued by the possibilities of the programs included in *Designing and Programming Personal Expert Systems* (TAB Book No. 2692), you should definitely consider having the ready-to-run disk containing the software applications. You get the complete Prolog knowledge system developed in the book—plus a Forth language system you can use to enter, run, and modify it! Not only will you save the time and effort of typing in the screens, the disk eliminates the possibility of errors that can prevent the system from functioning. This software is guaranteed free of manufacturer's defects. (If you have any problems, return the disk within 30 days, and we'll send you a new one.) Interested?

Available for Apple II-series computers (II, II+, *IIe/IIc*) with 48K, or IBM PC and compatibles with 128K, at $24.95 for each disk, plus $1.00 per disk shipping and handling.